# Devil's Playground

## By Simon Chambers

GW00381818

**PERCY**
PUBLISHING

*This book is a factual account of real events. Some of the names
have been changed to protect current live operators, family members
and current live operations.*

Enquiries should be addressed to
Percy Publishing
Woodford Green,
Essex. IG8 0TF
England.

www.percy-publishing.com

1st Published October 2014
1st Edition

ISBN: 978-0-9571568-7-6

# Dedication

To my long suffering wife Carol who put up with my mood swings and my bad temper, who nursed me through broken limbs and bullet wounds but who continued to encourage my writing despite the disruption to her normally peaceful and organized household.

Thanks love; I couldn't have done it without you.

Simon Chambers Served 22 years in the British Army and now operates as a Private Contractor anywhere in the world that pays the money.

# For all those who didn't make it home…

# Acknowledgements

I'd never written a book before and was horrified to see the amount of paperwork that was required once it was completed. It's not just about the book itself, but the synopsis, dedications, permissions, covering letters and more.

Finally, acknowledgements: where was I going to start? I was given some good advice by an experienced writer. 'This is a thing written from your heart, as well as a social thank you to colleagues, editors, publishers - anyone who has read your work in draft and given you helpful comments.' Good advice, so here goes!

I must have driven my wife Carol mad with the long hours and late nights I spent writing when I should have been using my time on leave resting and enjoying life with my family, but through it all she has supported and encouraged me. In fact it was she who suggested I write a book in the first place. My son Andrew and his partner Sarah, my younger son Simon, my daughter Claire-Louise and her husband David all backed my wife and ganged up on me to force me to put pen to paper. What choice did I have!

As the story developed I contacted various operators I had worked with to check that I'd remembered certain incidents correctly, and to confirm the timelines. I also sent them snippets of my early work, knowing that if anyone was going to rip it apart it would be these blokes. I was pleasantly surprised when they agreed I was on the right track and gave me permission to use their names and call signs. Many of them are active operators working in some of our world's less hospitable places, so their names have been changed, or first names and call signs used to protect their identity. Still in the business myself, I have used a pen name for the same reason; I have also withheld the identities of those killed in action, in order to spare their families any further distress.

My whole-hearted thanks to so many who have made this book possible: to Alan, John, Rob and Dave, longtime friends and fellow operators; to Zeppelin, Joker, Bullitts, K9, JW and Thomas for their friendship, and for making my time in Karbala one to remember, and to the rest of the Blackwater Karbala team for their comradeship. Bill Paris, another friend working in the same line of business but with a different company, gave me much invaluable advice. Author of "The Making of a Legionnaire" and himself an operator injured in action, he was always available to discuss my early attempts and steadfast in encouraging me to hang in there when I was ready to give up.

Many of us took photos at different times and shared our snaps with each other. A huge dossier of team photos was built up, and I used many of these to help myself remember incidents and timelines. I would like to thank everyone who gave permission for their photos to be used in the book, including those who regrettably had to remain anonymous.

Since starting this project some of my team have been killed in action. They do not appear on a military casualty list. They are not classed as soldiers. They have not made the headlines and many get just a few paragraphs in their local paper. They don't get medals either, although many of them have carried out deeds worthy of such recognition.

The uninformed call such men overpaid mercenaries, and reckon they get what they deserve. Nothing could be further from the truth. They carry out many missions above and beyond the call of duty, often in places where the military have yet to take control. They are helping the poor people to achieve freedom - fighting to stabilize their country to bring peace. Many of the deeds they carry out are heroic in anyone's book, but you will be lucky if you read about them. Five of these heroes who made the ultimate sacrifice were personally known to me. Bruce, 'Sparky', 'Dingo', 'Mac' and 'K2', it was an honour and a privilege to serve with you. This book is my humble memorial to you, to the guys who died at Falluja, and to the many others killed since I started writing it and whose stories may never be told.

Last but by no means least, I couldn't finish without thanking Nigel Streeter of Airsoft Action magazine for suggesting my work to Clifford Marker of 'Percy Publishing', and of course a big thank you goes to Clifford, Ruth and all the staff at Percy Publishing for making it happen.

If there is anyone I have omitted to mention, I can only apologize profusely, and I hope it goes without saying that it has not been my intention to embarrass or insult any of my team mates, every one of whom I respect and admire.

To our enemies who read this, and who will definitely feel insulted, I can only say this. You obviously have me mixed up with someone who gives a damn about what you think! You can go to hell.

Simon Chambers

# Prologue

## The Twenty-First Century Mercenary

The sweat slowly trickling down his back went almost unnoticed as he moved his eyes left to right in a slow zigzag. Rooftops, windows and doorways were scanned in the slow steady movement he had used so many times in Northern Ireland. Belfast, though, was now but a distant memory. It was a lifetime away. Then he only had the IRA (Irish Republican Army) to worry about, but now there were so many different factions - the Militia, foreign insurgents from so many Muslim countries intent on Jihad, Al-Qaeda, tribal factions - and all with one purpose, to kill him and his kind. After all, he was only an Infidel in the pay of the Americans.

He strained to hear his team leader's voice on his radio. Not an easy task over the noise of the fifty or so Iraqi kids in front of him all wanting his attention at once. Some demanded Pepsi, others begged for water or food; all were as pushy as hell. Gimme food! Gimme water! They didn't know what 'please' or 'thank you' meant, they just demanded. Shouting 'Gimme' like that turned the soldiers off giving them anything. They were just seen as the greedy little bastards most

of them were. Most of these kids had no need to beg.
All were well clothed and clean; they didn't have that
sad pitiful look of the desert children, who in comparison to their city cousins had very little and lived a hard
life. They came from comfortably-off middle class
Iraqi families and from the better part of the town, but
this didn't stop them seeing what they could scrounge
from the soldiers and contractors; like any other kids
all over the world, they were just trying it on. One moment they had been starving, the next they had turned
into professional beggars. Some of them were enter-
prising and would sell the troops rusty Iraqi bayonets
and helmets. Now they hustled a few dollars by selling badly copied, pirate pornographic DVDs. To their
credit most of the soldiers and contractors chased
them away but they could always find one or two individuals to buy their wares.

Usually there would just be a spontaneously formed
crowd of kids reacting to the presence of foreign soldiers, but at other times it could be more sinister. The
enemy was not shy of using children to test the soldiers, watching how they reacted to the situation. Were
they alert? Did they relax and give the children sweets,
or did they just sit in their vehicles and ignore the kids?
All this information was invaluable to the Insurgents
and Militia, helping them to plan their next attacks.
In the case of PSD teams, (Personal Security Detail -
bodyguard team) children had been known to scribble
in the dust coating the rear windows of the Hard Car.
This would mark the car carrying the team's Principal
so that the attackers could identify their primary target. Children had even thrown grenades into unsus-

pecting Humvees because their occupants had become complacent and allowed them too close to the vehicle. The poorer kids would gather up the chocolate bars and water and scurry off home to give the booty to their parents. The Coalition Forces' bottled water was prized by the Iraqis because it was clean and disease free. Until the US Corps of Engineers started rebuilding and replacing the old water purification plants most of the water the Iraqis drank came from the Tigris and Euphrates rivers. It was contaminated with sewage and chemical waste and many people had died from drinking it. This was a problem in Iraq long before the Coalition invasion took place. Saddam had done nothing to ease the water shortage of his own people. He chose to give them very little so they could be more easily controlled.

"All Call Signs, Principals are moving to the second floor!" The message came through his radio ear-piece unheard by any of those around him. He twice clicked the pressel switch - his personal radio's 'send' button - to confirm he had received the information, and continued his scan of the area. His lack of military uniform, his loose-fitting sand coloured trousers, black 'softie' T-shirt and black body armour confirmed to those watching that he was not the usual kind of soldier; the 9mm Sig pistol nestled in his tightly strapped leg rig and the Bushmaster rifle held at the low ready position painted a different picture. He was a professional: a gun for hire. In the old days he would have been called a mercenary but now his trade was legitimate. He was not here to attack anyone; he was here just to defend his principals as they went about their daily work of rebuilding the infrastructure of a defeated Iraq. To any observant onlooker he clearly had a certain something about him. Unlike many of the US Army's National Guard soldiers, who had been in Iraq for too long and were just looking forward to going home, this man was fully alert and watchful. He hadn't been ordered to fight - he had volunteered. Not for the good and benefit of the Iraqi people, nor for Queen and Country; he'd done all that. Now he was here for the money: more money than he could earn in the army; more money than he could earn as a civilian. He was using the skills he had been taught in his country's armed forces, but this time it was for himself. He would take that money home and improve the life of his own family, paying off a heavy mortgage and the debts he had run up, many of them accrued whilst serving in the army. He had sold his soul for the Yankee dollar.

His trigger finger lay alongside the trigger guard of his rifle. He had full control of his weapon and would use it without a moment's hesitation if he, his principal or any member of his team was threatened. Maybe the eleven magazines of 5.56 ammunition packed into his assault vest and body armour and the three magazines of 9mm ammo for his pistol hanging on his belt rig told them he meant business and had come prepared for a fight.

To the watchers in the crowd who made it their business to notice these things, this man with his unmistakable air of professionalism was the equivalent of Saddam Hussein's Secret Police. He could be ruthless when the job required it and like the Secret Police of the old regime he was an unknown quantity. Ever alert to possible threat, his head turned continually from side to side, but at the same time he held a loose conversation, exchanging pleasantries with the less pushy and friendlier children around him. After all, they were not his enemy. His dark glasses with their mirrored lenses hid his eyes. You could learn a lot from a man's eyes. Was he tired, alert, distracted, or bored? No one could tell. He was not the easy target the terrorists sought, and the watchers had all the time in the world. They would wait for another target and another day. They were patient. If they waited long enough one would certainly come along: it always did.

# Chapter 1

## The Call to Arms

It was June 2003 and I was very pissed off with the world. I had retired from the British Army, having completed thirty plus years in the Regulars and the Reserves. Now that I was a civilian I looked around me and didn't like what I saw. Most of the Western World was convinced we had peace. Peace in our time: now where had I heard that before! Each country in turn was busy bending to the will of the noisy minorities demanding disarmament, while the silent majority stood looking on inactive. The tree huggers and the Loony Left were having a field day running roughshod over the majority of law abiding citizens. We had a culture where the victims of crime had fewer rights than their attackers; where the word 'multiculturalism' was used to give more and more rights to illegal immigrants and take away the rights of those born and bred in the mother country. Everyone was afraid to speak frankly in case they were branded as racist. In my book if you were black you were black, and if you were white you were white. What was wrong with that? Thanks to Brussels interfering in everyone's business, England - to name but one of many countries - was in real danger of losing its sovereignty. Its laws were being eroded by Belgium-based Eurocrats who had nothing to do all day but think up daft ways of screwing people and making it look like they were doing something constructive. As a result most European countries were downsizing their armed forces. It was true that more money was being spent on military technological advances but as any former soldier will tell you, when you've dropped your bombs and fired your missiles and the air force has gone home for a cup of tea and a sandwich it's not over by a long chalk. It's the PBI, (The Poor Bloody Infantry), the 'grunts' on the ground who have to go in with rifle and bayonet and winkle out the enemy hunkered down in their holes and bunkers. The militaries of the world were being run by faceless accountants: young financial whizz-kids, who had never served in the forces themselves but might have played a few games of Delta Force on their PlayStations. They thought they were qualified to tell the generals what they should spend their money on, and so everyone was going 'hi tec'.

Unfortunately the British Army was no different, and many good loyal regiments were being disbanded to save money. I found it depressing to see this happening, and so much military expertise being lost. Many highly trained combat soldiers were made redundant, adding to the rapidly growing numbers of unemployed. The average age of a 22-Year man on discharge from the armed forces is around 40 to 42 years old. Unfortunately the typical infantryman has problems finding employment at the age of 40 and he will struggle unless he takes a resettlement course that's going to give him a trade he can use. He is still a young man but considered by many employers too old to hire or retrain. So there we were with PEACE, and I was amazed! As a former professional soldier, I found it really frustrating that so many people thought we were living in a time of peace and didn't need a large military presence anymore. I only had to look around me or turn on the box and watch the news on TV to realise that wasn't the case. It was all over the daily newspapers for everyone to read. If I could see all the trouble in the world, why couldn't other people! There were clearly more flash points around the globe than ever before. Britain, America and their allies were involved in many of these trouble spots in one way or another - usually as the world's policemen, trying to clear up the mess or get two sides to agree to peace. Suicide bombers were blowing themselves up somewhere around the world every day, killing innocent women and children in the process. This was a worldwide problem and no country was safe anymore. We were at war, had been for some time, and most of the world was still asleep to the reality of it.

When the First Gulf War kicked off we struggled to form a decent sized fighting force. It took twice as many logistic vehicles and personnel as the planners had calculated to supply the fighting soldiers on the ground, and many of them later admitted they'd been wrong. Having won that one, the first thing our governments did was disband more regiments and units, and scrap ships and RAF squadrons: the very units that had won the war for us. Unfortunately, we *hadn't* really won that one, though, and along came Gulf War

2. This one had to be fought in the face of a struggle to get reluctant allies involved, and relying on the reduced expertise of a now depleted military to tackle the situation as we should have done the first time round. More problems started to show through the cracks. The defence cuts had been so draconian that huge numbers of logistical and rear echelon troops that had been available during the first Gulf War no longer existed. These soldiers would have been used to police captured areas and maintain law and order in the towns and villages. They would have been used to guard prisoners. They would have guarded priority targets such as water purification plants, hydroelectric dams and facilities, and of course hospitals and other vital organizations and buildings. Using teeth arm soldiers to carry out these duties meant a drain on the front line fighting man, drastically slowing down the efforts of our commanding generals to bring the war to a close as early as possible and stability to Iraq. It also made our troops a duty target for the Insurgents, hell bent on causing chaos and preventing us from finishing the operation.

The only option available for our various armed forces was to hire retired soldiers as civilian contractors and let them carry out all the rear echelon duties. They would be expensive but only for a short time, and they could be sacked in an instant once the generals thought the country was stable enough for its own troops and police to take over peacekeeping duties. In the early days of 2004 vast sums were spent on encouraging civilian security and defence companies to recruit for the contracts on offer. The personnel and expertise needed were ready and waiting in Civvy Street, put there by the last round of redundancies. They were only too pleased to get back to the work they enjoyed and were good at, and they knew they would be well paid for their services. Fighting as contractors, they wanted the type of money that reflected the risks they were now taking as civilians.

The problem now was how to make use of these people without being seen to employ mercenaries, which is what they were by definition. 'Mercenary' was still a dirty word to many people, and so the American Government brought in new rules of engagement to try to bring a bit of respectability to the situation. They wouldn't be allowed to go pro-active - that is, pursue the enemy. They would be allowed to fight only in defence of themselves, their equipment and their employers. Their own personal rules of engagement were deliberately left ambiguous to give them more manoeuvrability in the combat zone. In most cases they would and how deep his pockets were.

As in all times of crisis, men of vision stepped up to the challenge. Companies such as Blackwater, Aegis, Erinys, Blue Hackle and many others were formed by retired Special Forces soldiers. They knew they could make lots of money doing what they did best, and began recruiting from like-minded personnel. This was the second oldest profession in the book. Great kings and leaders had called upon this type of soldier throughout history, but somehow it didn't seem right to employ them in our politically correct, 'enlightened' modern times. The word 'mercenary' was not fashionable, and so the term 'contractor' was born.

As a former Paratrooper and retired 22-Year man, I considered myself very patriotic. I was originally recruited into the army in Cold War days, believing all the propaganda about the Russians massing for an invasion of our peaceful shores and gladly volunteering to fight for my country and keep the Russians from the door. I had kept myself reasonably fit, and had expected to be called up for Iraq. I knew my age would make a difference, but I could still be called up in a teaching capacity. In fact I was quite convinced - maybe naively - that I and many like me would be needed. In the event, the long awaited letter from the Ministry of Defence never landed on my doorstep, and out of sheer frustration I twice rang Manning and Records to volunteer. The person at the other end assured me I would be getting a return phone call but it never came and I was not called up. I had to watch the Second Gulf War on TV from the comfort of my armchair. Bollocks! Being a retired 'older soldier' was becoming boring. It wasn't what I wanted in life.

As the war was scaled down and President Bush declared Mission Accomplished, coalition soldiers were still being killed. Didn't these ungrateful bastards realise we were trying to help them? There were daily news reports of Muslims from all over the world flocking to the Insurgents' cause: they saw this as a Jihad. The western governments had yet to realise they had opened a Pandora's Box. I was still at home champing at the bit and eager to do something to help. Then one night out of the blue, a mate of mine with whom I had served in the Parachute Regiment called.

"Hey Mate, guess where I'm phoning from! Bleeding

Baghdad! It's a job creation scheme. You want the work, get your arse into gear and get over here!" He gave me some more details before the line became distorted and we were cut off.

Working on his advice, I eagerly pressed my home computer into service and started to research the Internet for companies working in Iraq. This gave me hope that I might get a job yet. The Internet gave me the names of lots of firms operating in Iraq on a range of security related missions. Most of them I had never heard of, but what the heck! - a job is a job. I had a choice: did I want to go as an unarmed truck driver working on the logistics contracts? Good money, but unarmed? No bloody chance! If I was going somewhere people were trying to kill me, I wanted to be able to shoot back. There must be other choices too. Thanks to my hobby of parachuting, I had many military friends in other countries, and most were retired or serving paratroopers like myself. I contacted a few of them that I thought might be able to help, and picked their brains for possible employment options. The 'Airborne Brotherhood' was very helpful. With loads of freshly gleaned information, I began to build a database of security firms and their contracts. Then I went on line and checked their company web sites to see which were actively recruiting security personnel. Some were a bit guarded about what they were doing in Iraq; others blatantly offered former servicemen and women the opportunity to work for big bucks.

I eagerly sent off several copies of my CV to firms that had requested it and contacted other firms directly by phone. I then took a deep breath and sat back to await their replies. Most companies didn't even bother replying. One or two sent back an email telling me they had nothing at the moment, but if I wanted to wait a couple of months they had contracts in the pipeline. One female administration officer from a well-known American security firm sent me what could only be described as a snotty email: "We are currently employed by the United States Department of Defence and are only employing American citizens. I see from your resume that you are not. Is this the case?"

Now, it's not a good idea to send this kind of mail to a retired paratrooper of any nationality who has just sunk two bottles of wine. The red mist came down and I had this urge to strangle the stuck up bitch. I sent back a blistering reply. It went on a bit, as I was in full flow and I was so bloody angry. A couple of the passages were: *So this is our US/UK 'special relationship'!* and, *We're good enough to stick our arses in the shit alongside our American friends when there's a war on, but not good enough to be employed when the war is over!* For some reason I didn't get a reply, but I had made my point and I felt a little better for it.

Then out of the blue Armor Group, an American firm with its UK HQ in Buckingham Gate, London, invited me to come to their offices for an interview; it would include an all-day presentation. A friend of mine, John, was going for the same interview. This was good: the two of us could watch each other's backs and share any information we picked up. It was a typically English cold, grey morning when I took the train to London and arrived suited and booted, wearing my Parachute Regiment tie and clutching my very extensive CV.

It was a short walk from the tube station to Buckingham Gate along an old street full of large, imposing Regency, Victorian and Edwardian buildings - the history of British architecture in a single street. Most were posh hotels or VIP conference rooms. It was easy to imagine our captains of industry busy in private rooms, making the crucial behind-the-scenes deals that would ultimately affect our country and whole way of life. I was entering an unknown territory and I had a bit of a nervous knot in my stomach as I approached the address. I counted the door numbers down and found the right hotel a few hundred yards along the street. A uniformed doorman directed me to the conference rooms to the rear of the building.

I walked in at the open door to Conference Room 3 where the meeting was to take place. There were a lot of similarly 'booted and suited' people milling around talking to each other, but after a quick sweep of the room I spotted John. I didn't feel too bad now I'd seen a friendly face, and then as I went over to join him I noticed another retired paratrooper friend of mine.

"Hello, Alan!" He looked up in surprise from the conversation he was having with another candidate.

"Hello, you old bastard! What the hell are you doing here?"

"I wasn't sure," I said, "but now I see you're here I guess I'm slumming!"

John, Alan and I shook hands and then quickly made our way towards the front of the room and took three chairs in the front row. I thought we might as well go for the best seats in the house so we could see the speakers' faces. You can tell a lot by people's mannerisms and facial expressions and we'd be able to get a good idea if these people were going to bullshit us.

There were about thirty retired servicemen attending, and judging by the excited chatter they all appeared keen to get back into the type of work they felt they did best. Without warning, a side door suddenly opened and the place went quiet, as if on cue. Everyone stopped talking at the same time and watched with interest as one guy and two females entered, made their way down to the front of the room and seated themselves at the long table facing us.

To begin with they ignored us as they quietly conversed and shuffled papers, and then the guy loudly cleared his throat and I guessed that meant the meeting was now in session. Taking it in turns, our three speakers proceeded to explain the work the company did and where they saw us in the great plan of things. From the way they spoke you could be forgiven for thinking there was work for everyone in the room. We were subjected to a couple of hours of company bullshit on how good they thought they were, during which I found it hard to stay awake. The glare of the fluorescent lighting and the closed windows making the room hot and stuffy didn't help, and I wasn't interested in how well they were doing on the Stock Exchange: I just wanted them to cut to the chase and tell me if I had a job. Looking around me I could see quite a few other people were suffering from nodding dog, their eyes wanting to close. To the trained ear the company representatives came over as nervous and hesitant; they were trying to convince us how good their company was, but it sounded like they didn't believe their own bullshit. To me it sounded like a firm that was in a little over its head, trying to recruit the type of people they hoped could pull off the operation and save their bacon.

My gut feeling was telling me these people were incompetent and would unwittingly be doing their best to get me killed. However, I wanted a bloody job. I wanted it so much, I'd be their bloody tea boy to get a foot in the door! OK, maybe I was a bit over eager. I hated being a civilian and this was my way out of a life I didn't like, didn't want and couldn't fit into. The main speaker, who introduced himself as Nick, was a tall, lean guy, mid-thirties, with the so-obvious air of an officer about him. Every inch a 'Rupert', he was trying to put himself across as an all-singing, all-dancing cool dude. He knew he had an assembly of senior noncommissioned officers in front of him with more experience of soldiering than he could ever hope to gain in his whole lifetime, and he wanted to convince us he had been there, seen that, done that. If he hadn't tried so hard, we might have believed him.

When I first received the interview letter I googled Armor Group to find out a bit about them. During my research one of my commando friends had given me some background on this Nick character. He was reported to be a retired Royal Marine Reservist officer, a bit of a bullshitter who talked a good fight but hadn't got a clue. He had seen no active service and had a habit of flying into Iraq on administration missions and then out again so quick he had scorch marks on his boarding cards. As I sat there listening to him drone on I was convinced he was living up to his reputation, and I imagined the worst case scenario of him being in charge of my team on the ground. As he rambled on, completely oblivious of the fact that he had bored to death everyone in the room, I began to see holes in his description of the job. Other candidates were asking him about the weapons that were available to the operators. Did we have armoured cars? How long did the contracts last? What life support systems were in place? What about phone calls home; email availability? All these were relevant questions to the modern contractor - we don't mind sticking our necks out, but we do like our luxuries! - but mostly undreamt of when I first joined the army.

Our friend Nick was evasive on all subjects. He twisted and turned, never giving a straight answer to any of the more searching questions put to him. This boy would make a good politician. As far as I was concerned, I was selling my soul for the Yankee dollar. Fighting for Queen and Country was all well and good, but it wouldn't pay the bills. As long as the money was good I could take any crap they dished out. After all, that was what I was here for: the money. When at long last the presentation was finished, Nick invited us to retire to a side room for tea and biscuits. It was all very civilised, but the room was hot and stuffy and my mouth was dry. I didn't think a cup of tea was going to do it for me. Right then I would have preferred a nice cold pint of beer.

We were told to relax and we would be called forward one at a time for an interview. I poured a cup of coffee from the jug provided and followed John and Alan to a quiet corner of the room to compare notes. "What do you think John?" I asked, taking a sip of hot coffee.

Without hesitation he answered straight back. "Our friend Nick is feeding us a load of company shit. All I want to know is have I got a job? How much am I getting paid for risking my neck, and for how long? Is that too much to ask the boring fucker! I don't want to buy shares in the bloody company, I want to get out on the ground and do the job." No one had been very impressed by the presentation, but what the hell - a job is a job.

Alan was a bit of a ladies' man. A short, fair-haired, typically cheeky Liverpool lad, who could charm the knickers off a nun. He had been an enthusiastic member of 4 Para until the Government started on its first rounds of defence cuts, and he saw the writing on the wall. Until that moment he had been prepared to volunteer for an S-type engagement attached to one of the regular para battalions in Northern Ireland. Realizing that was not going to happen and thirsting for the adventure the Parachute Regiment had promised him, he looked around for an alternative. Becoming a mercenary seemed like the right thing to do, so he jumped on the first plane out of Liverpool's John Lennon International Airport and flew off to Africa. Armed with a list of dodgy companies hiring former soldiers, he first joined a civilian security company and gradually fought his way through various skirmishes from one side of the African continent to the other. Things started to quieten down, so jumping on yet another plane he got himself caught up in the war in Yugoslavia. Despite being involved in a few nasty incidents he managed to get through that conflict too, and make it back home to Liverpool. He knew a few people running security firms and through them was able to get some door work. Over the next couple of years he did the rounds of the close protection circuit, on one occasion working for the Barclay twins in the Channel Islands. Finally he ended up working for his brother as a doorman on the Liverpool club scene. Like me he hated being a civilian, and like me he missed the excitement of surviving in a hostile environment.

We first met while working together on one or two security jobs, and soon discovered that we shared a hobby - parachuting - and that we both belonged to Pathfinder, a veteran paratroopers' parachute club. Apart from the parachuting, it was a good place to compare notes about security and civilian defence jobs around the world. The club attracted former paratroopers and Special Forces soldiers. Many had their ear to the ground and passed on anything they heard about interesting jobs in interesting places. Alan and I had become firm friends, but although we'd swapped information on potential security work in the past, neither of us had realised the other was applying to join this firm. It came as no big surprise, though. In this type of work it's a small world and you keep bumping into the same people.

John had a similar story. Slightly bigger than Alan, dark-haired with a weathered complexion, he was also more matter-of-fact and serious. He had first joined the British Army as a combat medic and served with distinction in Northern Ireland. Several years into his unblemished career, a serious problem developed at home and John had applied for compassionate leave. Now, any self-respecting commanding officer would have granted compassionate leave, as no soldier with home problems is a happy soldier. Not this one, though: he decided that he needed John for an upcoming exercise, and as far as he was concerned John's family could sort out their own problems.

This was the wrong decision. Definitely not good man management. After jumping over the OC's desk and punching him to the floor, John was dragged off by the Chief Clerk and Squadron Sergeant Major, thrown into the unit jail, put under close arrest, and charged. A short time in the glass house at Her Majesty's pleasure was followed by a military discharge. His discharge book read, "Services no longer required."

At his court martial it was considered that his OC had acted unfairly. In the circumstances they could understand John's frame of mind, given the extreme pressure he was under because of his problems at home. However they could not condone striking a superior officer, and so he had served a minimum sentence and was subsequently discharged. His papers didn't read "Dishonourable Discharge," as in the court's opinion there were mitigating circumstances. "Services no longer required" was still considered an honourable discharge by British Army standards. To put it politely and given the situation in which he'd found himself, he didn't give a fuck.

John was still a soldier at heart, though, and had followed a similar path to Alan's. He ended up on the front line in Bosnia on the opposite side to Alan, working as a medic. Like Alan he had been in some of the heaviest fighting, and at first he had played by the book. His Kevlar helmet bore the Red Cross identifying him as a medic, and he wore a medic's armband. On several occasions the enemy decided that this was too good an opportunity to miss and used his distinctive medic markings as aiming points. After these near misses John developed sense of humour failure. Picking up a discarded AK-47 assault rifle, he tossed away his armband, fought with his militia unit and then tended the wounded after the battle. Many a time, he even found himself treating the very soldiers he had just helped shoot.

I first met John when I was preparing to leave the army and we both attended the same close protection course with Excel Security. I was entitled to over £10,000 from the army for resettlement training. This was to be used for a demob course to help me gain the qualifications I needed for my new career. I had completed twenty-two years of service, and my last few years had been with 63 Parachute Squadron, Royal Corps of Transport. I had all my driving licences and I knew I could easily walk into a driving job. It was a case of use it or lose it. I begrudged the army having that money, so I decided to let them spend it on something I could use as a fallback job.

Excel was not stupid. It was a one-week, fully residential course which came to exactly the full resettlement entitlement due to the soldier, down to the last penny. It was run by retired service personnel. Why wasn't I surprised? The course itself was a good one for the average civilian. It was more of a selection course than a course of instruction, and tended to weed out the faint of heart and the idle, muscle-bound doormen pretty quickly. Many of the latter thought they could just use brawn to achieve results. By the end of the second day that had whittled down the number on the course by a third. This saved a lot of money for Excel, as there were no refunds for voluntary failures, and it also gave them more time to concentrate on the serious customer.

Most of the instructors were good at their job, except for an ex-marine called Andy. He was a bit of a muscle buster who really fancied himself and was something of a motor-mouth too. He talked a lot about action, but never quite got around to telling anyone who he'd served with, or what action he had seen himself. The civilians on the course listened to his every word, whereas the military personnel let it go in one ear and out the other. He wasn't hurting anyone and it sounded good for the company.

My own most vivid memory of the course concerns Peter Consterdine, of *Martial Arts Magazine* fame. He came in one day as a guest instructor to teach a few techniques of hand-to-hand combat. One of his demonstrations was of an up-close and personal flat-handed punch. I was the unfortunate guinea pig in the demonstration. Peter gave me six polystyrene floats to hold to my chest as protection and told me to brace myself. This I did by stepping back with one leg and leaning into the punch. I distinctly remember him smiling. I didn't see his hands move, but the next thing I was aware of was making contact with the wall about five feet behind me and sliding down in a heap. For the first few seconds I couldn't get my breath. God, my chest hurt! Peter bent over me, genuinely concerned. "Are you Ok?" he asked. "I didn't mean to hit you that hard. I'm sorry." Not half as sorry as I was at that moment! To loud applause from the rest of the class, I got to my feet and pulled up my T-shirt. I could see a perfect red hand print forming on the surface of my skin. I decided at that moment to concentrate on improving my shooting skills and never let anyone get close enough to hit me that hard again; I also decided never to piss off this particular instructor!

A couple of days into the course found us on the pistol range at Minsterley Ranges near Hereford, run by the famous Mitch of SAS fame. John and I found ourselves paired up on many of the exercises we underwent, and got on well. The practice was a straight forward pistol shoot with Czechoslovakian-made 9mm CZs. John, I and four others made up the detail on the firing point. And then came the mistake. I didn't catch what it was, but John had made it. It couldn't have been anything too serious, as at that point we had only obeyed the orders to load and make ready. All weapons were facing down the range and in a safe condition.

Andy was one of the safety coaches on the range, standing immediately behind John and me. He went ballistic. His face was just inches away from the back of John's neck, and foam and saliva from his ranting covered the back of John's collar. Being careful to keep my weapon pointing down the range, I turned my head to the left to take in the scene. I could see the muscles in John's face twitch. A red mist had come down as he turned round, bringing his pistol to bear on Andy.

To this day I firmly believe John was going to shoot him. As he turned, I reached across with my left hand and held the action of his automatic pistol in a death grip. This successfully prevented John from firing the weapon; he glanced at me and then fixed Andy with an icy stare. "He's not worth it." I said. The two men were eye to eye and I saw Andy gulp. Something in John's expression told Andy he was in a world of shit. It had gone deathly quiet on the range and you could have heard a pin drop. I'm sure more than one man secretly hoped John would pull the trigger. Suddenly he relaxed and turned back to point his weapon safely down the range. Not a word had been said between the pair, but John had made his point. As he turned, I released my grip. My knuckles were white and my hand ached from the exertion. Andy, now visibly shaken, turned and stormed off the range without saying another word, and a different instructor took his place. The shoot then went ahead with no further mishap.

That evening I returned from dinner to find John packing his kit. He had no hope of passing the course because the other instructors would go out of their way to fail him. I knew that and so did he, and he wasn't prepared to give them that satisfaction. We swapped addresses and promised to keep in touch. If one of us got the word on a job, he would let the other know. That's how these things work - it's jungle drums. I watched John shoulder his Bergen and walk down the drive towards the waiting taxi at the main gate. It was Excel's loss.

The course started again in the classroom the following day. John's name and the incident on the range were never mentioned again, although everyone was aware of how quiet Andy had become. Maybe he had learnt a valuable lesson. John and I kept our promise to each other, though, and we worked together on many occasions afterwards. He always struck me as level headed, with good business sense. He was a good soldier, and I considered him wasted as a medic.

\*\*\*

So here we were at Armor Group's presentation, passing the time with small talk and waiting for our turn to be interviewed. John was called first. He walked into the interview room and the door shut behind him. After about fifteen minutes he emerged with a big grin on his face. "I got the job as team medic. That'll do for me!" he said. He'd been told he would be escorting convoys. The supply convoys in Iraq were getting hit daily, and were suffering a lot of casualties. They needed good medics and I had no doubt that in John they would be getting a good one. He was going to have to run to catch his train, so he wished me and Alan luck and told me to phone to let him know how we got on. "It's a piece of piss, Mate! You'll walk it," he said as he left. I was beginning to feel more confident. It wasn't as if I was young and foolhardy; I was a mature older soldier with a ton of experience, so why would I *not* be given a job?

While I waited my turn I got to talk to some of the other hopefuls. The majority were Territorial Army soldiers, similar to United States Reservists, and most were senior Non Commissioned Officers. Most had not seen regular service, although for today's Territorials that is not considered the norm. They were all keen as mustard but personally I didn't think many of them had much of a chance. This work called for experienced combat soldiers, and I was feeling confident: I had definitely seen a lot of combat. "Don't count your chickens before they hatch!" my dad always told me, and I wish now I had listened more to his advice.

Alan was called for his interview next. He told me later that he thought things had gone well, and he had been promised a PSD (Personal Security Detail) job. He had shaken hands with Nick, who told him he would give him more details over the phone in a couple of days. As he rushed off to get a train back to Liverpool he made me promise to call him on his mobile the moment I got out of the interview. With any luck we would be on the same team.

Then it was my turn, and I entered the interview room. One of the women, whose name I later learnt was Caroline, was already at a desk, talking to another hopeful, and I had drawn our friend Nick, who was sitting at a small polished table of light wood. Without looking up, he motioned for me to take the chair opposite. Stacked on the table was a large pile of completed application forms. I was obviously supposed to feel I was being picked from a cast of thousands. He checked my name off his list and then, without looking at my CV on the desk in front of him, he asked me about my time in the service. He outlined some of the work that was supposedly available, mentioning at intervals that I was the oldest applicant there.

After he had stressed this more than once I began to feel uneasy. I was in good shape for my age and had kept my skills up to date as a guest instructor on courses run by the WASF (World Wide Association of Special Forces), of which Alan was the Secretary. I had also kept my hand in as a Regimental Weapons Instructor with the British Army's Reserve Forces. My track record should have spoken for itself. Nick waffled on about the contracts they had. They were mostly convoy escorts, with a few teaching jobs. He stated that he could not see me carrying out convoy escort duties because of my age, but he thought I could be invaluable teaching Iraqi policemen how to drive and use small arms. If he had bothered to read my CV, which he obviously had not, he would have seen that I had transferred from the Parachute Regiment to 47 Air Dispatch Squadron, Royal Corps of Transport, and on from there to various other RCT units. Convoys were my bread and butter - every bloody aspect of them from carrying the loads, to anti-ambush drills. I was a driver maintenance instructor: I could teach a soldier to drive and maintain his truck, and how to recover it. I was a Warminster-trained weapons instructor: I had been trained to take a civilian off the streets and turn him into a killing machine, and now here was this jumped-up, part-time bootneck more worried about my age than anything else.

I was mad as hell and struggled not to show it. However, a job is a job and if teaching Iraqis was the only thing on the table, then I would take it. I bit my tongue and nodded my head in agreement with his suggestion. Nick smiled and said I had made the right choice. However, the teaching contract was not yet in place and he would be finalizing the small print in a few days. Would I mind waiting and he would phone me at home with the details? We shook hands on the deal and he welcomed me to the company. As I turned to walk out the door, he handed me his business card, but I still had a bad feeling about this.

A short while later on my way to the tube station I called John and Alan in turn on their mobiles and voiced my concerns. They both reckoned I was worrying over nothing, but a few days later my fears were justified when a letter arrived in the morning post. It was from Armor Group and I just knew it was not going to be good news. I tore open the letter and quickly scanned the single page. "Dear Sir, Thank you for attending … blah, blah … do not have a place for you in our organization … blah, blah … wish you luck in your future endeavours." No explanation. It was not even signed by Nick, but by the Human Resources Department. It was about as final as you can get.

Bastards! They had given me the bum's rush and I was not happy about it. I sat at my dining-room table, brooding. Luckily the family was out at work so I just fumed in silence. Then I remembered Nick's business card, his big mistake. It was not going to get me a job, but I might be able to find out why I had been rejected. I suspected it was to do with my age, but I still couldn't understand why someone with my qualifications had been turned down and TA soldiers with very little experience had been taken on.

The phone rang three times. "Hi, Nick here! Can I help you?" came the cheerful voice at the other end, and I reminded him politely who I was. He seemed briefly nonplussed, and then stammered, "I'm in a meeting at the moment. I can't talk." I told him not to hang up, as I would just keep ringing him. I wanted an answer *now*. Why had he as good as promised me a job when he clearly had no intention of employing me? "The police job is still being negotiated. You're pencilled in for it. I don't know when it will be finalised." I told him about the contents of the letter and he tried to assure me it was a mistake; the letter should not have been sent. I hung up.

My next call was to the Human Resources lady whose telephone number was at the top of the page. I informed her pleasantly who I was, but omitted to tell her I had already been in touch with her boss. "I'm awfully sorry," she said, "but it's your age." She lowered her voice as if to hide what she was saying from others around her. "I'm afraid the company doesn't hire anyone over fifty, otherwise, they have to pay extra insurance premiums." I thanked her for her honesty and asked her to pass on to her boss that I thought he was a lying turd and that I hoped to meet him in Iraq one day soon. I hung up.

A few days later John phoned to say he had received his plane ticket. His job didn't start until the 1st of February, but at least he had a definite date and could plan ahead. His job was confirmed, but he wasn't happy with the way I had been treated. I told him not to worry, shit happens, but if this was how they worked he'd be wise not to trust the company. Shortly after, Alan rang to tell me that he'd been sent the same sort of letter as mine, with no explanation of why he had been rejected. Maybe Nick just didn't like paras.

\*\*\*

Two of my American Military friends, Rob K and Dave S, had kept me up to date with information on potential security work. One name, 'Tom', had cropped up a couple of times so I decided to email the guy. Tom was a retired U.S. Army senior NCO who had been doing this kind of security work for a number of years. He was on a subcontracted job from an American firm I had never heard of, Blackwater. From the outset, I never received anything but honest answers from this guy. He gave me no bullshit or sob stories.

His best bit of advice was to hang in there and not to give up. Contracts were coming up for renewal and nothing would be happening until January at the earliest. If any firm told me different, it was crap. Something about Tom's honesty and positive attitude got to me, and I warmed to the guy. His advice was to get a civilian job for the time being and keep in touch. He promised to contact me the moment he had any news. I believed him.

Christmas was coming and bills had to be paid, so I reluctantly went back to driving trucks for a living. Tom mailed me with updates and occasional pleasantries, but things were moving slowly even for him. In the meantime I was receiving mail from the other firms I had contacted. "Thank you for applying. We now have you on our books." This usually meant they were bidding for a contract and just wanted as many names on their books as they could get, to impress the potential client. It was not a guarantee of work. Tom had told me the firm he was working for had bid for a big contract in November and would have an answer by January. It seemed a long way off, but I knew these things took time. The pay for this type of work was good, and there was no way I could earn that kind of money as a lorry driver, so it was worth waiting for.

My wife was justifiably scared for me. I tried to explain that I had done this kind of work as a soldier for less money and that the reward was worth the risk. She was not convinced, but knew I would be able to pay the bills, get rid of my overdraft and take a big chunk off the mortgage. My wife deserved something better than living from hand to mouth. I had dragged her round the world as the wife of a paratrooper and we'd had some really shit postings and grotty married quarters. I wanted to give her a better, easier life. If that meant risking my neck, then so be it.

Christmas came and went and there was still nothing definite. Suddenly out of the blue an email arrived from a bloke called Cory, who introduced himself as a mate of Tom's working out of the same company. "Hi Roy, Tom put me onto you. Are you still interested in our type of work?" Bloody right I was! I typed the reply so quickly I swear there were friction burns on my keyboard. "OK," came the reply. "Your plane ticket is on its way. You are to report to our training facility in Moyock by the 10th of February. Look forward to meeting you." I was in a bit of a daze. After months of crap and being lied to by company reps I had finally got something positive. Mind you I had been told by a mate not to believe a word of it until I felt the camel shit oozing between to toe straps of my sandals. Something pretty deep and philosophical for a former para!

When I emailed Tom in Iraq he was as surprised as I'd been. He wasn't aware yet that things had progressed that far, and guessed that the major contract must have been finalised early. I was the first British National they would put through the American vetting system. They would be using me to test it out and see what problems arose, and with the know-how gleaned they hoped to be able to speed up the process and take on more foreign nationals. The company wanted to hire British SAS, paras and marines. Our troops were used to urban warfare after so many years in Northern Ireland, and would be an asset to their organization. I would be the first of many. In their own words, I was their 'Crash Test Dummy'. Tom wished me luck and said he might be in the States at the same time as me, and would look me up. I was glad I'd got the job, but not sure I liked the job description: 'Crash Test Dummy?' Mind you, I had been called a lot worse. I was on my way at last. I resigned from my job with the Driver Hire driving agency and spent the next few days getting my affairs in order. If anything happened to me, I needed to know my wife would be okay. I had to make sure everything would run smoothly for my family while I was away, as I didn't know when I would be able to contact them next. Within a couple of days Blackwater was as good as their word, and the airline ticket duly arrived. Carol drove me to Heathrow with my youngest son, Simon. It was a long quiet drive; neither of us felt like saying much. Naturally she didn't want me to go, but wouldn't dream of trying to talk me out of it.

We said an emotional goodbye in the terminal and I went on into the departure lounge. I hated goodbyes: we had been through more than our fair share in my army career and they never got easier. That familiar knot in the stomach suddenly took hold, and I felt choked. I wanted to hurry through to Departures as soon as I could, but at the same time I hated leaving my wife and family like this. Each time we knew there was a good chance I wouldn't make it back. Why would any woman marry a paratrooper, knowing we are always in the worst trouble spots our country can find, and that there is always a real chance we could be killed? Carol was a wife in a million. She had stuck with me through thick and thin, and after all these years she was still looking out for me. Unfortunately I had not always made it easy for her. I had tried to make this departure as painless as possible but it was still hurting, and I only hoped Carol would be okay.

Once fully boarded by its mixture of tourists and Americans going home, the British Airways flight for New York took off on time. A mood of finality settled over me. I'd made the decision to accept this job for better or worse, and now it was up to me to make the best of it and try to live long enough to collect my wages. Several hours, two feature films and a couple of inflight meals later, we landed in New York. Through the cabin window I could see snow drifts around the airport and I wished I had brought a heavier coat. What happened to sunny America! There was no extra stress involved, as Blackwater had once again done their homework and I knew my connecting flight was to leave in forty-five minutes. Clearing Customs, getting my bag, walking through the terminal, and the coach ride to the small jet airliner took all of that. I produced my ticket for the flight attendant to check, and no sooner had I taken my seat than the aircraft was taxing down the perimeter track towards the runway. Just as suddenly the pilot opened the throttle, the aircraft hurtled down the runway and we were airborne, winging our way through the night sky towards my final destination, Apache Security's training camp. The lights in the cabin were dimmed so I settled back in the seat and shut my eyes, listening to the steady drone of the engines until I finally nodded off into oblivion.

It was still early evening when the aircraft touched down. I'd had time to cat-nap on the flight but it was a restless sleep because of all the questions buzzing around in my head. What was I letting myself in for? How legal was what I was doing? How good was the company I was working for? I had suddenly realised how little I knew. Oh, well! In for a penny, in for a pound, as the saying goes. It was too late to think about turning back now.

As soon as I entered the airport building I could see its naval connections. A large portrait of U.S.S. Norfolk proudly dominated one wall of the terminal lounge and young ratings in uniformed blues, their kitbags stacked in neat piles, sat around waiting for their rides back to the base. According to my joining instructions I was supposed to meet six other blokes, all arriving at different times. I was next to last on the list of names attached. The others would already be waiting for me, and together we would go to the hotel where Blackwater had booked rooms for us. Each group also had a hire vehicle allocated to it, to be picked up from one of the many hire firms at the airport. I hoped someone else had a driving licence, as I was still tired and jet lagged and not looking forward to driving at night on the 'wrong' side of the road in a strange country while looking for a strange hotel.

Walking over to Vehicle Reservations, I asked if my group had contacted them. The clerk behind the desk confirmed they had, but there'd been a change of plan. The others had arrived early and gone ahead with another group; I was to wait for two latecomers whose internal flights had been delayed. I was also asked to sign for a set of keys, and then the helpful booking clerk led me through a side door to the car park. I had been handed the keys to a Suburban SUV without a clue as to what the vehicle looked like, or how it handled. The clerk pointed to a large, gleaming black vehicle the size of a small bus. To make matters worse, it was an automatic, and I hadn't driven an automatic for years. There I was jetlagged, in charge of a very expensive rented car in a strange country at night, and with only a dubious looking tourist map to help me find my way to an unknown hotel in a strange town. This was not a good start! All I wanted was a bed and some sleep.

I went back to the airport lounge to wait for the other blokes. I tried to study the wall map showing the local area and tourist attractions, but my eyes were doing their best to close and I was having trouble concentrating. Luckily, it wasn't long before one of the late arrivals flew in. He was a short, stocky black guy and, as it turned out, a retired U.S. Marine. We shook hands, he introduced himself as Ben, and yes - he had a driving licence! I threw him the keys and breathed a sigh of relief: I'd got out of that one nicely. We packed our gear into the vehicle and sat back to await the last man. I had now been at the airport for nearly three hours and he still hadn't shown up. We checked with the flight desk and discovered that his aircraft had landed, but there was no sign of him. It was about half an hour before the arrival of the next internal flight he might be on. We gave it all of that and some more, and then decided to call the emergency number we had been given. There was no reply. It seemed to be switched off and a recorded message asked us to try later. This was not turning out as well as I had expected. It looked like the last man had changed his mind, so we decided enough was enough and called it a night.

With Ben at the wheel, we negotiated the exit ramp of the airport car park and drove down the highway towards the hotel where we were to stay. We got there in no time at all, thanks to Ben. This was a seaside town and a busy resort at the height of the Season, but now there was hardly anyone around and it was cold, wet and windy as we turned into the main drag leading to the hotel. In summer the place would be teeming with life, but on this winter's night it was a ghost town. Neon lights advertised the pleasures and wares that could be sampled inside the various establishments, but shutters on the windows told us these were false promises. 'Come back when the sun is shining and the tourists are here!' they seemed to say, with one or two signs swinging precariously in the wind, as if threatening to fall on any unwary pedestrian. We passed many expensive and luxurious looking hotels that were obviously full in summer but now only partially occupied by salesmen and suchlike, and then we spotted ours. We stopped at the lights for a few seconds and I noticed movement in the shadows ahead. A drunk staggered out of the dark and across the road, singing to himself. Oh well, there must be some entertainment around here; maybe we would get the chance to sample it. The lights changed and our SUV bumped over the ramp and into the sheltered car park of the hotel. We had arrived at our destination and all I wanted was a bed.

**While I was busy getting myself in country, other contractors working in support of the Coalition Forces were already dying in Iraq, and in ever increasing numbers.**

*Iraq Coalition Casualties: PSD, Convoy, and Site Security. JAN. 2004*

| Date | Name | Nationality | Incident |
|------|------|-------------|----------|
| 05/01/2004 | Richard Flynn | Canadian | Killed by IED |
| 06/01/2004 | Unknown | French | Killed by small arms fire in Fallujah |
| 14/01/2004 | Unknown | Unknown | Convoy attack in Tikrit |
| 14/01/2004 | Unknown | Unknown | Convoy attack in Tikrit |
| 25/01/2004 | Habibur Rehman | Pakistani | Convoy attack in Tikrit |
| 26/01/2004 | Arthur Linderman Jr | American | Convoy attack near Tikrit |
| 31/01/2004 | Francois Strydom | South African | Killed by a suicide car bomb in Baghdad. Francois was a PSD Bodyguard working for Erinys Security Consulting, protecting the Iraqi Labour Minister, Mr. Sami Azara al-Mujun. |

# Chapter 2

## Boot Camp Revisited

I had been put in a quiet, spacious double room by my-self; Ben was sharing with another team member. The bed was comfortable, and there was a coffee-making kit - as long as I had my coffee I could face anything. I had fallen asleep as soon as my head hit the pillow but now somewhere in the background of my mind my alarm clock was ringing, desperately trying to wake me from the sleep of the dead. I had set it for early: it wouldn't do to be late on my first day. I woke with a mouth tasting like the inside of a gorilla's armpit, wondering what the day was going to bring. I showered and shaved and hurried down to reception to meet the rest of the blokes.

There were about thirty of us milling around in the lobby, and some hurried introductions were made. I was useless at remembering names but I hoped I would get to know who was who as time went on. The hotel didn't have its own restaurant and one of the blokes asked what we would do for meals. Another of the recruits said not to worry; Blackwater would be sorting that out. I certainly hoped so, as I hadn't eaten since yesterday's in-flight meal and my stomach was beginning to think my throat was cut. The leader of our group was Julius, a very big guy whose call sign I would later find out was Shrek. He was a member of a PSD already working in Iraq and would be acting as an instructor on our course. He led us into the hotel car park where several Suburban SUVs sat waiting for us. We formed an eight-vehicle convoy as we bounced out of the covered hotel parking lot onto the road and headed for the freeway.

I was impressed. A lot of money had already been spent on hotels and rental cars, and we'd been told we would be reimbursed for any expenses, including gas and tollbooth payments. You'd have to fight most companies tooth and nail to get any expenses out of them. It was winter, and Blackwater would have been able to cut a deal with the hotel, but a place like that on the beach of a tourist area wouldn't come cheap even out of season. All the hire vehicles we had picked up from the airport would be used for training on the course, as well as transporting us on the 45-minute drive to and from the hotel every day. With Ben at the wheel, I sat back and relaxed as we sped down the freeway towards Blackwater's own training camp. We drove through the toll and off into a small, spread out farming community, passing through the town of Moyock and on into open country. We turned down a side road and about a mile further on passed through the electronic gates that guarded the entrance to Blackwater's ranch. Another three miles further and we came upon the main complex. These guys believed in maintaining their privacy. We had finally arrived at the headquarters of the world renowned Blackwater.

The place was a small township in its own right: 7000 acres of private military training area. To anyone who knows British Army training camps, it was Bulford and Tidworth rolled into one. Disney world for the SAS would be an even better description. It consisted of twenty-two individual target ranges and two killing houses, one of which was designed to be attacked by helicopter or by boat through the swamp to its rear. There were two 'unknown distance' target ranges for sniper training, and they had their own tin city of two dozen assorted houses and several streets, which enabled most scenarios to be played out. To one side was the hunting lodge, a deluxe, single floor wooden construction with two high-class lounges and the capacity to sleep sixty trainees in comfort. Next to this were the main headquarters complex and the cookhouse. On the other side of the complex were two dozen assorted cabins housing the stores, ammo bunkers, workshops and classrooms. It was a military camp in everything but name. I knew British regiments who would give their right arm for a training establishment half as good, and I was excited at the thought of using these facilities. We had nothing anywhere near as elaborate in the UK.

The vehicles parked up next to the main building and we debussed and followed Shrek down through the maze of cabins and huts to a long, single floor lecture room. The group of candidates assembled in one of the trailers, which was to serve as both teamroom and classroom. We had a total of 42 men of all ages, shapes, colours, and cap badges. This was the first large group of its kind that this security company was to deploy. As I was to find out, most of the hierarchy were former SEAL team members. The rest of the staff were retired Special Forces with a few police specialists retained for additional specialist subjects. For anything else that needed to be taught, qualified people would be brought in from the outside world. We were split into two groups, each with a designated senior instructor. After a pregnant pause of just a few minutes while all the instructors got their briefing for the rest of the day we started with a roll call and personal administration, followed by a whistle stop tour of the facilities. After filling in all the usual banking forms, next of kin forms, medical declarations and several other forms of a similar nature we began the six cents tour. We started with Blackwater's 'bread and butter', their ranges. These covered every conceivable type of shoot you could think of and which we would need to practice - falling plates; ETR (electrical target range); moving targets; CQB (close quarter battle) and FIBUA (fighting in built-up areas), plus a few more especially tailored for the Special Forces. The two 'killing houses' had an overhead gantry, so the instructors and your fellow team members could see what you were up to and could give you an 'End Ex' report at the end of the exercise. They would of course be merciless.

At the other end of the facility was the CQB village where FIBUA and CQB could be taught, as well as motorcade ambushes. It was an impressive construction, the size of a small rural village. Paint ball guns were used here to simulate actual hits. You don't get hit that often because you quickly learn to move fast and keep low, 'duck!' being the operative word. Even a paint ball hurts when you get hit, and no one wants that!

In the main complex there was a full military specification cook house, and we were told that all trainees were provided with three square meals a day. The ladies who prepared the meals took pride in their cooking and nothing was too much trouble for them. The food was good, healthy and freshly cooked on the premises. As a foreign national, I had a few early problems trying to identify some of the dishes, but in true airborne fashion I soon learned to survive.

Just before the tour had brought us full circle we were shown the company's own K9 section. As I was to find out later, these highly trained animals would be worth their weight in gold in Iraq.

Back in the classroom, each man was asked to stand up and say a few words about himself. The first thing I noticed was that no two people had exactly the same specialist qualifications. It was as if someone had handpicked this first group with as many different skills as possible to test which formula would work best in the field conditions for which we were heading. Apart from the one or two obvious arse-holes that you'll always get in a group of this kind, the majority were good blokes and I made a few new friends. I was the only British bloke there in fact, I was the only foreign national in the group. Cory was right; I was the "Crash Test Dummy." I had a lot to think about and so the drive back to the hotel was a quiet one. I went to bed early.

Day two was to be crunch day. No one had mentioned a test week but I had expected as much. Although I had not been told there was to be a selection process to survive, I had worked it out from all the PT (physical training) kit included on the list I'd been sent. It seemed to come as a surprise to some of the candidates, though, and there were a few worried looks. I was slightly nervous myself and I had good reason to be. I had neglected to inform the company that I'd broken my back parachuting eighteen months previously and this would be the first physical exercise I had performed since then. I had passed my GP's medical and he'd signed me off as fit because I told him I was about to do light security work. Okay! I stretched the truth a little because I knew it would have to be all or nothing. I wanted the work and needed the money and so I was going to give it my best shot.

To a certain extent I'd come prepared, having purchased a Neoprene sports back support and a big supply of good old 'soldier's friend' Ibuprofen tablets. I knew from experience that you could run through most pain after taking a couple of those little blighters, and the brace would help too. Just to be on the safe side, I swallowed four of the pills at breakfast. That was two too many but I thought, what the hell! In for a penny, in for a pound!

The PT test was the standard American military one, very similar to our own and graded by age groups. We would be on a U.S. Department of Defence contract, which required we be at the same physical standard as American soldiers, which seemed only fair to me. Men over fifty would have a slightly easier time on pull-ups and sit-ups, but it was still going to hurt. If we had the timed run first and then the PT test, I reckoned I was in with a chance - and it would give the painkillers time to kick in.

Cory was to be our instructor for this phase. He was a retired Marine Corps NCO. Short, muscular, and a no-nonsense type of guy, he had been through a lot of shit in some nasty places and was a very experienced operator. He gathered the group together and outlined the programme. Then he split us into age groups. There were seven of us in my age bracket, so at least I was not the only 'older' soldier there. As it turned out, we were scheduled to complete the PT test first. Shit! I would have preferred the run, and I was convinced I was going to struggle. I discreetly tightened the Neoprene sports brace to give as much support as possible to my weakened back muscles, and I had worn a baggy t-shirt to try to hide the fact that I was wearing it. I wasn't doing anything wrong because my doctor had signed me as fit. I was just taking precautions, I told myself.

The first test was to drag a human-sized dummy over a 50-metre course. It weighed about the same as the average adult. All the limbs were jointed, which meant it would be limp like an unconscious human. This made it extremely hard to pick up, just like the real 'dead weight'. The best way to complete this task was to grasp the dummy under the armpits, lock your hands together around its waist, straighten your back and then drag it backwards for the distance. I watched one or two of the others struggle with different methods before it was my turn. I only hoped my injured back would hold out.

I bent my knees, grasped the dummy under the arms and locked my hands tight. Gritting my teeth, I straightened my back. The tablets were working and I was able to lean back and support the weight. The angle was good and as soon as I was given the word, I stepped back and got a rhythm going. The ground was flat with no obstructions and so all I had to do was keep moving. "Stop! Well done!" Cory said, and that part was over almost as soon as it had begun. So far, so good! I then had to complete as many sit-ups, push-ups and pull-ups as I could for one-minute durations. It was just a case of dig in and go for it. I had always been weak on upper arm exercises and I didn't do too well on the pull-ups, but luckily I wasn't the only one, so I didn't stick out like a sore thumb and I managed a pretty good score on the rest of the exercises.

Next came the run, which was over a mile and a half of road. Cory waited until we were all ready and then started his stopwatch. "Go!" I started off at a steady pace but was soon left behind by the younger, faster runners. It was a bit embarrassing really, when you consider how much I used to enjoy a good cross-country run. There were several runners behind me, though, and I was determined they were going to stay there. I most definitely was not going to be the last one in.

I soon started to sweat badly. I think maybe my body was trying to sweat out all the extra medication I'd taken. Every step onto the concrete road surface hurt, as if the cushioning between my spinal vertebrae was non-existent, and I felt every thump of my training shoes on the iron-hard ground. As the pain became ever more excruciating I could feel my eyes watering and the tears welling up, and my breathing was rapid and painful as I sucked in lungsful of air. About a third of the way round the course the younger group up front developed stragglers. Some of them had been over confident and had started too fast. I was overtaken by one or two of the guys behind me, but I could tell by the way they were running that they wouldn't last. Feeling much more confident now in myself and in my ability to finish the run, I put my head down and dug in.

By the half-way point I had managed to ignore most of the pain in my back and switch off, something we'd been trained to do in the Paras: forget the other runners; just dig in for the end; mind over matter; no pain no gain. I was opening up my lead on the guys behind me and gaining on a couple of those in front. I knew I wouldn't be able to catch them, but if I could just gain a bit of ground I could improve my time. After all, we were not really competing against each other, just trying to beat the clock. I was sweating like a pig with the exertion but the end was in sight. I could see Cory looking at his watch while another staff member took the runners' names and timings. A few were doing warm down exercises, one or two just lay on the grass, and at least one was throwing up in the bushes. The last couple of hundred yards I really pushed and finished well. Cory smiled and said "Well done!" as I passed him, but by then I'd lost interest in everything except trying to stand up and breathe. Blimey, that hurt! I had really let my fitness slip and I knew it wasn't just down to my injury. I'd become lazy and would have to do something about it if I wanted to succeed in this tough new environment.

Cory came up behind me and said, "Good job! You worked hard for that," and patted me on the back, his hand contacting the sports brace I thought I had hidden. I hesitated and then thought honesty was the best policy under the circumstances.

"I suppose I'd better come clean about this," I said reluctantly. Cory gave me a stare as I started to explain. "It's a recent parachuting injury that's still giving me a bit of trouble."

He just smiled and held up his hand to stop me before I dug a hole for myself. There were different ways to earn respect, he said, and I had earned his for the effort I'd just put in. I had passed fair and square - no problem! I didn't know it then, but Cory later reported me to the bosses, as he was duty bound to, but told them I was doing okay, and it was worth keeping me in the program. On the strength of his recommendation they all agreed, but the instructors were told to keep a watchful eye on me over the next few days to see if my injury would stop me from doing the job. Thanks to my painkillers I was able to carry on normally, and I guess I must have impressed them.

We dried ourselves down in the trailer, which now stank of sweaty bodies and socks, a familiar smell to us all. Unfortunately we were going to have to put up with it. We weren't paying guests, and therefore not allowed to use the showers in the lodge. We would just have to wait till we got back to the hotel. As we were changing back into our day clothes a couple of the recruits who had come in last were taken outside by a member of staff and didn't re-join us. This was getting like P Company, the Parachute Selection course you have to go through to become British Paratroopers. In the event, our numbers would be whittled down each day until the instructors were left with the best of the bunch, or at least the survivors.

Another instructor came in and asked us to take our seats. He handed out more paperwork for us to read and we filled in more forms, this time requesting information for passport renewals and visas. All the over-forties would be having an electrocardiogram, something that was required by the insurance company. This was a first for me and I wondered how I would fare. Those of us who had been called forward for this procedure assembled in another trailer that served as the company's Medical Centre, with two doctors and a nurse in attendance. When it was my turn, the nurse asked me to take my shirt off and lie on a couch. She heated a few contacts and attached them to my chest and head, and I was wired up to the monitor and told to relax for a few minutes. I should have brought a book to read. After a short while, the nurse removed the pads and said I could put my shirt back on. As I did so, the doctor was looking at the readout.

"How did I do, Doc?" I asked, genuinely interested.

"No problems, perfectly normal." Now that was a first for me. Normal!

Two of the older guys had not done so well on the ECG. One was found to have an irregular heart beat and the other suffered from high blood pressure. Both were told that for their own good they could not continue with the training. You could see the disappointment in their faces. They were good soldiers, but their bodies and age had let them down, and they were sent home that evening: I considered myself lucky. Our group was getting smaller by the minute now, and at this rate

Blackwater would soon not have enough bodies for a team, but I guessed they knew what they were doing.

On the company staff list Blackwater had a psychiatrist whose door was always open if you had any 'issues'. I thought this was a waste of money: we all had to have a screw loose to be here! One afternoon one of the younger ex-SEAL team members asked for a consultation. As we heard through the grape vine afterwards, he told our lady psychiatrist that he was having a recurring nightmare in which he could see all the team getting killed. I had a recurring dream where I won the lottery, but it had never happened to me. He was sent home immediately. We couldn't figure out what had possessed him to tell her that, even if it was true. Maybe he'd had second thoughts about the line of work he was about to let himself in for, and wanted to get out without losing face - who knows! Maybe he was the sensible one.

Shrek had a discreet word with a few of us. "Ok, Guys! The selection process is over. Now we're gonna train you up the way we want you to do things. No one else gets sent home unless they're stupid or just plain unlucky."

After a light lunch we reported to the armoury to be issued with our AR-14 Bushmaster rifles and Glock 17 pistols. The rifle would be altered to fit our needs. The company used a lot of equipment made by Blackhawk Industries, one of the world's leading manufacturers of law enforcement and military specialist equipment. It therefore followed that we would be issued with the best the budget would cover; after all, we would become a walking advertisement for them so everything had to be on the ball. We were shown how to remove the old shaped Armalite hand guard and replace it with a rail system. This in turn would allow us to fit all sorts of extra equipment to our weapons, and most of the rifles were fitted with EOtech sights. Everyone was issued with night vision goggles or scopes which could be fitted on the rifle or worn on a headband, whichever you felt the most comfortable with. A lower pistol grip and Sure-Fire flashlight were added for good measure.

Somewhere in the company it had already been decided who was earmarked for which jobs. Many of the ex-army guys were pissed off that all the SF (Special Forces) and SEAL team members had already been selected for PSD duties, while the rest of us got the scraps. I understood why they had done it but I still wasn't happy with it. The company was run by retired SEAL Team members and it was understandable they would favour guys from their own system. I was earmarked for site security, not the most glamorous job but for the money I was being paid I could grin and bear it. Many of the young SEALs had never seen a shot fired in anger, so in my book they were an unknown quantity. As it turned out, the site teams were to see more action than the PSD.

As we got used to working in our groups the days were filled with first aid lessons, weapons handling lessons and range work. We fired from windows and doors. We fired prone, kneeling, standing and sitting. We fired at targets from every conceivable angle, static and moving. To cap it all, we were already on the payroll and being paid $100 a day, with food, lodging and transport thrown in. I was getting paid to enjoy myself, and I was.

Our one and only night familiarisation shoot was from the building fronts on Range 8. These were two-story facades like something you might find on a film set. They had a staircase in the middle and then stairs left and right. A shooter could practice firing from upstairs or down, and from the doors or windows. Working in firing teams, you could cover each other while other shooters ran the 50 metres to the second house. This range had everything from falling plates to moving targets, and all had to be neutralised to complete the exercise. The only illumination was provided by hand-thrown flares, and we had three magazines of rifle ammo and three magazines of pistol ammunition. It was up to the shooter which weapon he used first, but both weapons were to be utilised until all the ammunition was spent.

We arrived on the range just before dark, having had our evening meal earlier, and began preparation for battle by cleaning and lightly oiling our weapons. Then as darkness was falling, one of the other instructors came rushing up to tell us there was a cock-up with the range bookings and we would need to wrap up within the hour. The senior instructor swore out loud. He had worked hard on this evening's time table and now it was well and truly fucked. He thought for a moment, and then ordered the entire group to take up firing positions in the two building fronts. He tossed several hand flares out onto the range to illuminate the targets and gave the order to fire. Everyone opened up at the same time on everything illuminated to our front. Forty shooters took 30 minutes to take out every target on the range and totally expend all their ammunition. The noise was deafening and the local civilians must have thought they were in the middle of a terrorist attack. It was an exhilarating shoot, though, and I definitely got a buzz. I felt my heartbeat quicken and I knew I had a big grin on my face. It was the nearest the new boys could get to the feel of a real fire fight, and I don't know about them, but I had enjoyed the exercise - even if it was a bit short.

We finished earlier than had been expected, and the range was cleared. Someone suggested going for a beer. Now that sounded like a good idea! Every available vehicle was pressed into service, and the entire course and a few instructors drove to the row of pubs back at the beach front. We all hustled into the bar opposite the hotel we were staying in, as that way we wouldn't have so far to crawl back to our beds. Preparation and Planning Prevents Piss Poor Performance as my old Sergeant used to say. 'Always remember the six P's!' The young barmaid didn't bat an eyelid as we all piled into what had been her quiet bar; the orders for beer and food flew thick and fast, but she and her cook just took it in their stride.

No one tore the arse out of the beer drinking. I suspected we were still being assessed, possibly to see who got on with whom within the group. Despite my initial reservations, it was turning out to be a pretty good night. All those present seemed to be getting on well together as they chatted about guns and equipment. It looked as if the powers that be had been good judges of character, and all the guys seemed to be of similar minds. One or two were trying a bit too hard to fit in. Hal and Mike were ex-Navy and had known each other in a previous posting. Hal was of Puerto Rican descent, about 25 years of age; Mike was Mexican and the older of the two by a couple of years. I had noticed during training that Mike was going out of his way to impress the instructors, but it was having the opposite effect and he was just making himself look stupid. Sometimes it pays just to be the 'grey man' and keep your head down. Some of the other blokes had already made comments about him, and he was getting noticed for all the wrong reasons. Mike and Hal were sitting at a table with me and two others. I'd ordered a shrimp platter and they thought it funny that I was now facing several pounds of the bloody things. I like shrimp, but didn't realise how large a 'large' portion was. They kindly volunteered to help me eat them and soon the table was covered in shrimp shells. Mike said there was another bar down the road where there was a break dance contest on; these were normally good for a laugh, he said. I looked around the crowded bar and decided it might be a good time to get a bit of fresh air, so we paid the bill and the three of us walked out into the Night.

It was cold outside and I pulled up the collar of my jacket against the evening chill. The other bar turned out to be a few hundred yards along the main street and was just as full and noisy as the one at the hotel; two very large doormen said, "Good evening, Gentlemen!" as we went in. This kind of place wasn't really my scene but I was out to get to know the guys in the team and so I was being sociable. I ordered three

Millers and carried them down to where Mike and Hal were watching the dancing. It was pretty noisy, but entertaining watching the competing dancers spin around on their heads and do things with their bodies that I am sure will come back to haunt them in later life. After a short while I noticed Mike had gone. "Hey Hal, where's Mike?" I asked.

Hal was preoccupied with a young lady who was body popping along the floor. He nodded towards the door. "He's gone to get some fresh air I think." I'd noticed Mike had been going pretty heavy on the Tequila - every beer we'd had he'd followed with a chaser; it was starting to affect his speech. I knew he was going to suffer in the morning, so I told Hal I was going to check on Mike, and pushed through the crowd towards the street.

Just ten feet outside I could see Mike was about to get into serious trouble. He was facing down two of the biggest bouncers I had ever seen, and I could hear him gobbing off even above the din from the club. So far he had managed to insult their mothers and most of their families and was attempting to force them both into a scrap. From where I stood, the bouncers were being pretty controlled but how long that would last was anybody's guess. If we got into a fight, we would be thrown off the team. If I walked away and was seen by one of the company staff, I would probably be accused of leaving a team mate behind. I was damned if I did and damned if I didn't.

It looked like it was all about to kick off, so I stepped in front of Mike and the doormen with my hands up to show I wasn't carrying anything that could be mistaken for a weapon. "Whoa! Hang on blokes! He's had a hard day and too much to drink. We don't want any trouble!"

A crowd was beginning to form and Hal had pushed his way through to stand beside me. The doormen were happy to see the end of the incident and advised us to take our pal home and put him to bed. Mike, on the other hand, now thought he had back-up and wanted to take on everyone there. I exchanged looks with Hal, apologised to the doormen, spun Mike around and grabbed him by the arms, and then between the two of us we frog marched him towards the hotel.

The fresh air and alcohol took their toll, and it was no problem getting him into his room and dropping him onto the bed, where he promptly passed out. We put him in the recovery position with a pillow behind him so he couldn't roll over during the night and choke in his own vomit. Hal said he'd check on him and make sure he got up in time to go to the ranch with the rest of us, so I grabbed a cup of black coffee from the machine in Reception and went to my room. I thought we were very lucky to have got away from that with no bloodshed. Despite their suits, those doormen looked a couple of hard bastards, and I had no doubt we'd have had a job getting Mike away from them had it all kicked off. Next morning Mike appeared looking decidedly the worse for wear, and wasn't saying much to anyone. He slept most of the way to the camp: I guess he needed it too! As I looked at his dishevelled appearance I made a mental note to keep Tequila on my 'Things Not to Touch with a Barge Pole' list. Now that we were familiar with the route it was taking less time to get there, and I was soon punching in the code numbers on the gate key-pad as usual. The gates swung smoothly open, I jumped back into the front passenger seat of the SUV and we swept through, with the gate shutting automatically behind the last vehicle. Today though, I wondered if there were going to be any repercussions from last night. I felt pretty sure we had stopped any problems before they started and I didn't remember any faces in the crowd from the course, so I thought we might be lucky and get away with it. Having come this bloody far, the last thing I wanted was to get 'binned off' the course. We would just have to wait and see.

Once inside the camp we quickly parked up and made a mad dash to get in the cookhouse queue, ready to help ourselves from the well stocked hotplates. Judging by the amount of food the Blackwater ladies provided, they must be used to cooking for an army! In the British Army it used to be a chargeable offence not to eat breakfast, and it was classed as Scale A parade: everyone had to attend. But if you were involved in the type of physical activities we were going to be put through, you really *needed* a good breakfast before starting the day's training. We would certainly be burning the calories off before the day was through.

I had just sat down to mine when I saw Cory beckoning me from the doorway. Reluctantly leaving my steaming plate of eggs, bacon and hash-browns I followed him through into the main office area. "I want to have a chat," he said seriously. I accompanied him into the reception area and sat down on one of the sofas opposite him. "Have a good night?" he asked. I could see immediately where this was going.

"Could have been better," I replied. "Could have been a lot worse!"

"I hear you did a good job of defusing the situation." I nodded sort of noncommittally and tried to leave it at that.

Then Cory asked me what I thought of Mike. I replied that I thought he was okay, and that last night had just been down to the effect of the drink on an empty stomach. "Funny," he said. "I thought he ate quite a lot in the bar earlier." I was running out of excuses. I couldn't remember seeing Cory in the bar but then there had been quite a few of the instructors in there and it was crowded.

"What do you think we should do with the guy?" he asked. I thought that an unfair question. I was not going to be responsible for getting another bloke sacked, and told him so. "OK, let's make it easier on you. If you were making an assessment on the basis of last night's antics, would you pass him?" I paused, trying to think of a way out of this. "OK, let's make easier still! Based on last night's performance would you feel safe with that guy watching your back in a fire fight? I want an honest answer."

I had to admit it. "No, I wouldn't trust him to watch my back."

Cory smiled. "Right answer! I just wanted to hear you say it. But don't worry - the decision's already been made. Just wanted to see how you'd handle it." Bastard! I thought.

I didn't feel like finishing my breakfast after that, so I just had a coffee in one of the plastic disposable cups and sipped it as I took a slow walk to the classroom. I didn't feel very good about the situation. As the others started to trickle in, Hal came over. "Guess they asked you the same questions," he said, and without waiting for an answer he went on. "It's his own fault. He never could hold his drink - it got him into trouble in the Navy a whole lot." I think we both realised at that moment that we would still have to watch out for each other in future. There was no telling how long they would continue to assess us.

Cory later told me that because Norfolk is a small town everyone knows everyone else. Both bouncers were ex-SEALs, despite their size, and had only held off ripping Mike apart because they'd been told he was from Blackwater. The whole thing had been witnessed by Cory and a few of the senior instructors, so Hal and I had been seen to do the right thing. We had been lucky, as Blackwater appeared to have eyes everywhere. Well, it was their home town after all.

The lessons that day were going to be mostly on self-defence, with or without a weapon. We were shepherded into one of the classrooms near the K9 compound and the first lesson was to be unarmed combat, so the room was totally devoid of furniture. We had been split into two groups because of the large numbers and placed in separate rooms: there were about 20 individuals in my class. Our instructor was a small, smartly dressed man in his late thirties with a shock of black curly hair. He struck me as being a bit effeminate but I knew better than to judge a book by its cover. He introduced himself and his assistant, who turned out to be his brother, although they looked completely different. The brother was a short, squat, muscular type, who looked well-suited to throwing troublemakers through the windows of pubs. Must be adopted, I thought to myself. They both ran Police courses in fighting, and had a number of qualifications in various unarmed combat techniques. Both were experts in street fighting, which as anyone will tell you is downright dirty. I was pleased I hadn't voiced my initial thoughts aloud: pissing off either of these two could have been painful.

It was to be a typical military-style course of instruction. EDIP - Explanation, Demonstration, Imitation, and Practice. The demonstrations were fast and furious, a blur to the naked eye. The brothers kept apologizing for being too quick, and had to keep slowing down the moves to an almost painfully slow speed so we could follow their instructions. Most of the moves they taught lacked the finesse which is normally associated with martial arts. There was no meditation, no deep meaningful explanations. This was dirty fighting, solely designed to disable an attacker. You don't fight to lose, you fight to win and by any means at your disposal. Anything struck got hurt. We were taught different techniques for disarming an attacker who was in too close to us and pulling a pistol on our principal. This could be achieved from different angles, and up very close and personal. Shout, "He has a gun!" Grasp the pistol - not the wrist - turn into the attacker's body, forcing him to release the gun, then follow with a jab to the throat.

In a short space of time we were all sprouting bruises on our face and arms as we misjudged distances and inadvertently struck each other. Nevertheless, it was very good training. I learnt more unarmed combat and dirty fighting moves in two days in this camp and with these instructors than I had in my entire career in the British Army. One of the more interesting moves which I had never seen before was defending yourself from an attacker while on your back on the floor. This was achieved in two phases. First you kicked at your attacker with both feet in a windmill fashion, as if you were trying to ride a bike. Secondly, you spaced your elbows apart to give a sturdy base and pushed your body around in a circle away from the attacker. This was completely knackering, but it gave you the few seconds needed to pull your pistol and shoot the guy. Working in pairs we played both parts, attacker and defender. We quickly found out how tiring it was to be the defender, but it also proved how difficult it is to get at the man on the ground with a knife if he's defending himself properly. It was an exhausting exercise but we enjoyed the adrenalin rush that always comes in the moment of danger - particularly if some bastard is going out of his way to kill you. At the end of these sessions I was black and blue and I ached from head to foot, but I had the satisfaction of knowing I'd learnt some new tricks and could now handle myself in a tight spot a bit better than before. It was all about giving us confidence when the shit hits the fan.

By this time we had lost quite a few people off the selection course. Some went for medical reasons, some for safety infringements on the ranges. All weapons were carried live on the range, with one round up the spout. The Americans refer to this as 'carrying hot'. We would be carrying our weapons like this most of the time in Iraq, so we had better get used to it now. No mistakes could be tolerated or someone would ultimately get injured or killed. If you can cock up in training then you can do it in a real situation and no one wanted a friendly fire incident. There had been too many of these in Iraq and Afghanistan already.

One or two of us were having documentation problems. All our passports had been sent to the Kuwaiti Embassy through an agency that specialised in this sort of thing. Blackwater had paid a lot of money for this to be done right, but so far their local representatives had managed to screw up most of the vital admin. One guy's passport had been lost and others had been wrongly processed. Mine did not come back with the batch it had been sent with and there was a danger I wouldn't get in-country at the same time as my team mates. At the rate this was going, it would be a miracle if any of us got there by the contract start date. This was a big government contract for Blackwater, but they were getting little or no help from their Departments of State or Defence. One of the biggest problems was the individual operators' contracts. No one had seen one. Everything we had been told about the job was by word of mouth. Some of the guys who had carried out this type of work before asked about the contracts and insurances but were told the company was having problems with the wording, and all contracts had gone back to their legal people to be reworded. We were told this was because the work contract we were supposed to be on for the DOD had changed again for the umpteenth time. Without proper contracts we had no way of knowing if we would get adequate medical care if we were wounded, or if our families would get the Defence Contract Life Insurance should we be killed or badly injured. We were assured by one of the company representatives that we were not to worry and that we would get the finished contracts well before we were to be deployed. They were being altered to give us the best possible cover in case of injury. This was my first foray into the Mercenary World and I suppose I was a bit naïve, a bit too trusting for my own good. I had come from a military system that looked after its own, and I had no idea how the corporate world looked after its soldiers. This was not the world of mercenaries I had read about where you made up the rules as you went along; where there was no back-up and you relied on your own wiles and initiative to survive. This was the modern world and we were legal now. We were contractors. I had believed the Company's patter hook, line and sinker and would live to regret it. A couple of days later my passport arrived back at the ranch. It cost the company an extra hundred dollars because I was a foreign national. Just for a rubber stamp.

Most days were a mixture of lessons on medical training, security lectures and half a day on the ranges. With the number of gadgets attached to our Bushmasters we were beginning to resemble storm troopers from *Star Wars*. The Company tended to favour an elasticised sling on the rifle with a snap hook on one end, which came in handy on the range when practicing 'transition'. This was something I had not been taught in the military. It involved simulating running out of ammunition for your rifle, letting it drop to your side, and then drawing your pistol to continue the fire fight. It was not the sort of tactic you could use very successfully in open countryside, but was very effective in a built-up area because it would give you a breathing space. You could draw your pistol and keep up a steady rate while you got to cover, and then reload. Most of us were able to practice this until we could manage a seamless transition from rifle to pistol.

Another piece of training I enjoyed was the killing house. This was a good exercise for concentrating your self-control and fire discipline, while at the same time testing your aim and reflexes. It was also good fun. Everyone likes a challenge, and in the army I used to get quickly bored with firing at stationary targets on a range. Instead I much preferred what we called a 'tin city'. This was where you would walk down a simulated street with buildings either side of you and targets would pop up in the most unlikely places. It was sheer snap shooting with no real time to aim, and it certainly honed your reflexes. The killing house had the same effect, giving you only a split second to identify and kill your target. Similar in construction and design to the SAS killing house in Hereford, the walls could be changed around to form differently shaped rooms and hallways. An overhead gantry allowed pairs of your team mates to watch your progress through the house, and then assist the instructor with your critique at the end of the practice.

The beauty of this system was that you used your own individual pistol and rifle, not training weapons. We simply replaced the ammunition with plastic capped, low-power training rounds known as 'simunition'. These would still penetrate the paper targets and record direct hits, but only give you a bruise if you were accidentally shot by your mate. Of course, the general idea was *not* to get shot by your mate.

At a given command we positioned ourselves in pairs on either side of the entranceway to the building. On the word GO! We moved in rapidly, heading alternately left and right. To get us warmed up we were brought face to face with life-sized 'armed' targets as soon as we entered the building. Two rounds to the body mass and one to the head for good measure was the method favoured by the Blackwater instructors. My partner and I took out the first two with our Glock 9mm pistols and cleared the room. The next room was at right angles to our position and we had to check the doorway prior to gaining entry. This time my partner's target was to the left but mine was behind the door. He hit his with all three rounds; I missed with the head shot, but got my first two rounds in the body mass. "Well done, Heroes!" the instructor shouted as the building echoed with the last burst of fire. "You just took out a friendly." My partner's target had been unarmed. Oops! Shit happens. At the debrief everyone was once again berated about the vital need for positive identification of targets before engaging.

Another interesting lecture was on IEDs, (Improvised Explosive Devices) the favourite weapon of a cowardly enemy, just like in Northern Ireland. Unlike Northern Ireland, though, where everything was smuggled in from abroad, in Iraq there was an abundance of discarded explosives lying around for anyone to pick up. The Coalition Forces had tried to secure all the ammo dumps and recover battlefield ordnance too late, and much of it had found its way into terrorist hands.

Any of it could be turned into booby traps. Some of the concoctions were downright overkill, like 120mm artillery shells buried at the side of the road, triggered by an anti-personnel mine or hidden inside the rotting carcass of a donkey. Some could be triggered by using a cell phone. The many ways to kill our forces were ingenious, and at the same time use of the suicide car bomb was on the rise.

How gullible could a would-be terrorist be? If an eighty-year old cleric told me that by killing myself and my enemies I would go straight to Paradise to be waited on hand and foot by 74 virgins I would definitely smell a rat. Apart from the impossibility of finding all those virgins, if heaven was such a sure thing how come he was still alive, and eighty into the bargain! Shouldn't he set an example and be one of the first to blow himself up? No, the suicide bomb tactic was devised simply to cause terror, enabling the potential martyr to take the maximum number of victims with him. It was not a well-aimed weapon and usually succeeded in killing and maiming many innocent passers-by - and all in the name of Allah.

I had read a bit of the *Koran* and if I remembered rightly, in many ways it echoed the New Testament. A gentle book, it spoke of protecting others' faiths and beliefs. Nowhere did it say you would get to Heaven by killing innocent women and kids, or by chopping the heads off unarmed civilians. This was the fanatics' interpretation and it was completely twisted. I could only hope they'd discover that when they passed through the gates of Hell and discovered not a virgin waiting for them, but a devil.

Our instructor had several gory pictures to accompany his lecture and obviously relished his work. His descriptions of the photos were graphic and left a lasting impression on those of the group who had not come across this kind of warfare before. Hopefully, it would make them more alert in-county. Apparently MREs (Meals Ready to Eat), or 'compo' as we call them in the British Army, were causing a problem out there. Soldiers were throwing some of their rations to starving children begging at the side of the road, but the cartons were being recycled as booby-traps and left near military vehicles. Several soldiers had been maimed with this type of device, but it had killed many more innocent civilians and in particular children. The simple rule was, 'If you didn't drop it, don't pick it up!' Anything could be an IED, no matter how big or small. This lecture was followed by a lesson on searching for devices on vehicles. Everyone was very attentive; no one wanted to be blown up. We had already been given clothing and equipment so that we were uniformed up to a point, but now we would be required to wear our body armour for the rest of the training to get accustomed to the weight. This was a good idea for those of us who had never had to wear body armour before. It does tend to make you feel restricted at first but you soon get used to it. The most uncomfortable feature was the heat: it could get unbearably hot wearing body armour.

The FIBUA village was an experience all of its own. I had been set up in response to some extremely difficult and unique problems arising in the wake of a couple of horrific school massacres. It was an intensely serious area where every conceivable scenario we could face could be played out to its ultimate conclusion, and was a very popular training ground, used by many of America's Police SWAT teams. Three cars were positioned in the parking lot opposite the main building. The first squad was given its positions and we were then shown the procedure recommended by the State Department for getting in and out of cars with a principal in tow. Most of us had done similar work but had evolved different ways of doing things, so the company instructors had to ensure we were all working on the same wavelength.

Next came walking drills and the formations required to give all-round protection while moving to and from the venue. Once the instructors were happy with the drills they began throwing in scenarios.

"Attacker with a knife from the rear!" He is quickly dealt with by one of the team, with the others closing ranks around the principal.

"Gun right!" Two guys on the right flank kill the assailant while the others form a human shield and bundle the principal unceremoniously into the waiting car.

Then we were issued with paintball guns and eyeglasses. The cars were driven through the streets, where we played out more scenarios.

"Principal's car disabled!" A second car pulls alongside to recover the Principal. (If the crew of the disabled car can get in as well, it's a bonus. If not, you're on your own).

"Ambush from the front!" Reverse, turn, rear car falls in behind and blocks, and you speed away.

The only thing we didn't like was not being unable to fire back. When you're in an armoured car, for instance a level 14, the windows don't usually wind down, so all you can do is get away from the site of the ambush. This is known as 'getting off the X', the X being the immediate point of ambush. We had to be reminded constantly that our job in an ambush is not to take the fight to the enemy but to protect our principal, who has to be removed out of harm's way. This was the hardest part of all because it went against all the military anti-ambush drills I had ever been taught. The only car in the formation able to fight was the CAT car. 'Counter Assault Team' to give it the correct name. The crew of this vehicle *could* fight. Their car was usually a 'kit' car, partially armoured but with gun ports and a rear machine gunner, so that it could attack and defend the principal's vehicle.

Now that we had mastered the basics, a full ambush was sprung. A simulated burning car was pushed into the end of the street blocking our way. Our three vehicles attempted to reverse out, but a pick-up truck with gunmen on the back blocked our escape. "Debus!" the team leader called over the radio. "I have a blue door right!" I identified our escape route and moved towards it. Paintball shots rained down from snipers in upper windows as we removed the principal from his vehicle and headed for the identified door. The first two members of the PSD to enter the building cleared the room. "Room clear!" The principal was pushed into a corner with the senior bodyguard shielding him while the rest of us returned fire. Meanwhile the first two men cleared the rest of the ground floor and looked for a way out. You don't want to get bottled up in one place. The idea is get into cover, and then keep moving from house to house, cover to cover until help arrives or you are able to get other transportation out of the killing zone. *How* you get the extra transport is up to you. 'Hijacking' is such a nasty word - whatever it takes to survive! We had just reached the third building, moving at speed and killing a couple of bad guys on the way, when "End ex!" was called. All the guys regrouped around the cars, feeling quite pleased with themselves.

The instructor told us we had done well. The drills had been good, cover was well used, return fire had been swift, the principal had been extracted and protected correctly, and we had indeed killed more than our fair share of the attackers. However…and he paused to look at our team members. I followed the direction of the instructor's stare and noticed how many of us had red splotches of paint on our bodies from enemy weapons. I'd been hit twice and didn't even remember it happening: one on the arm and one on the leg - not killing shots but I would certainly have been disabled and probably wouldn't have made it to cover. It wasn't good knowing that in 'real life' I would be still out in the street being used as the 'duty target' by enemy snipers. Not one person remained unscathed. One of the team, an ex-Marine, had been hit right in the centre of his forehead and a large golf ball-sized lump was starting to show. He was reassured that since he was a Marine the shot had missed his brain by five feet and everyone laughed, but it was the nervous laughter of people who were not comfortable. We all knew this would soon be the real thing. Our only bonus was that the principal had not been hit. However, the principal's bodyguard had about six hits on his back, which brought home to everyone just how risky this business was: all we were replacing was a good old-fashioned sandbag. This had been a worst case scenario, but we had been put through it to make us all aware of how dangerous this job was, and to sort out once and for all anyone who might be having doubts.

That night two more candidates went home voluntarily. They had obviously thought about it and decided their chances of survival in Iraq wouldn't be that good. Our numbers remained about 40 strong on paper as other operators joined us from previous contracts. On one of the Operations Room walls was a list of places in Iraq with names written against them. These names changed daily, so it was not yet set in stone who would be going where. Contracts had already been finalised in three main locations, and it looked like I was earmarked for somewhere called Karbala. I didn't know anything about the place, so I spent that night reading the last company situation report on it that we had on file. It was a highly religious centre in the Muslim world with two important Mosques. Annual pilgrimages to these Mosques had traditionally been made on foot by several million Muslims, but were banned during Saddam's reign of terror. Now they had apparently been revived and Karbala was a hotbed of anti-American, anti-Christian activity. It was beginning to sound like it was going to be a case of 'never a dull moment', and thoughts flashed through my mind of Charlton Heston as General Gordon in the film Khartoum. I shook my head to banish them! If the Company was to be believed, we had a lot more back up than poor old Gordon. It could never happen to us - could it!

About this time we were joined by fifty Chileans. All were retired Special Forces men of one kind or another. Some were marines, others were army, and there were a few police personnel who would make up the remainder of our site security teams. Their qualifications mirrored our own. As one of four team leaders on our site I would have a platoon of about fifteen under my command. Great, I thought! I didn't speak a word of Spanish: all those years of watching Speedy Gonzales cartoons had been wasted. I only hoped I'd get one or two who spoke English.

I needn't have worried, as all the Chileans proved to be good guys, very nationalistic. They were extremely proud of their homeland, and keen to prove they were professional soldiers and could do the job. A few were in their mid to late forties with years of experience in counter terrorism, but the majority were in their late twenties. Many - as paratroopers, SEALs and SF - had the same skills as we did. Most, although young, were very enthusiastic and couldn't wait to get stuck into the job. A number of them had seen action on the Peruvian and Bolivian borders and they had come to work for Blackwater because it offered better wages than they could get back home.

Quite a few had served under General Pinochet. The Socialist Government he handed his country over to, had replaced him quickly and fearing the military and what they were capable of, had reduced the size of the armed forces virtually overnight. The fact that the soldiers demobilised voluntarily and peacefully should have proved to the government they had nothing to fear from them; however, the deed had been done. Yes, there had been human rights violations, but these had been perpetrated by a few soldiers only. It was easy to forget that the people now in power, who had been the so called pro-democracy movement, had in their turn blown up government buildings killing innocent civilians, and had executed without mercy those police and soldiers who were found to have infiltrated their movement. As the saying goes, one man's freedom fighter is another man's terrorist.

Unfortunately, all Pinochet-era soldiers had been lumped in the same barrel as the few bad apples. For many of them, the chance had come to show that they had been wrongfully sacked; that they were first and foremost loyal to their country, that they were professional soldiers and not the thugs some people had made them out to be. But although the Socialists were the minority party in Chile, they made the loudest noise, and the people who had been the enemy of Pinochet's forces when he was in power saw this mercenary recruitment as a new threat. The former soldiers were now poor and downtrodden and treated as second class citizens in their own country, but if they got back into combat and came back with money in their pockets there was no telling what they might do! The Chilean government needn't have worried, though. The money these former soldiers would be making would be much greater than anything they could hope for at home, but the dollars they earned would be sent back to Chile, bringing much needed currency to their country. Like the rest of us, they just wanted to improve things for their families. It had been declared illegal under the Chilean constitution to be a mercenary, but after seeking advice from lawyers within the Chilean judicial system Grupo Tactico hired them perfectly legally as security guards. To reassure the government and people of Chile still further, a statement was published in all the media declaring that their sole purpose in Iraq would be to guard buildings and facilities belonging to the lawful government of that country.

Nevertheless, because of the adverse publicity their recruitment had caused in Chile, a Socialist parliamentarian by the name of Navarrete was starting proceedings to have these men jailed as mercenaries. He saw this as a way to get himself noticed, and a way into a possible soft job with the UN. He figured kicking up shit over the so-called mercenaries and the hiring of former military personnel would get him noticed by the right people. His main argument seemed to be that it was morally wrong for former military personnel who may have been involved in previous human rights issues to be hired in any security roll. He hoped this was just the issue that would ingratiate him with the United Nations and its Human Rights Commission. Not many people in the present government took him seriously, after all the men were being hired as security guards and they would be bringing their wages back to Chile to spend. This would get a lot of unemployed people back into work. Where was the problem?

In all fairness to Blackwater the company was fighting in their corner, and had sent a legal representative to Chile insisting once again they were only being hired in a protective security roll. Triple Canopy, another top American Security Company was also hiring Chileans and had made their own representations to the Chilean government. The Chileans themselves were not too bothered either: it was only politics and they were doing nothing wrong. It was considered by all of them to be worth the risk to give their families a better life and they figured they had right on their side. I had to admire their guts. There had been some people within Blackwater's management that thought the hiring of former Chilean military was not a good idea but the company owner Erik Prince, himself a former SEAL, thought otherwise. He had served in Chile and respected their soldiers, and he was well up for hiring them. When the chance for overseas security work was advertised in Chile over 800 former Special Forces soldiers applied. Many who had been sacked from the military that had supported Pinochet had been living on the bread line ever since their discharge. For them this was their one chance to make a bit of money and drag themselves and their families out of the gutter where they had been dumped.

The recruiter was a guy called Mike Pizarro. He had his fingers in many South American pies and was a well-known wheeler dealer on the South American Security scene. A former Chilean officer himself, he had worked for the US Government and then CNN. Originally he had served as an officer in the Chilean Army, and then resigned to join the US Marines. He wanted to see action and didn't think he was going to get that with the Chilean Military. He had dual nationality so it was an easy move from one to the other. Once in the Marines he adopted the name 'Mike'. He was soon granted his wish for action and moved through the Latin American countries with the US Southern Command, working as a translator, and brushing shoulders with some of the highest ranking officers at that time. On leaving the army he saw a golden opportunity to offer Blackwater a source of cheap but highly trained former military personnel from his own country's armed forces. His first attempt was brushed aside, but in due course he managed to get an interview with the company owner who told Mike to put his money where his mouth was. They agreed that Pizzaro would pick a group of his candidates, train them up and have them ready for a pre selection. If the owner liked what he saw, he would consider a contract.

Mike set up an office in Santiago and started recruiting. An advertisement in the Chilean daily El Mercurio started the ball rolling, but unfortunately rumours started circulating as well. Some said that Grupo Tactico was offering between $2500 and $3000 US a month. When you consider that the average wage for a Chilean soldier was $400 a month it was not an offer to turn down lightly. Many officers in the Chilean Military resigned in order to apply and this didn't help Mike in his efforts to keep out of the Chilean Legal System's bad books. Other rumours said he was working for the CIA. Mike hadn't really thought out his public relations and advertising too well, causing the volunteers and himself a lot of unnecessary bad publicity.

Despite all this, Grupo Tactico still managed to present their first 300 pick of the bunch at a secret location in Chile. Under Chilean law the guards could not be trained in their own country, so Mike had simply evaluated the candidates himself and then picked the best - those he considered already sufficiently trained and with the specialist knowledge needed to do the job. Luckily for him his choice of candidates was spot on. The Blackwater evaluation team liked what they saw and reported back favourably to their HQ. From the 300 tested, the first batch of 100 former Chilean military personnel were called forward by the company to their ranch for further assessment and training, prior to deployment. Of these, seventy-eight and Mike finally arrived. Of course at the time we knew very little of this. There were small articles about them in the News, but we were too busy getting ourselves ready to be worried about the foot soldiers. That was someone else's problem for the time being.

About this time a new addition to the office was nailed to the wall. This was The Battle Board, where all our group names began to appear. Blackwater had nominated team leaders for each contract and was building the teams around them according to the skills that were needed in each location. We still didn't know where we were going, though, as each location had a single code name. At this stage it was all on a 'need to know' basis, and we didn't need to know. One team leader had the call sign 'K2'. Names had already appeared underneath his, and mine was added to the bottom of the list. The name of one location disappeared overnight because the company had not succeeded in securing that contract, and the names underneath the code words disappeared and reappeared elsewhere on the board. Karbala, Samawah, Hilla and Diwaniyah were some of the locations mentioned.

We didn't know at that time that in each location we would be looking after a politician and his administrative staff, and what the admin staff didn't know was that they were considered 'strap hangers' - in other words expendable. Our orders were to save and protect the principal at all costs, but his staff were secondary. I'm sure every effort would be made to save them in an emergency, but I hoped we'd never have to put it to the test. All these politicians belonged to the negotiating teams working for Mr. Paul Bremer the head of the Coalition Provisional Authority (CPA), whose task was to negotiate a settlement between the warring Iraqi factions and thereby bring peace and stability to the area. It was a noble cause, but I thought a bit like 'pissing in the wind'. It was an impossible task in the present Iraqi political situation.

Early on in the training, during one of the many briefings on the country and places we were going to, we had been advised to grow facial hair and a full beard if possible. It seems our Arab friends respected anyone with a moustache and beard as showing age and wisdom. I was not convinced, and apart from the usual 'Mexican' moustache worn by most young British paratroopers in the '70s, I had never attempted to grow a beard. The fact was I could grow hair anywhere except my head. I'd always had thin hair, probably due to wearing a beret from an early age. I had started off as an army cadet and always seemed to be in the army wearing military headgear after that. Years of wearing helmets while driving armoured personnel carriers, jumping out of planes and performing similar military activities had taken its toll on my follicles and I doubted if I could grow a full set even if I was sprayed with compost. It had been a few days since I had stopped shaving and I was starting to look like a poor man's George Michael look-alike. It itched like hell, and I was beginning to wonder if it was worth it. The things we do for money! I thought.

***

*Iraq Coalition Casualties PSD, Convoy, and Site Security FEB 2004.*

| Date | Name | Nationality | Incident |
|------|------|-------------|----------|
| 08/02/2004 | Tomasi Ramatau | Fiji | Killed by Mortar Baghdad |
| 16/02/2004 | Ray Parkes | American | Killed in Ambush Baghdad |
| 23/02/2004 | Al Clayton | American | Killed by IED, Unknown |

# Chapter 3

## Days on the Ranch

There was still no news on the start date for our contract. The U.S. government had not released the money to Blackwater's bank and the CPA contracts were changing by the second, inciting disagreements and necessitating re-writes. We had yet to see our own personal contracts as promised; these had still not been finalised and the start date was getting closer. Blackwater decided to send the teams on unpaid leave and call them forward when they had a definite date. It was only expected to take a few more days, and their families would be glad to see them home for a short break. My case was different, though. It would cost too much to fly me home and back within a week, so I was asked if I would like to spend the time putting the team equipment boxes together. I wouldn't be alone, as Kerry, Ed and Caesar had also volunteered to stay. We would be working under Cory and Shrek's directions and on the payroll at $150.00 a day plus food and lodging.

To save money for the Company and travelling time for us, we were moved from the hotel in Norfolk to the shooting lodge in the grounds of the camp. The lodge was the very lap of luxury: people on courses paid good money to stay there. Without transport I was stuck in a place which could have been a lot worse. Outside the weather turned nasty, with storm warnings being issued all over America. I'd picked a bad time to come to the States - but then within a few days I hoped to be moving to sunny Iraq!

There was really no need to go out of camp, as the entertainment system in the two lounges would keep even the most easily bored person occupied. The rooms were pretty Spartan by comparison, but spacious enough to allow for a team of four in bunk beds with plenty of floor space for team boxes and equipment to be stored. The bathrooms were tidy and cleaned daily by a small staff. Blackwater had plans to build a gym and fitness room, but of course I wouldn't be there long enough to benefit from them.

The same day I arrived five of the blokes on the K9 course moved in with us. They were mostly retired policemen who had been dog handlers before. One dog handler with one dog would be joining each team in each location. Every dog was worth in excess of $20,000 and had been specially trained in the former Czech Republic, which meant the handlers had to learn some of their commands in Czech.

For the first five days we busied ourselves building the team boxes as more much-needed equipment arrived from the manufacturers. A lot of it was still on order and the suppliers had let the Company down with delivery dates. It was just as well we'd been delayed because getting this stuff to us once we were in Iraq would have been a logistical nightmare. Each box contained additional communication equipment, lap tops, and DIY tools for improving or repairing our precious kit in-country. Blackwater was going out of its way to make sure we were well equipped. It was the first time they had put large PSD teams into Iraq and they were breaking new ground. They were staking their good name and reputation on getting this right the first time, and from where I stood they were doing a good job. The Company had spent over $2,500 on each man's personal equipment, and that didn't even include his weapons.

The five days turned into ten, and we were roped in to help issue the Chileans with their equipment. Early every morning they would run past the lodge as a large squad, chanting like an American training unit. They were trying to impress us with their enthusiasm! It would start with a noise in the background disturbing your sleep. Then, still only half-awake, you'd hear a distant chanting growing louder and louder as they ran in a group towards the lodge. I tried pulling my pillow over my head but it didn't help. Mike would deliberately run the squad past our window, shouting out their chant in Spanish at the tops of their voices - just to make sure we were all awake, which by now we definitely were. They would then about turn as a squad, their boots stamping into the concrete as they marked time, and jog off in the opposite direction singing loudly. As they disappeared into the distance down the other end of the camp with the singing gradually receding, I used to wish I knew the Spanish for Noisy Fucking Bastards and only hoped the novelty would soon wear off! I like my sleep in the morning, at least until 0600hrs.

Before long the Chileans were moved into the lodge to save the Company money, and the lads and I put up extra beds for them in the far wing. We had one end of the hunting lodge and they had the other. There was no deliberate segregation; it was just more convenient that way. They had the free run of the place, so we got to know them in our off duty time. Blackwater didn't skimp on the Chileans' gear either, and they were issued with the same equipment as us. A lot of money was being spent on this operation and boxes and boxes of Blackhawk tactical gear were delivered to the camp. We moved it all into one of the briefing rooms, split the boxes and shared out the contents into identical piles. Our Chileans filed through one at a time, called out their names and were ticked off on a clip board list, and then passed down the line of tables. One of us stood behind each table, ready to hand over the necessary clothing and tactical rigs. By the time everyone had filed through we were left with great piles of empty boxes, while outside the Chileans staggered away under the weight of their newly issued equipment. I was impressed at the time with the gear provided, but the improved body armour and helmets that had been promised never materialised, though I was reliably informed that the US government had been billed for them. If the stuff *was* delivered, we never saw it: I was starting to see a slight crack appearing in what had seemed a smooth operation.

I telephoned Carol from the lodge. She was getting concerned because the contract didn't start until I was in Iraq, but I told her not to worry - I was still being paid. Until I could get some money to her she was living off our overdraft, so I only hoped it wouldn't be for much longer. I wanted to reassure her, but the truth was I was getting worried myself; the last thing I wanted was any more debt.

The next batch of FNGs (fucking new guys) arrived. Another forty hopefuls! The Company was chomping at the bit to get its operations started, and one of the staff singled me out. They had seen that I was a weapons instructor, so could I take the new guys on the range with the M240. In the US Military only the Marines used this machine-gun; in the British Army it was known as the GPMG or Gimpy, and we had used it successfully for many years in Northern Ireland. I had no objections to training anyone: it would keep me busy and help the time to pass quickly, and I enjoyed a good machine-gun range. Everyone had to be familiar with the gun anyway and if I taught them, at least I knew they would be able to handle it properly.

As I was on the company payroll I was covered by their insurance, so there was no problem with me teaching. The new group turned out to be a mirror image of our original one, all from different walks of life and military backgrounds, and all as keen as we'd been to get stuck into the job. I began by organizing them into two smaller groups for easier control. There were a couple of marines who were very familiar with the weapon already, so I decided to use them as gun coaches and for range safety. This would make life easier for me.

We piled into the vehicles and drove to the machine-gun range. Ski, one of the range staff, had asked me to make sure the gunners only fired short bursts at the targets and tried not to hit the frames. They were running short of the frames the metal targets hung on and he had another class the next day. I had every intention of teaching the British Army system, and assured him not a frame would be touched. The Americans have a habit of firing long bursts, but we tend to conserve ammunition by firing short aimed bursts - two to three rounds, keeping both eyes open and watching for the fall of shot. This makes for more accurate shooting and wastes less ammunition. Of course, if truth were told, the British Army probably just didn't want to spend the money on more ammunition!

Once on the range, I lined both guns up about 50 feet apart and detailed off my coaches to a gun each. The shooters were then told to line up behind the gun and dress back off the firing point. While they did this, I carried out a quick walk around the range and a safety check behind the butts. When I was happy it was safe to shoot, I hurried back to the firing point to give the range briefing. The ammo liners were broken open and everyone was issued with a belt of 200 rounds, each man's quota for this practice. There was nearly twice that much and I had been told to use it up.

"Right, you lot! Today this range will be run British style. This is not a 240, it's a GMPG. Anyone calling it a 240 gets ten push-ups, is that clear?" This brought laughter from the group and broke the ice.

"Shit, Man! I'll never remember that," said one of the marines I had given the coaching job to, and got down and gave me ten on account.

This was another good bunch of blokes with a good sense of humour. "All orders will be given in the Queen's English. Any problems with that?"

One of the other guys, of Mexican origin, replied in Spanish. "Ok!" "Down ten!" More laughter as he dropped and pushed out ten in a cloud of dust.

"Right then, Gentlemen, line up behind your guns! First two down, take command of your gun and test and adjust your position. Load! Ready! Targets to your front, in your own time - go on!"

Nothing happened. The gunners and their coaches looked over their shoulders at me with puzzled faces. Oh, bugger! I thought. This was America, and British fire control orders might just as well have been Klingon. I definitely heard sniggering. "Lock and load, and bloody fire!"

Both gunners turned back to their guns, racked the cocking handle back, opened the top cover, slapped a belt onto the feed tray and closed the cover. There was a short delay while they got used to the site picture and then the two men fired simultaneously. Both missed their respective targets, but this was normal while the gunners got over the initial noise and recoil of the weapon. The second burst brought a satisfying pinging noise down range as the bullets struck the hanging metal targets and sent them spinning wildly on their chains.

It was at this stage that the British system of short bursts went out the window as each gunner warmed to the weapon. Longer bursts sent up great spouts of earth into the air as the first metal frame disintegrated under the onslaught of 7.62 rounds. This brought a cheer from the waiting students. "Right you bastards, that's a beer you owe me!" Unfortunately, this now set the standard of shooting for the rest of the day as each gunner did his best to destroy the target and frame. Shit! As long as they were enjoying themselves and hitting the targets, I was achieving my aim I reasoned to myself. I pretended to fine each successive man more beer as each target was hit. At this rate I'd be owning a brewery.

It was then I noticed two guys hanging back. Both were obviously a bit nervous about using the weapon and I couldn't have someone scared of a GPMG, as anyone of us could be called upon to use it. It would be our main support weapon, and without it we could be seriously outgunned by the enemy. I pointed them out to my two assistants, who immediately encouraged them to take a prone firing position behind the guns. With the marines coaching and with a bit of encouragement from me, both men ended up relaxing and firing the GPMG confidently by the end of the shoot. A good job all round: everyone had now fired the weapon and I was fairly happy that most of them would be able to hit what they were aiming at. The entire group had now fired the GPMG, but we still had some time left on the range and we still had a lot of ammunition left. I'd be told to use up all the ammo, so it was split up among the guys and they rattled off the remaining rounds in a more relaxed manner than when we had started the day. As a bit of a reward for all their hard work and support, the marines acting as my assistants got a bigger share of the spare ammo, and thoroughly enjoyed themselves putting rounds down range. Both admitted they hadn't fired the machine-gun enough when they were in the forces and they had really enjoyed the chance to turn so many highly polished 7.62 rounds into so many empty cases. The general consensus was that it was a most enjoyable day's shooting.

If I'd got all the beer I was owed in fines, I'd have been drunk for a month.

We cleared the range and picked up the empty cases and then I examined the frames, which had all been shot to shit. They had so many holes in them they looked like a piece of Swiss cheese. How was I going to explain this to Ski? One of the blokes produced a roll of masking tape and we decided to see how many of the frames we could reassemble. After much swearing and struggling, twelve hanging target frames were standing, if somewhat precariously, back in their original positions. They would look the part and be okay as long as no one hit them. I could imagine Ski's surprise later when he put his course on the firing point, gave them the order to open fire and most of the target frames fell over. Sorry, Ski!

Back at the armoury we cleaned the guns and returned them to their racks. I had just started walking towards the lodge when Cory caught up with me to give me the good news. We were moving out to Kuwait in a couple of days; the other team members were being sent their flight details as we spoke. Tom had arrived in camp on his way to another contract, so at last I got the opportunity to thank him for helping to get me the job. That night Tom and his missus, Cory and I and a few of the lads went downtown for a meal and a drink. It might be a long time before we could have a night out again.

I phoned Carol again that night and told her the news. She was pleased I had a start date but naturally very worried about me going to Iraq. It was not too late to come home; we could manage without the extra money. I disagreed. No we couldn't! I was fed up with soldiering for Queen and Country for a pittance. I had done that for nearly 30 years as both a reservist and regular soldier. What had I got to show for it? - a few medals and a sergeant's pension. I wanted to give my family something better, and this was no time to have second thoughts. Like most people, I had a mortgage that was killing me and this was a chance to pay off a big chunk and be able to relax from our money worries, at least for a while.

The plan was for the team to fly via the UK, stopping over at Heathrow for 14 hours before our connecting flight. Carol said she would take the day off work and meet me in London. I had been paid by cheque and I cashed it locally. I would give the money to Carol to put in the bank: I wouldn't need much in Iraq, and at least she would be able to pay the bills until my first wages went into our account a month later.

Two days later I was ready to roll. I shook hands with the K9 teams, Caesar, Bruce, Tiny and the other guys I'd been working closely with - not forgetting our Chilean friends! - telling them I'd see them again in-country.

I was on the move again, but this time it was to re-join my team.

# Chapter 4

## Have Gun, Will Travel

Kerry had the unfortunate call sign 'Gabby'. He was a former 82nd Airborne Paratrooper, born scrounger and another of our base team, and had been tasked with driving the kit to Dulles Airfield. I would be going as his co-driver. The truck Blackwater had hired would take us about four hours to get there and I was the only one of the rear party to be joining his team at this time. I guess Blackwater wanted to see some return for the money they were spending on me. My team were being recalled from leave, and would be given the RV times at the airport; the rest would be coming over later. Kerry and I had an uneventful drive from Moyock to Dulles, stopping half way for a meal and to refuel the truck - all paid for with the Company's credit card. I was glad to be moving at last. Like everyone else I'd been going stir crazy waiting for everything to kick off, and now we were finally on the move. As well as all the team kit, equipment boxes and weapons bundles, we were carrying a thick sheaf of documents in a sealed envelope. Our instructions were to give this only to K2. On arrival at the airport we realised there was nowhere near the entrance where we could park for unloading. There were no parking zones anywhere, which was bloody frustrating as we needed to be close to the main doors to maintain the security of our sensitive load. I stopped the truck outside the terminal anyway, and Kerry went to find a security guard to explain our problem. Within a couple of minutes he came back with two guards in tow. Once he'd told them who we were and where we were going they allowed us to park right outside the main entrance: Blackwater had a good name in the American security world. Kerry had phoned the team earlier to tell them we were arriving, and most of them were waiting just inside the terminal building ready to unload the equipment boxes. Kerry stayed with the vehicle while I found K2, briefed him on the equipment, and then gave him the large package of documents. Everyone formed a human chain and we unloaded the boxes into the main terminal foyer in quick time.

As we were the first group to be mobilised we were carrying extra team boxes and heavy equipment for two other locations. These would have to be checked in detail through British Airways. All the paperwork had been copied to the airlines in advance; Customs had copies of everything, and the Company had been given reassurances that everything was in order to help with a speedy transition through the airport and onto the aircraft. With so much advance planning what could go wrong, I asked myself? We had the weapons for three teams, so the paperwork had been checked meticulously to prevent cock-ups. The team retired to the coffee shop at the airport and grabbed a brew as K2 broke the seal and opened the package of documents. I could see by his face he wasn't too happy with its contents. Still, he was the team leader and it was his job to look worried. I was sure he would share his concerns with us if necessary. In the meantime I could do with a cup of coffee.

As well as the weapons and equipment Customs sheets, K2 had everyone's contract, finally produced by Blackwater's lawyers. There were sixteen pages of legal mumbo jumbo for each of us to read. I had a quick flick through the pages, but didn't understand a word of it. Then just as everyone was leafing through their contracts a British Airways representative hurried up to K2 and told him there was something wrong with the paperwork for the weapons. Great, I thought! Here comes cock-up No1. K2 had a slightly animated conversation with the official and then turned towards us. "Hurry up and finish your drinks!" he said. "We have to go sort the weapons out. Apparently there's a problem with Customs."

"What the fuck's all this legal shit?" One of the guys asked loudly of no one in particular. "I thought this contract was going to be easy to read?"

Someone else commented, "We've only got half an hour to get on the plane!"

One of the other contractors, a veteran of some experience, wasn't happy either. "We're supposed to have a company representative here to answer any questions on the contract, and if there's anything we're not sure of, we're entitled under United States law to have ample time to have it read by a lawyer. I don't know any lawyer in this God-damn country that could make sense of sixteen pages of this shit in half an hour!"

K2 was getting visibly angry. First he'd had to sort out a problem with the weapons, and now some of the guys were questioning their contracts, as was their legal right. Not having a clue about contracts, I was completely out of my depth: it was all new to me.

"Do you want the job or not?" he rapped out. "You have two choices it's as simple as that. Sign and get on the plane, or stay here and sort it out with the company! It's your call."

"Aw, fuck it!" someone said, and as if an invisible order had been given we all scrawled our signatures on the two pages marked with a cross. Shit! I needed the money, and I was not going to lose the job having got this far. Everyone else must have felt the same way as they all signed and gave the contracts back to K2, who sealed them in another envelope and passed them over to Gabby. It would be his job to deliver them by hand to the administration staff back at Moyock.

I could see more cracks appearing, though.

"Don't worry!" K2 said, as if reading my mind. "I've worked for this company a long time. They're usually pretty good on the paperwork and they'll be sending copies out to you later. It's just been a rushed job, that's all. Now let's go sort these weapons."

We were all under pressure, but being the professionals we were we followed K2 out to where the weapons bundles were now stacked under the watchful eye of one of the security guards who'd been so helpful earlier.

Despite all the phone calls from Blackwater to the airport and back, as well as the assurances given to the company by the airport Customs Office, the relevant information had not been passed to the Duty Security team. They couldn't reach anyone in authority to sort out the problem, so they quite rightly asked us to unload every weapon so they could check the serial numbers against the manifest. It was worth it to see the look of horror on ordinary civilians' faces as weapon after weapon was laid out on the terminal floor for inspection in full view of the general public! If Blackwater had any idea of moving discreetly and covertly from the States to Iraq, that cover had now been well and truly blown. I half expected our faces to be splashed all over tomorrow's tabloids!

Luckily my British accent worked like a charm on the American lady at the British Airways desk, and with her help we soon had ten security staff helping us re-pack the weapons, secure the gun cases and rush them onto the aircraft. They could not have been more helpful and apologetic. Our flight was being called just as we finished the paperwork. I shook hands with 'Gabby' and promised to keep in touch, hoping I would see him in Iraq. He was an easy guy to work with and he was a good soldier to boot. That made him okay in my book. The team boarded the aircraft with minutes to spare and the plane took off on schedule. We received a few strange looks from the other passengers: they must have been wondering who the hell we were. They needn't have worried, though - hijackers don't normally check in their weapons with security.

I relaxed into my seat and took a deep breath. Well, it was finally happening and who knew what the future might hold for me. It wasn't long before they served the in-flight meal and it tasted good, so I must have been very hungry! I thought I'd get some shut-eye, but my brain was hyper-active and wouldn't let me sleep. After fiddling with the screen controls on my arm rest I finally worked out how to change channels for the films, and plugging in my head set I settled back to watch. After two feature films back-to-back I was finally able to close my eyes. It was a long flight of several hours and I felt well and truly jet-lagged by the time we reached London and began our descent into Heathrow. In contrast to my snowy arrival in America the sun was shining over London and it was clear blue skies. As we spiralled in on the holding pattern I could clearly see the Millennium Dome from about 12,000 feet. It looked just like the opening title scene from *East Enders,* one of our better-known British TV soaps.

The aircraft made a smooth touchdown and taxied to its gate. As we started to leave, one of the cabin crew wished us good luck in Iraq. I hoped we wouldn't need it. We cleared Customs quickly, as apart from our hand baggage everything else would be transferred from aircraft to aircraft without us touching it. We wouldn't see the heavy gear until we arrived in Kuwait. The rest of the team hurried into the airport lounge and booked in. If they had to spend fourteen hours there, they wanted to do it in comfort.

I had phoned ahead and Carol was waiting for me as I left Customs. It felt so good to hold her in my arms again as I gave her a big hug. I hadn't realised how much I'd missed her. "Before I forget," I said, "put this to good use. I won't need much where I'm going," and I passed her the money I'd saved for her. She looked relieved as she put it in her handbag. Money must have been getting tight, but she wouldn't admit it. It was not in her nature. As an army wife she was used to struggling by on a soldier's pay.

"I've booked us into a hotel," she said casually. If I'd suggested that, she would have murdered me! You just can't tell what women are thinking, but we had better things to do with our precious last day than sit in the airport lounge playing video games and watching TV. Our car was in the long-term parking lot and we wasted no time in getting to the Travel Inn hotel just outside the airport perimeter. Carol confirmed our reservations at the desk and I noticed we were getting a few strange looks. Then I realised it was because we had no bags. People had jumped to the wrong conclusions. I didn't mention this to Carol, wanting to spare her the embarrassment. We had a meal in the hotel and passed pleasantries about the family. Neither one of us was keen to talk about where I was going. We retired to the hotel room and enjoyed each other's company for the short while we had together. It was definitely a case of a few stolen moments. I eventually fell asleep with Carol cuddling into my back. She felt warm and reassuring.

For a few seconds after the alarm went off I couldn't figure out where I was. I got out of bed, went into the bathroom and splashed cold water on my face to wake myself up. The alarm had been set to wake me in good time, giving us a clear hour to get ready and say our goodbyes all over again. I hated this bit, and although we'd been through it many times over the years, it didn't get any easier. We drove to the airport in silence.

Carol dropped me at the entrance to the Departure Lounge. I didn't want to prolong things any longer than I had to; it was hard on both of us. I kissed her goodbye and waved as she drove off. I could see the tears in her eyes and I suddenly felt guiltier than I had ever done before for putting her through all this yet again.

I dialled my home number on my mobile and Simon, my youngest son, answered the phone. "Hi, Dad! How are you?" I spoke to him for a few minutes making idle conversation, and then told him his mum was on her way. She would be home before my aircraft had taken off and I wanted him to phone me and let me know when she had safely arrived. He assured me he would and made me promise to be careful. Walking into the airport lounge, I found the guys scattered around looking bored out of their heads.

"You look like the cat that got the cream," one of them said.

"Yeah - looks like I had a better day than you did!" I replied smiling, and I sat and had a coffee as they started to get their gear together.

When K2 was sure he'd gathered everyone together and they all had their personal belongings, we set off at a brisk walk to book in for the flight to Kuwait city. We still had two hours until take off, but the airlines liked you there two hours early because of the extra security checks. It was a necessary evil if you wanted to fly unmolested. Not every country's security was as diligent as it was in the United States and the United Kingdom, and aircraft were still being hijacked. Nowadays, though, there weren't as many as in the 1970s when it was an all-too-common occurrence. Yasser Arafat and his PLO (Palestine Liberation Organisation) had started a new phase in terrorism that was to plague the West right up until its 9/11 culmination. That was to be the civilised world's wakeup call, and many innocent people had to die before anyone really took serious notice of this new terrorist threat.

Our passports were checked and the team leader confirmed with Customs that our baggage and weapons had been cross-loaded. It wouldn't do to lose anything at this stage. The team moved through into the departure lounge and grabbed yet another coffee, and then we sat watching other aircraft taking off to destinations unknown. Heathrow was a busy airport; I had read somewhere that one aircraft took off or landed every two minutes, and couldn't help imagining the chaos that would result if one plane was out of sync.

When my mobile rang I was so deep in thought that I jumped and nearly spilt my coffee. "Hi love!" came Carol's voice. "Simon said you wanted a call."

"Just wanted to make sure you were back okay!"

It was a short call as we'd already said everything that had to be said, but I promised to contact her once I got in-country. I wasn't sure whether it would be by phone or email, as I didn't know what life support would be in place. I expected the worst, though - anything better would be a bonus.

As Carol hung up and my phone went dead we were called forward to board our flight. Through another airport gate, through another tunnel, down to another aircraft: check our boarding cards and we were on our way yet again. Once on the British Airways aircraft I settled down straight away and slept the sleep of the dead most of the way over. I only woke for the in-flight meal. My body clock was well and truly screwed up and didn't know if it was night or day. By the time we landed at Kuwait International Airport many hours later I was feeling extremely jet lagged.

My first impression of Kuwait was of a clean, if somewhat sterile city. Everything seemed to be in its right place and just so, creating a sort of ersatz Western environment. I couldn't quite pinpoint the feeling it gave me, but if pushed, I would say I thought it lacked atmosphere. On the plus side it was living proof that Muslims and other religions could live side by side without wanting to cut each other's throats. Well, on the surface anyway.

Everyone in the Arab World seemed to be skimming off the top; everyone wanting their piece of the pie. The first problem was that Kuwaiti Security asked us to break open the American Customs seals on the already secured weapons cases, so they could check each weapon's serial number against the manifest. We tried to point out that this had already been done, but they would hear none of it. Next they decided that the oxygen cylinders in the vehicle medical kits constituted a bomb hazard. This was despite the fact that they were empty and labelled as non-pressurised, and with all the international paperwork necessary to prove they were non-lethal cargo. We finally gave up arguing and just did as they asked. Then came the crunch. We couldn't board Blackwater's chartered Casa aircraft because we didn't have the correct visas for passing through Kuwait. After all those weeks of waiting for the visas and passports to come back, it turned out they were not worth the paper they were printed on. The female courier the company employed arrived on the scene, and after much heated argument with the officials she announced that all could be resolved if Blackwater paid for new visas. Now there *was* a surprise - more money greasing more palms! Couldn't these Arabs do anything legally? Our team leader agreed to make a payment and went into a nearby office to sort out the details. I don't know how much money changed hands, but within ten minutes of the deal being struck our passports had new visas and we were being ushered through the airport by happy officials who couldn't do enough for us. We got VIP treatment through Customs with no further checks, and found ourselves out on the aircraft pan next to the Company's rented Casa aircraft.

The pilots and load master greeted us and showed us where to stow the equipment, and the uniformed baggage handlers we'd picked up en-route brought in trolley after trolley with our equipment and personal belongings. All the kit was stowed on the tail ramp of the aircraft and secured by freight straps, with a large cargo net thrown over the top for good measure. Before securing the load we had opened up our kit and removed our body armour, and we now put this on prior to take off. Our weapons had to stay secured all the time we were inside Kuwaiti airspace; only the load master exempted from this rule, and he was armed with an AK-47 assault rifle.

The pilot's safety brief was short and sweet: "If we get hit by a SAM (Surface to Air Missile) we'll all be dead;

if we get shot down by small arms fire you will most likely die in the crash; in the unlikely event of engine failure and a crash landing, you will probably die in the desert. Apart from that, this is a very safe aircraft and there is nothing to worry about. We would like to thank you for flying with Kamikaze Airlines!" He was joking, right?

The load master completed his checks as the pilot started the engines, went to the rear and partly closed the ramp; his secondary role was as rear gunner. He occupied an old office chair secured by freight straps attached to several strong points on the aircraft floor, wore a parachute for good measure and was attached to the aircraft by his aircrew safety harness. As we took off, he sat tight with his AK-47 and watched the ground recede into the distance, and then at a safe height he closed up the ramp and went to sleep on the cargo. I could see he had done this before.

It took a couple of hours of uneventful flying to reach the border. The Iraqi desert sprawled below us like a giant children's sand pit, and Baghdad soon swam into view through the hazy blue sky. It was nothing spectacular - the usual miles and miles of featureless buildings like so many LEGO building blocks, broken here and there by a mosque or minaret. We came into the airfield perimeter from a height of 12,000 feet, and the pilot told us to hang on to our breakfast as it was going to get interesting. A cargo aircraft had been hit by a SAM a few weeks earlier while taking off from Baghdad International Airport. I remembered seeing it on TV, one wing burning as the pilot calmly turned the aircraft around and got it back on the ground in one piece. A good bit of flying by anyone's standards! Since then every take-off and landing, even by civilian airlines, had to be a tactical one.

Some of our team were not airborne trained and therefore not familiar with the term 'tactical landing'. Our aircraft circled above the outer marker on the airfield waiting its turn. When the air was clear of any other aircraft, the pilot was given permission to land. He cut back on the engines, dropped a wing and lost several thousand feet in a few seconds. People pay good money for a roller coaster ride like this. It brought back happy memories of my days as an air despatcher at RAF Lynham, only then it had been in a C-130 Hercules. The light, two-engine Casa bucked, creaked and groaned as the pilot executed a couple of high speed G turns. He levelled off and revved the engines, and no sooner had the uninitiated in our group recovered their stomachs than he rolled the opposite way and lost a few more thousand feet. The ride might have been a wild one, but was designed to throw off the aim of any terrorist trying to get a lock on with a SAM, or hoping for a lucky hit with an RPG, (rocket propelled grenade). I looked over my shoulder at the rest of the team; a few like me were enjoying the exhilarating ride, but most of them didn't appear too happy. Some had turned a distinctly funny shade of green. There was a bump followed by a pause, and then another bump and we were down. We were still a target though, so the pilot kept the speed on and taxied along the runway towards the airport terminal to one side of the airport. For an international airport it was fairly quiet. Dust and bird shit covered most of its surfaces.

It was obvious that normal services had not yet been resumed, and the airport was still under military control. Two or three aircraft stood on the tarmac where once many had parked. The walls were pock-marked with bullet holes from the Gulf War, and no one was to be seen walking about in the open. It looked like a ghost town.

From out of nowhere one of the guys managed to commandeer an airport bus with an Arab driver. All our gear was loaded into the belly cargo compartments and we piled on board. There was more dust and shit inside the bus than there was outside. After much raising of voices and waving of hands the driver finally seemed to understand that we wished to be taken to the military side of the airport. As no one in our party had any idea where that was or how to get there, we were completely in the hands of our Iraqi driver who, after completing a couple of 360 degree turns, sped off across the concrete aircraft pan. This didn't reassure me with any confidence in our new found driver and his ability to get us anywhere.

The bus rattled and shook as it bounced across the cracked and potholed perimeter track. We appeared to be approaching a sand-bagged single floor building of some kind, when all of a sudden three Humvee's hurtled out of a side compound, screeched to a halt on either side of us and half a dozen U.S. soldiers leapt out. They quickly surrounded the bus and called for us to dismount and keep our hands up, all their rifles pointing our way. Our driver completely lost it, and was babbling away to himself in Arabic. I caught a "Hum da lala" mentioned a few times. He was obviously convinced he was about to be shot, and to be honest I thought there was a very good chance of that happening. Despite the fact that not one of us looked like a bloody Arab, we were ordered out and into a single line, told to face away from the soldiers and hold up our ID.

While we were held at gunpoint one of the soldiers came up behind us and gave our ID a cursory check. The lieutenant in charge was now satisfied that he didn't have some mass incursion of bad guys and told us we could put our hands down. Now we were all friends again. He explained that they didn't get civilian transport on this back road very often and that they had come under quite a lot of small arms and mortar fire. They were justifiably nervous: apologies for the misunderstanding, but better safe than sorry! I understood his viewpoint but still suspected he was just trying to look good in front of his men. The upside was that we now had a military escort that quickly took us to our check-in point. This made it much easier to clear Customs and find our vehicles and escorts. We shook hands with our young military companions, and they wished us luck in return. They reckoned we would need it. Did they know something we didn't?

Immediately outside the terminal we found our welcoming committee. A pickup truck and a mixture of black and white Suburban and Pajero SUV's were waiting for us. The Blackwater guys on the ground looked the part, easily identifiable in their Royal Robins sand-coloured shirts and trousers. All wore sunglasses as protection against the glare of the Iraqi sun; Bushmasters as well as an assortment of Soviet weapons were clearly on show and openly carried, and pistols were slung where they felt most comfortable. Cross draws, shoulder holsters and low leg rigs were evident as were a few beards, proving some of the men had been in-country longer than others. They were very happy to see us. For one or two our arrival meant they were now able to go on leave, but the rest were happy simply because we were the reinforcements they had been waiting for. We would now be taking some of the pressure off them.

Eager hands helped us load our gear into the back of the pickup truck and we were assigned seats in each vehicle. The vehicle commanders briefed us individually on our arcs of fire, responsibilities, and actions in the event of an ambush. We were each handed an AK-47 with two 30-round magazines because our own weapons were still in the sealed weapons cases. These guys were thorough, even though we were only going to be 15 minutes en-route: the airport road was probably the most ambushed in the country, and more people had already died on this five-mile stretch than anywhere else in Iraq. It was soon to become labelled the most dangerous road in the world.

"Ok! Lock and load!" the vehicle commander called. Each man checked his weapon and then slapped a magazine in place. Unlike most other weapons, the safety catch on the AK is left in the 'off' position. As long as there's no round in the chamber it can be left like this, which prevents negligent discharge; to have a round ricocheting about inside a vehicle would be potentially lethal to the occupants. Some operators don't like this system because with the safety off the weapon could be cocked and made ready to fire in the seconds it took to dismount. But even in war you must try to be as safe as possible: it's embarrassing enough being hit by the enemy, let alone by friendly fire.

We were ready for business, and our high speed convoy of vehicles pulled out into the heavy traffic of Baghdad. "Push through!" came the convoy commander's instructions over the vehicle radio. The lead car pushed out into the traffic at speed, causing other drivers to swerve to avoid him. Then the rear car pulled out. "I'm blocking," came the radioed message from its commander and its rear gunner showed his Russian-made PKM machine-gun to the traffic. The other drivers respectfully stopped dead in the road and allowed the remainder of the convoy to pull out. To ignore him would mean a burst of automatic fire into their engine block, or worse, as all coalition forces were authorised to use deadly force if they felt they or their passengers were in danger. This still gave the local Iraqis an easier time than in Saddam's day, when his convoys would shoot innocent people for the fun of it, and he had been known to wind his car window down and shoot someone just to test a new rifle. Our drivers pushed their cars nose to tail through the heavy traffic, the idea being to stop any other vehicles from getting in between them. Many a PSD or military convoy had been taken out in the early days by suicide bombers who got into the middle of a convoy and detonated themselves, killing the principals and usually many innocent passers-by as well. VBIEDs (Vehicle Borne Improvised Explosive Devices - driven by suicidal insurgents) were the hardest thing for the teams to fight against and would prove to be the most nerve-wracking part of any PSD operator's job, a daily nightmare to many. Sometimes an operator would crack up under the pressure and ask to be released from his contract. When this happened it was no use reasoning with the guy. His nerve had gone and that was all there was to it. No one I know would blame or ridicule an operator who has just had enough. Shit happens. I would meet many such operators as my time in Iraq went on. Many were very good former SF guys who had been in action plenty of times and who you would definitely not call chicken, especially to their faces if you wanted to keep your teeth. However, one shooting or explosion too many and a guy would resign and go home, reasoning that his luck was about to run out. It could happen to any one of us at any time so there would be no recriminations. We all understood the problem. Post-traumatic stress disorder was still being investigated by the Military and had still to be fully recognised as an illness in certain quarters. Many a good soldier had been affected by it, often with tragic consequences, murder and suicide being two of the most common.

# Chapter 5

## Downtown Baghdad

It didn't take too long for the convoy to reach the Green Zone, or US Military designated safety zone. I failed to see what was so safe about it though, when you considered the number of car bombs and mortar rounds that still managed to explode within its boundaries. All the same, you could breathe a sigh of relief when you got there, as you could relax a bit. After all, it was someone else's job to stand next to the blast walls and check for suicide bombers. It was easy to recognise the entrance: a large camouflaged concrete tower stood in the centre of the road, flanked by armed sentries and two Humvees. A few of the guard were Iraqi police or army, but most were American military personnel bristling with weapons. A vehicle park was situated some distance from the palace entrance to prevent car bombs gaining entry to the inner compounds. Beyond that you ran the system of concrete slabs that formed a chicane up to the sentry posts. Identity cards were checked, and if you couldn't be identified you didn't get in. In fact forgetting your ID was a good way to get yourself shot. Just past the sentry tower we hooked right across some waste ground and entered a typical Baghdad side street. At the corner were mountains of rubbish and human excrement that must have lain there for several days. The stench was overpowering. Cats, dogs and the local residents sifted through the pile of crap for anything they could eat or use, stirring up the billions of flies that covered everyone and anything. The first few houses were pretty basic, most being square buildings with very few features, but in contrast the next couple were quite expensively designed with high-walled gardens and bright, colourful brickwork. Two young Iraqi security guards stepped in front of our cars, their AK-47s held at the ready. They looked alert and ready for instant action. Recognizing the vehicles and drivers they smiled and waved to us as we drew to a halt and debussed in the street. Other guards were in evidence on the roof tops and in the garden of the safe house, which bristled with barbed wire and security lights. No one was going to get in here unannounced! To some extent it gave us a feeling of safety, but at the same time we all knew that if this amount of security was needed, this place was anything but safe

We were met by Mark, the resident Mr. Fix it. Mark managed the safe house and was unusual in that he was a dwarf. When he first walked out to greet us everyone bit their lip and tried not to laugh. A dwarf with a Glock in a low slung rig was a surprise and I wasn't the only one to think this must be some kind of joke. It was no joke, though. Mark had been in Iraq for a few years already as the only Western representative of one of the big American parcel delivery services. He knew people, and more importantly he knew Baghdad like the back of his hand. When Blackwater recruited him as their gofer and Mr. Fix-it they knew exactly what they were doing: he was exactly the right man for the job. Now he welcomed us all, showed us around, and explained the few house rules.

Inside, the building was surprisingly large. It went back further than it seemed to from the outside, with three floors and a roof level. Downstairs was the kitchen with several Iraqi staff, together with a large, comfortable and tastefully decorated lounge and a couple of smaller rooms that served as bedrooms. In one corner of the lounge was a big TV, the main entertainment. Upstairs were several bedrooms housing from four to six men on bunk beds but with plenty of space to stow kit. The safe house was not really designed for permanent occupancy, more as temporary transit accommodation for operators moving up country. Blackwater also had a large contingent of guards and PSD teams housed in Mr. Bremmer's residence. All around Baghdad there were similar sites occupied by our company personnel, including their helicopter crew based at the International Airport. The helicopters helped with the nightly CAP (Combat Air Patrols) of the surrounding area, flying in night vision goggles to avoid being an easy target for SAMs (Surface to Air Missile) and small arms ground fire. Their 'night suns', large extremely bright searchlights mounted on the fronts of the helicopters, were used to light up any identified targets when requested. Their main job was to give top cover for Bremmer's cavalcade when it went out on meetings. This they did well, being fast and highly manoeuvrable, the racing cars of the helicopter world. The Company's own door-gunners were ever ready to fire their machine guns in support of the guys on the ground, and they were a formidable asset - not many security firms could boast their own air force. Most of the pilots were Vietnam or Gulf War vets and well used to flying combat missions under fire.

Soon after we arrived everyone lent a hand to unload the team boxes into the store rooms, and the usual human chain was formed to transport all our own personal gear upstairs to the rooms which were to be our homes for the next few days. There was a short break in the work when the Iraqi cook made coffee for everyone. The team leader chose this moment to introduce us to the dozen or so Iraqis working at the house. We were informed in front of them that they were not the enemy, but loyal, trustworthy members of the Company. Everyone shook hands and our Iraqis beamed - apparently with sincere pleasure at being introduced to us in this fashion. With the number of kidnappings going on from so called safe houses, no one to my knowledge was ready to go house visiting with them, though in the event they did turn out to be friendly, helpful and genuinely nice people. The security guards had been trained intensively by the Company to its own high standards and were extremely keen. They were well paid by Blackwater and were proud of their training. They considered themselves far superior to similarly trained Iraqis. Maybe they were, but I didn't have much to compare them with at this stage. There was one thing they did which I noticed and commented on at the time: they kept their finger alongside the trigger guard of the rifle, unlike the Iraqi police who had a habit of walking around with their finger on the trigger. As a result, the Iraqi security forces suffered more casualties through friendly fire than through enemy incidents. Our guards, however, showed they were confident and safe whilst carrying their weapons in the course of daily duties, and that went a long way in my book.

I slept well that night, but the 9mm pistol under my pillow might have helped some. I awoke to the familiar smell of a Full English being produced by our Iraqi cook. Nothing was too much trouble for her and by the end of the meal she had a large fan base of happy, well fed customers. Unlike most of her countrymen she had no problem cooking our bacon, but that might have been because she followed one of the most persecuted religions in the Middle East. She was a Christian.

Our instructions were to chill out for a few days until orders came in to move to our new locations. The resident PSD team had laid out a large batch of rusty, unserviceable AK-47s and other old Iraqi weapons which Blackwater had been given by the US Army. A couple of the guys who were trained gunsmiths were busy stripping, repairing and assembling the weaponry to see how many good ones they could produce. These were intended as fall-back weapons for the Chilean guards coming out after us. Despite emails back to our base, no one could tell us if they would be bringing out their own rifles, or if we had to equip them in-country. Our teams on the ground had to be ready for the worst case scenario and to equip them locally. Not the ideal situation, but one we had to be prepared for. A lot of us gave a hand, and soon there were thirty weapons ready for action laid out on the front lawn. Next to them a huge pile of scrap parts accumulated, not worth turning into paper weights let alone serviceable weapons. Many were museum pieces.

We sat down to a hot meal that night, and afterwards crowded into the lounge to watch the TV. CNN was showing the usual bombings and shootings when suddenly the house shook with a great shock wave. The windows rattled, and then the lights flickered and went out. "Bugger!" someone exclaimed in the dark. "I was just going to put a film on." In their scramble to get their weapons, people bounced off each other and off the walls. The click of magazines snapping into place and the unmistakable sound of weapons being cocked resounded through the building, and Surefire, Maglite and head torches stabbed through the darkness, the beams crossing each other like some crazy Star Wars fight scene. Most of the operators had gathered in the garden looking for the direction of the bomb when an Iraqi guard rushed in and gave a garbled report to one of the permanent PSD.

"OK guys, stand down! It was the North Mansour district again - car bomb and a large one, but not near us. We'll get the details in the morning, or better still watch CNN when the power comes back on. The media guys seem to have a habit of being in the area when any shit goes down."

We'd already noticed that certain TV reporters had an uncanny knack of being in the right place at the right time when it came to shootings and car bombs. It had long been suspected that many such incidents had been orchestrated by the Media. On other occasions they had been tipped off that something was going to happen. One or two reporters had passed this information to the Coalition Forces, who had then been able to react early and avert a potential terrorist attack. Others had protested that they had to protect their sources and had then been on hand to film soldiers getting killed. Many of them couldn't understand why the military was hostile towards them, but considering they tended not to show us in a good light, it was no wonder we had no love for them.

Back in the lounge the lights flickered and came back on. By the time I was inside again "Apocalypse Now" had been put on the DVD player, and somehow it seemed appropriate! As the film came to an end everyone drifted out of the room, and slowly the house settled into an uneasy quiet as each man finished his tasks for the day and went to his bunk. The atmosphere was electrically charged. We'd been close to a bit of action and then had come the anti-climax, but I guess most of the guys were still wired up waiting for something to happen. I lay in bed for a while my rifle loaded and cocked under it, and my pistol likewise under the pillow. Outside I could hear the Iraqi guards talking to each other in low voices. In the distance I could hear the occasional stutter of machine gun fire, and as I started to drift off a low rumble signalled yet another explosion. But it was in the distance - someone else's problem not mine, and with that last thought I promptly fell into a deep sleep.

I awoke to bright sunlight streaming through the curtains. The room was already starting to feel hot and uncomfortable. Outside in the garden the birds were singing in the trees, and the noises of breakfast being cooked and the clank of cooking pots being moved around on the stove drifted up. The other guys started to move around, and as there was a limited number of toilets I grabbed my wash kit and towel and made a dive for the one on our floor. I needn't have bothered: everyone else had the same idea and a queue had already formed.

"Stop having a wank and move your arse!" the front man called as he banged on the door to speed his mate up. The door opened and the red faced occupant came out wiping the back of his neck with his towel.

"Can't a guy have a shit in peace? Bastards!" This brought laughter from everyone else and then a mad dash as someone tried to jump the queue and a friendly fight started up.

Our team leader stuck his head out of his room. "Glad you've got so much energy, Guys! Once you've eaten there's some ammunition to distribute."

By now anyone who'd been a bit tense after our high speed arrival and the minor disturbance of the night before had settled down. Everyone joked and chatted at breakfast, and some ate in the lounge watching the news of the bomb blast the night before. Sadly, several innocent Iraqi civilians including children had been killed, but thankfully no Coalition Forces. Graphic pictures of the dead and dying were splashed across the screen, but it didn't seem to put anyone off their breakfast. Crates of 5.56 ammo and boxes of 9mm began to appear in the hallway, and each man carried ten magazines of 5.56 for his rifle and four magazines of 9mm for his pistol. Our team would be taking a crate of thirty AK-47's and a few hundred magazines with us when we left. These would be issued to the Chileans when they arrived, and if they didn't need them we would use them as back-up weapons. Each car carried one in the well, or 'boot' as we say in Britain, so we were being adequately prepared for all eventualities.

We were informed that there would be a delay going in-country. Some of the principals we were to guard hadn't arrived, and our cars hadn't arrived either. The main problem was that our Department of Defence cards would take time to process. These would be a big problem, as the department handling them had no sense of urgency. As I was to find out, this was why nothing ever got done immediately. It was the Iraqi way, and everyone seemed to go along with it.

One of the residential team asked if anyone wanted to go to the PX. Several of us were up for it. Most of us needed stuff like shaving foam, toothpaste, soap and the like, which are usually hard to get up country. And toilet paper, *soft* toilet paper, definitely had to get some of that! Even though this was a local 'milk run', we put on our body armour and locked and loaded our weapons. This was Baghdad: anything could happen at any time, and usually did. The entire group squeezed into three Suburban SUVs and we pulled out of the street, past our Iraqi sentries and did a left turn onto the main road. Humvees and Iraqi police vehicles rushed past in all directions going about their usual daily business. We filtered into the Green Zone traffic, made our way around the inner ring road, past the palace and main vehicle park, and then turned right towards the PX. One of the resident team had to vouch for us as we still hadn't received our DOD cards.

I was a bit disappointed in the PX, which normally has a better honesty rating than our own NAAFI, as their prices were every bit as high. Funny how organizations supposedly providing a service for soldiers in a wartime situation don't seem to have any qualms about ripping off their customers; we were a bit of a captive market really. A couple of the guys purchased personal DVD players, as there would be a severe lack of entertainment where we were bound for. Everyone replenished their toiletries and paid in US dollars, the accepted currency throughout Iraq. Across the road was a 'hajji' market, or souq to give it its proper Arabic name. A few bargains could be bought there, such as pirate DVDs going for a couple of dollars - not always the best copies in the world and a few wouldn't work, but for the price we paid who cared! Everyone piled in there and everyone came away with a few bargains, ranging from wall carpets to DVDs. One guy even bought a 'hubble- bubble' pipe; he swore it wasn't for personal use, but would be an ornament and a talking point in his flat back home. If the locals didn't like *us*, they certainly liked our money and happily exchanged it for local souvenirs and tat. After all, we new boys were no different from tourists and didn't know when we were being ripped off. Shopping trip over, we drove back to the safe house through increasingly heavy traffic. What we didn't know as we left with our purchases was that only a short time later the market would be blown up by a suicide bomber, who had gone out of his way to hit a soft target. Most of the dead were women and children, and the bomber would have known who his targets were going to be as Iraqi men don't shop for the daily groceries. That's women's work. When the bomb went off the blast and shrapnel ripped through the stalls as if they were made of paper, killing many of the people who had just served us and spreading body parts across a wide area. It would be yet another day of carnage for that long-suffering city.

Our vehicle pulled away from the market. "Anyone want to buy some beer?" the driver asked.

Someone asked the question that was on everyone's mind. "Where we gonna get beer in Baghdad?"

"Thought this lot were Muslims and didn't drink?" another voice piped up.

"They are," he replied, "but the booze shops are run by Iraqi Christians - and most of their customers are Muslims!"

With this surprising information we pulled up next to a brightly painted hut. From the outside there was nothing whatsoever to show what it sold, but once inside it was clearly a very well-stocked Iraqi off-licence. There were shelves and shelves of gin, rum, and other spirits and liquor, and in the corner were crates of Carlsberg and Holsten Pils. For thirty dollars a crate of beer became mine. That would do nicely thank you! Things were looking up. Our shopping trip was now complete and some very happy customers stuffed their purchases into the vehicle. As we turned into the street, machine gun fire could be heard fairly close by. "It's outgoing," someone said. "Hope they hit some deserving bastard!"

That evening when we'd had our meal and retired to the lounge one of the resident team leaders gave a briefing on the day's activities in Iraq. A bomb had gone off in such and such a location and killed some children; another had blown up an Iraqi police checkpoint; a vehicle-borne IED had hit an American convoy and destroyed two trucks, luckily no casualties - and so it went on for at least half an hour. Was there any good news in this country? There was a lap top computer with an internet connection belonging to one of the team and he kindly allowed each of us a few minutes on it to send messages home. At least we'd be able to tell our families we had got this far in one piece. There was a hiss and clicks as someone cracked open the first beer of the night. Now that was a good idea, and several of us followed his example. A suitably 'blood and guts' film was on the TV so we settled back for another quiet night in Baghdad. Once again drinking was in moderation and we were more than half expecting a similar disturbance to last night, but by the end of the film we realised it was going to be a quiet night and a bit of an anti-climax. Slowly we all drifted off to our beds and crashed for the night, with the occasional rattle of automatic fire in the distance. The last thing I heard before sleep took hold of me was a couple of shots from a rifle, followed by a longer burst from a 50 cal. I remember thinking, "That'll teach the bastard to play with the big boys!" and then I sank into a grateful oblivion.

The following day we had the call to go to the local ID card issuing department at the palace, where we queued for over two hours before getting into the office. Typical civil servants with no sense of urgency sat at their desks sipping coffee and acting like they were on a go-slow. When I finally got my turn it was a simple case of a ten question form, finger printing and sitting in front of a digital camera. I waited five minutes for the card to be made on site and then walked out. What a drama over nothing! But then this was Iraq, and as I soon discovered nothing in Iraq is done in a hurry, not even getting us in-country where we were urgently needed. The urgency clearly hadn't filtered down to the pencil pushers, who were still treating their work as a 9 to 5 job regardless of the people dying outside the wire whilst they continued with their protected civilian occupation inside it. Iraq can be a very frustrating place and it's hard not to let it get under your skin.

As part of our orientation we were all taken to the main palace, which served as the Coalition HQ. Here we would be given the chance of an historical tour which only a few westerners had been treated to before the overthrow of Saddam. Like many other security companies we had our Operations Room within the palace complex, so that was as good an excuse as any to have a nose around. Our vehicles pulled into the coalition forces' car park in front of the palace and we debussed, ready to negotiate the checkpoints and barriers necessary to gain access to the inner sanctum. Once again we had to show our Department of Defence identity cards several times before we got through the main security, first to American army personnel and then to a Ghurkha from Global Security. The palace looked pretty imposing from the outside, but once you stepped through the main entrance you were spellbound: this place would give even the Sistine chapel a run for its money. Every wall, every ceiling oozed intricate patterns edged with gold leaf, much of the work having been commissioned from French artists by Saddam in his glory days.

After the bad workmanship I had seen on buildings all around Baghdad this was nothing short of spectacular. Every mural, every pattern had been painstakingly finished by craftsmen. The floors were tiled and covered in mosaic, and nearly all the stairs were made of marble or some other expensive stone. The corridors which Saddam's followers had once so softly trodden now echoed to the sounds of many combat boots stamping irreverently up and down in the normal daily hustle and bustle of a military headquarters. This must have been one hell of an imposing place in its day: it was still an imposing place now. Every nook and cranny held a military or civilian government office. Civil Rights organisers rubbed shoulders with generals and politicians, and civilian contractors and close protection teams moved through the halls on their everyday business. Combat equipment and body amour littered the place. Notices on offices doors written in English and Arabic proclaimed the department, with every military and government department necessary to rebuild a country represented. People rushed by in a hurry, pushing and jostling in an effort to get their jobs done. Everyone had an official ID card around their necks or clipped to their shirts to prove they had every right to be there, and the place hummed with activity.

We were shown to our operations room tucked away to one side of the Palace. The duty crew were friendly enough and allowed us all to send an e-mail home using the company computers. One or two of the guys didn't have computers at home and so they were allowed to make a phone call. This was always seen as a privilege rather than a right, so no one tore the arse out of it. It was just good for morale to be able to contact the family now and again and let them know you were okay, even if only for a couple of minutes. We were given yet another briefing on area activities, but this time the main places of interest were pointed out to us on a large scale map pinned to the wall. Baghdad was a rabbit warren. Half the streets in the residential areas shown on the map no longer existed, partly due to the bombings and partly due to bad workmanship. As one of the team said on examining a house that had been finished a couple of days before, "It takes great skill to make a new building look like a six hundred year old ruin!" Once deployed, we would have to gather as much detailed intelligence on our local routes as we could, mapping alternative escape routes in case of ambush. With the lack of a clear route it would be hard if not downright impossible not to start following a pattern, but the same route every day would quickly be sussed out by the Insurgents and we would very soon be ambushed and wiped out.

We were invited to eat with the local boys before returning to our safe house, so we broke for lunch. The main cookhouse was situated in the central hall of the palace and several hundred people could sit down to eat at any one time. For those military personnel who were in a hurry and were still carrying their weapons there were a couple of ante-rooms in which they could eat in safety. Even these small rooms could seat fifty people and were covered in ornate carvings and bright, intricate patterns. The caterer tried to produce food for the majority of nationalities present in the coalition, and managed to keep ninety percent of the people happy, though I didn't see one Yorkshire pudding anywhere. Still, I didn't mind making sacrifices - after all there was a war on!

As well as our DOD identity cards we had been issued with weapons cards. These informed anyone who needed to check your status, which weapon you were allowed to carry, its serial numbers and what condition you were allowed to carry it in. As part of Mr. Bremmer's personal bodyguard detail I was allowed to carry my weapons with a round in the chamber at all times. Common sense prevailed, and you normally only carried your pistol in this state if you were in friendly offices; when visiting other locations every weapon you carried would be 'hot'. This is what all the training at Moyock had been for - to ensure that no one in the Company's employment was sent into the field in any way unsure or nervous about carrying a hot weapon. By now we were all comfortable with this. With the rest of the team I joined the dinner queue. As we slowly shuffled towards the hot-plates each of us took a set of 'diggers' and a plate from the racks provided. Like everyone else I craned my neck past the line to try to get an early warning of what food was on offer. A tap on my shoulder and the rather posh voice that only a British officer is capable of producing brought me back to reality.

"I say!" said the posh voice which I now identified as belonging to a British Lieutenant Colonel dressed in desert camo. "You're still carrying your pistol?"

"Yes, Sir!" I replied, always courteous to anyone wearing the Queen's Commission. I realised that because I was wearing my old Parachute Regiment sweat-vest he must have mistaken me for an off duty British soldier, although what this idiot thought an off duty soldier was doing in civilian clothing in this mess hall was beyond my comprehension. It was against regulations for starters.

"Are you carrying a live round in there?" he asked, raising his voice so that it echoed around the hall. You could hear the chink of cutlery on plates as the place went quiet and everyone present took an interest in what was unfolding. I replied that, yes, I was indeed carrying a round up the spout. He started to go off on one, shouting that I was an idiot for breaking rules by carrying my weapon, and that having a live round in the chamber was a cardinal sin. I listened with amusement to his ranting, half expecting to hear I was to be shot at dawn, and at the same time removed my weapons authorization card from the back of my ID holder. I don't suppose the smile on my face helped the situation but I was trying hard not to laugh. He stopped in mid flow, a look of total surprise on his face as I held my card up.

"Hold on, Sir, before you get your knickers in a twist." I explained that I was part of Mr. Bremmer's personal bodyguard team and not a British soldier. I was therefore completely within my rights to carry my weapon in the government building, and to carry it live. He coughed and spluttered as if he was about to have a heart attack. I turned away before he had a chance to answer, but not before I had the satisfaction of watching him turn bright red with embarrassment. There were sounds of sniggering, and I could see the shoulders of the people in front of me in the queue going up and down as they tried not to laugh out loud: the old saying 'please engage brain before opening mouth' sprang to mind. I reached the front of the line and helped myself to chicken and chips as my new found officer friend grabbed his food at the gallop and rushed off to hide in one of the ante-rooms while I sat down to eat with the rest of the team .We all looked at each other and burst out laughing; there are always lighter moments in war and this was one of them.

"So that was a British Officer," one of the guys said ironically. All I could think of was 'God save the Queen'!

We spent several more days in the safe house, and it was getting boring. Every night we listened to someone else getting hit with mortar rounds and small arms fire - okay, it was good it wasn't us, but we just wanted to get to our job site and start working. The sooner we all got into a routine the sooner we could finish the job and go home. I managed to borrow a mobile phone from one of the group, as mine wouldn't work from Baghdad. I couldn't be on for long but just to hear Carol's voice would be enough. There was a slight echo as the signal was bounced off a satellite, but we had a cheerful conversation. Carol said she had told our grandkids that I was working for a security firm in the USA - a necessary white lie when the BBC and ITV were showing beheadings and bomb attacks nightly. With so much TV coverage it would be hard to explain to young children that Granddad was nowhere near the fighting.

By now Cory, our instructor from the Blackwater ranch was in-country as Second in Command of the Bremmer detail and came round with some of his team to see how we had settled in. Our main concern was the quantity of ammunition we had. It seemed a small amount to be shared out between what were effectively supposed to be three teams. Cory said he could get us some more and maybe a few other bits and pieces, such as smoke and fragmentation grenades. This was heartening, and good as his word he was soon back with a couple of boxes containing several thousand rounds of assorted ammunition. Some of it was Egyptian and unreliable so we sat on the living-room floor of the safe house, each man with a large pile of loose ammunition in front of him sorting out the good from the bad. Two of our team, Stingray and Hollywood were ex SEALs and knew a few of the team stationed on the other side of the airport. They set off on a scrounging mission, confident that if there were any spare 'bangs' to be had these guys would have them. They came back a couple of hours later with a rosy alcoholic glow and more ammunition than we had originally been issued with, not to mention a couple of 84 mm rocket launchers. Given the opportunity, we could put them to good use. Hollywood said the SEAL team was having a Bar-B-Q tonight and we were all invited. Problem was their hooches were within mortar range of the local bad guys. What the hell! - a party is a party. We were warned to go easy on the booze as they regularly got incoming fire, but encouraged to have a good time as we didn't know when we'd be getting another chance to unwind like this. It would give us all a chance to make some new friends, and you never know when you are going to need friends in a war. That evening we all piled into the available spare vehicles and set off for the other side of the airport where several air-conditioned trailers and a large brick and wood building were home to the SEALs. Various types of meat and chicken pieces spat and sizzled on a homemade Bar-B-Q, and we were invited to help ourselves from a couple of fridges in the main building holding a large assortment of beer bottles and cans. Parties are few and far between in Iraq, so our arrival was a good excuse. I was introduced as our 'limey'. Oh well, I'd been called worse names!

Everyone used the evening to get a first-hand account of the situation, and any tips and intelligence this team could provide us with. They were a mine of information and certainly helped us by briefing us on everything and anything they thought would be useful, much of which would help us in days to come. As darkness fell, so the sound of gunfire and explosions became louder and louder. It looked like it was going to be a busy night for the city so we decided to get back to the house before we got involved in anything. Goodbyes said, we raced back to base and got inside the building not a moment too soon. Two mortar rounds hurtled overhead and exploded in an adjoining street. Everyone grabbed their weapons, put out the house lights and took up positions on the roof, balconies and any other high points we could get to. After about an hour it was obvious that the bad guys had lost interest in us and were busy elsewhere.

Once we were stood down we gathered in the front room to have a coffee and discuss what we had learnt.

Most of it was hints and tips on how to stay out of trouble and what to look for. Also we had been promised more ammunition so things were definitely looking up. Our new found friends seemed to think that where we were going we'd need every round we could get.

The following morning we took delivery of four SUV vehicles and a white pick-up truck. The pick-up was the sort used by the local Iraqis and wouldn't stand out. Our main problem was the extra kit we had received while we waited at the safe house. Fresh equipment had been arriving from American daily. Each team now had a large tool kit and power tools as well as other necessary equipment, such as radios and charging consuls for the radio batteries. We were going to start fresh contracts in new locations, and we would need the tools for improving our living conditions and building defences. Three teams were being deployed at the same time to three different areas. Although these new locations had been briefly reconnoitred, we still didn't know what to expect and had therefore gone fully prepared for the *unexpected*, or so we hoped. To add to the load our SEAL team friends had turned up with a small amount of surplus kit and some more bangs for us. Then just as we thought we had worked out a loading plan Mark came in and informed us that an email had come through from the ranch. It was not known if the Chilean security guards were being allowed to transport their M4 rifles into the country with them, as there was a paperwork problem with Customs. This meant we now had to find room for thirty AK-47 Assault rifles and several hundred magazines, as well as the supporting ammunition just in case it was needed. We knew the assault rifles would work but they looked tatty and I felt uncomfortable issuing them in this state. The Chileans were professional soldiers and would resent being lumbered with what looked like a load of crap. They already had a chip on their shoulders about the Americans looking down on them, and this would only reinforce the idea. That's all I needed from day one - a pissed off site security team.

We turned our attention back to loading the pick-up truck. Things went in okay and stacked well. There was no problem with the payload either, but the kit bags and personal kit were slightly higher than the cab roof. This was solved by putting two planks of wood upright against the back of the cab so nothing could fall forward. "While we're at it, why not make it look like an overloaded Arab truck?" someone suggested. This seemed like a good idea, and several cardboard boxes were acquired from somewhere and folded flat. Next they were put alongside the wire fence like sides of the truck, successfully hiding the contents from a side view. Some old curtain material was draped over the back of the truck and tied down. Outwardly it appeared a loosely thrown together affair but was in fact a well secured and fastened load. Several dents already on the outside of the vehicle would add to the camouflage, and we even removed a couple of hub caps to add to its scruffy appearance. Both the driver and escort would wear shemaghs, so that from a distance they would blend in. Everyone was given their position in each vehicle. Each 'shooter' was briefed by the team leader, K2 on their arcs of fire and in the comfort of the safe house front room we discussed 'Actions on Effective Enemy Fire.' In the case of an ambush we would be in deep shit and we'd have to fight our way out. We had communications with the military but it was not the most reliable system in the world and there would be no back up, so we would have to rely on our own capabilities. Everyone felt confident that we could handle anything the 'rag heads' could throw at us en-route to Karbala. I just hoped we didn't have to test that theory. Tomorrow would tell. Before we turned in for the night everyone checked their chest webbing and filled every pouch with full M4 magazines; spare ammo was packed into our Camelback escape packs; all our weapons were stripped, cleaned and reassembled: nothing was left to chance. First aid kit carriers were placed on the individual's belt or rucksack where they could be easily got at by their buddies; if you got hit they were hardly likely to use their own first aid kits on you. Blood groups were stencilled with black marker on the carriers, and I made sure my Union Jack was tucked into the bottom of my pack. I reasoned that if we called in an air strike in an emergency I would place this on the ground near me to aid recognition. After all, a member of the Mahdi Army is unlikely to be waving a British flag around in a battle is he? It sounded like a good theory to me.

I fell asleep that night listening to the far away sound of a distant fire fight. It was somehow soothing. What would tomorrow bring?

*Blackwater HQ in Moyock.*

*The Karbala Blackwater team just after our arrival at Camp Juliett.*
*Front Left: 'Pops' (Simon Chambers) wounded. 'Tango' Bill (K9).*
*'Mickey' Killed in an RTA in Cyprus, 'Tank'.*
*Second Row left: 'Hollywood', 'Zepplin', K2 Rod Richardson, Team leader killed later on in an ambush.'Bullets', 'Dallas', 'Sparky Killed in an ambush.*
*Third row: 'Joker' wounded. 'Dingo' Killed. 'South Side' Single figure up:' Monkey'*
*Top: 'Stringray'*

*APC visitor.*

*A soldier with multiple injuries but still on his feet is helped out.*

*Karbala internet cafe.*

*Iraqi army and mentors at Saddams Square.*

'Tango' poses next to the Bulgarian armies recoilless rifle.

The armour was not penetrated but the unarmoured back windows were.

*Truck remains.*

*CPA Karbala bombing. Remains of a Police 4x4.*

*Our Chileans going to their tents.*

*Er! Abdul you're firing at the wrong camp!*

*Some of the US Camp defence team.*

*Polish gunners position on the roof of Juliett.*

*Dingo' and Roy pose for the camera near the back blast wall.*

*ID and weapon Cards.*

# Chapter 6

## Road Move to Karbala

Karbala is the second most holy site for Iraqi Shiites. It contains the shrine of Imam Husayn ibn Ali, who was martyred there in the year 680, and has over one hundred mosques and twenty three religious schools. The Shiites make pilgrimages called Ashura to Karbala twice a year to commemorate Husayn's death, first on the tenth day of the Muslim month of Muharram and forty days later in the month of Safar. They were forcibly prevented from celebrating either of these anniversaries by Saddam Hussein and his Ba'athist government. In 2003 it was estimated that the city had a known population of 527,300 people.

I once again woke to the sound of birds singing outside our window and the sun streaming through the gap in the heavy black curtains. One or two individuals were still snoring as K2 woke each person in turn. "Breakfast's on! Grab something to eat on the run - we want to be off as soon as possible." Bodies coughed and spluttered awake and tumbled from their beds looking for their clothes.

"Who's got my bloody trousers?" someone asked.

"They're where you left them, you stupid bugger!" came the reply.

"You're fucking helpful," the owner of the lost trousers said, as someone else found them and threw them across the room, smacking him on the side of the head. "Thanks for nothing, Bastard!"

What may have looked to an outsider like the beginnings of a fight was just the friendly banter of soldiers letting off steam and trying to hide their nervousness. We had no way of knowing if we would be ambushed on the way out. Even then, back in early 2004, ambushes were an everyday occurrence in Baghdad, and we all hoped for a chance to get used to our surroundings before our first contact. The teams were professional enough to take on all comers, but an edge was a nice thing to have and we wanted one badly. That we'd eventually be involved in a fire fight of some kind was never in doubt. It was not a case of *if*, but *when*.

I grabbed a sandwich and a quick coffee, and with the help of a few of the others started moving all our personal equipment out of the room, down the stairs, and onto the patio at the rear of the house. Soon a pile of body armour, weapons, and associated equipment littered the ground as we 'first paraded' the vehicles, and the team leader and drivers pored over the maps and set their GPS. We all gathered around K2, who spread a large-scale map on the bonnet of the pick-up. We would be driving through at least two villages that were openly hostile to Coalition Forces. One had a right-angled, heavily congested junction in the centre; we could go round it, but that would mean some cross-country driving, which would attract the attention of the locals. The Mahdi Army had eyes everywhere. We all decided to go for it and bluff our way through, though we did discuss 'actions on'. If any vehicle were hit and disabled, the crew of that vehicle would fight to hard cover in the shape of the nearest building. They would then fight through to the next building and keep moving till they could reach a road or side street where they could be recovered by the rest of the convoy. Hijacking a local vehicle would be another option - whatever it took to save lives. All these scenarios had been practiced at Moyock, so we were pretty confident we could react to whatever was thrown at us. At the moment we had to cope with the fear of the unknown, though maybe 'fear' wasn't quite the right word, as we were all highly trained soldiers. I guess if anything it was a bit of apprehensiveness, which we knew would vanish the moment a fire fight kicked off.

Mark and the house staff had made everyone a packed lunch of sandwiches and fruit, which we stowed in pockets, pouches and anywhere else we could find that was not already full of ammunition and other necessary items. We were eager to get on the road, so we said our hurried goodbyes and pulled the vehicles out into the street. Once our Iraqi guards were happy that the adjoining roads were clear, the barrier was removed and we drove out into busy, hectic Baghdad. We immediately had to close up nose to bumper to stop local vehicles from getting in between us; any one of them could have been a suicide bomber. It was instant chaos. Almost at once our driver had to push a scruffy, dented red and white taxi to one side so we could keep our place in the convoy. As if it was a contest, the vehicle in front of us rammed a battered white pick-up out of the way, its shemagh-clad driver waving his arms in despair and cursing us in Arabic. No doubt any donkeys or camels we owned had just been cursed, and now their offspring would be born with two heads or something equally nasty.

Reports on continual bumps and minor collisions went back and forth from the drivers via our personal radios as we pushed through heavy traffic towards the relatively clear road that would be our exit from the city. Everyone was tense and ready for a fire fight. In any other city, the police would have been called, or someone would have jumped out and started a fight. This, however, was Baghdad and as we were finding out, we were doing nothing out of the ordinary. It was Iraqi town driving at its best. I was convinced that all Iraqi drivers had passed their tests on the bumper cars at Southsea. Then suddenly we were through the heavy city centre traffic and on the exit road.

The traffic here was relatively light compared with what we had just been through. Gaps were allowed to appear between vehicles, although our speed and blocking drills still kept the local cars and trucks away from us. We shook out into a decent convoy distance and accelerated. "Going to a hundred!" came the lead driver's call over the radio. "Two, a hundred! Roger that!" came back Vehicle Two, and one by one all the drivers called in to show they had heard and understood the instruction. The convoy picked up speed and hurtled at a steady pace away from Baghdad and all its chaos and towards the countryside.

When we passed the occasional Humvee or Bradley parked next to sandbagged bunkers or hastily erected VCPs, (Vehicle Check points), the lead driver flashed his DOD card and held up his fingers to show the number of vehicles in our group. We were waved through by young, heavily armed U.S. National Guardsmen, acknowledging their wave as we went through. It was bad enough that they blew our cover by making it obvious who we were, but the alternative - heavy calibre friendly fire! - would definitely have ruined our whole day. A wave to show we were friendly was simply the lesser of two evils.

The larger, more majestic buildings and palaces of the Green Zone and the core of the city receded, and we found ourselves passing miles upon miles of square, red and sand coloured buildings, all badly constructed. Now *there* was an understatement! It was hard to identify which had been destroyed by Coalition bombers, and which were just falling down from bad workmanship. Despite their ramshackle state, most seemed to sprout a satellite dish on the rooftop; Al Jazeera, the enemy-favoured Arab TV station, would have many fans round here. The buildings looked derelict, but as we continued on our way our eyes were on doorways and rooftops, and anywhere else a sniper could be lurking. So far so good, though I didn't think we'd fooled any of the local hajjis into thinking we had Iraqi-manned vehicles.

Within twenty minutes or so the trees thinned out and the buildings closed in, the road narrowing as we approached the first of the villages. The black-topped highway had disintegrated into potholes and craters after years of neglect. A dead donkey, its legs in the air and its belly swollen with gas, lay at the side of the road where it had been struck and killed. The call from the lead truck to give it a wide berth and move out to the left side was relayed down the convoy. It was a favourite trick of the terrorists to pack an animal carcass with explosives and detonate it as a PSD team or Coalition Forces passed by. It was a pretty deadly tactic, which usually took out not only the target but also many innocent civilians. The Mahdi Army didn't worry about collateral damage the way we did. As far as they were concerned, provided they were killing infidels the deaths of any of their own kind that got mixed up in the carnage were justified, and the victims would become instant martyrs for the cause. We passed the dead animal at speed and Joker put his fingers in his ears.

"What you doing, Buddy?" one of the others asked.

"Just in case!" he replied with a smile.

Now that was funny at an otherwise tense moment. I could see how he got the nickname Joker.

As we passed the first few ramshackle buildings on the outskirts of the village the road became narrower and the side streets more cluttered. The whole scene was a health and safety nightmare. Rubble and rubbish of all shapes, sizes and description littered the streets. These were not just small piles, but half a ton at a time, showing it had been many weeks since anyone had taken the initiative to remove any of it. Power cables and telephone wires hung side by side from makeshift poles. Some almost touched the ground, forcing people to walk around them and drivers to use the centre of the road for fear of being electrocuted. Water ran from a broken pipe into the gutter. It was not that the local Iraqis were unable to help themselves: they just couldn't be bothered.

We approached a cement hut positioned in the centre of the road where a tattered Iraqi flag and a badly painted sign declared the existence of a police checkpoint. Over the vehicle radio K2 warned everyone to be careful, as these buggers could not be trusted - Police by day, local Militia by night. It was hardly a high tech checkpoint. To clear the post, each vehicle had to negotiate a chicane of oil drums, rocks, and piles of rubbish, any one of which could have hidden an IED. Everyone slowed while the lead vehicle drove through and checked out the position. "Ok, clear!" came the call. "Watch the guys on the right; they have AKs but no uniform."

As each vehicle passed through, the gunmen were covered by the shooters on the right-hand side. There was a small group of gunmen to the rear of the post, a couple of them sitting on boxes, others standing around smoking or drinking tea. AKs were held at the rest with gun hands around the pistol grip and the index finger inside the trigger guard. No one raised a weapon in our direction, which was very wise of them as the slightest movement towards us with the muzzle of an AK would have brought them a world of hurt from a dozen semi-automatic weapons. I would have said they were totally uninterested in us, if it had not been for a uniformed police officer to one side of the group talking rapidly into a mobile phone and looking in our direction. One of the others beat me to it and came up on the radio to report our observations. "Ok, Guys! They know we're in the area, and they know our direction of travel. Stay alert!" K2 advised.

Everyone tensed. Suddenly we ground to an abrupt halt on finding the road blocked by hundreds of hijab-clad women, snotty-nosed kids, goats, sheep, the occasional camel, and male Arabs in assorted dress. It was market day, and we had just driven right into the centre of a market that was being held in the main street. So much for Intelligence giving us a clear route to Karbala! "Keep to the left and push through! Use your horns!" came the instructions from the front vehicle. We pushed through. It was slow going but we kept moving, drawing more than one hostile stare as we nearly ran over locals and threatened to overturn market stalls while we progressed through the chaos. One youth looked in our direction and made a cutting motion across his throat - I didn't need to have that explained to me. I kept the barrel of my weapon pointed in his direction. If it kicked off, he would be my first target.

The stink and noise were unimaginable, and the strident Arab babble all too obviously directed at us could be heard over the throaty rumble of our engines. Our show of weapons made them think twice about giving us any grief, but we could clearly read the hatred in the faces of some of the men. We passed so close to the stalls that I could have reached out and picked up a couple of souvenirs: not that I could see anything worth taking. It took about ten minutes of shunting and careful driving for all our vehicles to clear the market. Meanwhile, I watched the roofs and upper windows, but saw nothing serious. One or two black-clad women were hanging out the family washing, but that was it. I suppose they must have been genuinely surprised to see us, and we had caught them completely unprepared.

Once clear of the market, we speeded up and soon left the village behind. Apart from a pack of dogs that appeared from nowhere, barking and snapping at our tyres, it didn't seem as if we had provoked a reaction. Another IP checkpoint on the other side of the village sprang into view, but we were waved through by a scruffy policeman who seemed completely uninterested in us. Next to the checkpoint was a 30-foot high, freestanding concrete picture frame. In days gone by an image of Saddam would have graced the frame, together with declarations of the local village's undying loyalty to his sovereign person. Now it held a badly painted likeness of a local cleric that didn't quite hide the hundreds of bullet holes that pock-marked the surface. Before he had been painted out, good old Saddam had been used for target practice by everyone in the area who had a weapon, probably including passing Coalition Force soldiers. I couldn't blame the villagers. I'd have done the same if I'd had to put up with years of persecution by his Ba'ath party. The road now led away from the village and back into the countryside. We bumped and shook our way along, trying our best to miss the potholes. Some of the damage could be mistaken for shell craters, but the truth was that the roads were just badly maintained, or not maintained at all, and no one in this God-forsaken country was in a hurry to do anything about it.

The smell and noise of the village receded as we once again increased our speed into the Iraqi desert. Date palms and bushes with razor sharp leaves dotted the roadside, along with the occasional rusty Iraqi tank so readily and eagerly supplied by their Russian friends, who had used the Gulf War as a means of field-testing some of Russia's armour and technology. They had equipped Saddam's Republican Guard with their latest tanks fitted with explosive reactive armour, an idea they had stolen from the West. Unfortunately for them, our uranium-depleted shells tore through it like a hot knife through butter, leaving hundreds of Iraqi tanks and soldiers destroyed and rotting at the roadside. 'DU' painted in large white letters on the sides of the dead hulks reminded the locals that it was not safe to linger, as the uranium shell fragments could still be a health hazard.

After several miles of erratic, bone-shaking travel the second village came into view. As we approached the first checkpoint, which was almost identical in design to those we'd already encountered, we became very wary. There was no Iraqi flag flying from the pole, and Arabic graffiti was scrawled over every available wall space on the security post and the police station opposite. Posters of Muqtada al-Sadr and other rebel clerics were pasted haphazardly on telegraph poles and the lone, long-disused lamp post beside the checkpoint; bullet holes were evident everywhere. Instead of uniformed Iraqi Police, a couple of local Militia wearing man jammies and shemaghs stood nearby, cradling AK-47 assault rifles in the crooks of their arms. They did not look friendly, and unlike the guys at the previous checkpoints, showed a definite interest in us as we navigated through the unmanned barrier.

"Gunmen right!" came the call from the lead vehicle.

"Eyes on!" came the reply.

Once again I believe it was our open show of superior firepower that got us through without any trouble. Our rear gunner covered both gunmen until they disappeared in the dust cloud kicked up by the convoy.

We entered the main drag almost immediately. It was the usual turmoil of cluttered shops, rubbish-filled streets, dented red and white taxis and other local transport, all fighting for co-existence. People were milling around everywhere, and suddenly a camel led by a young boy stepped in our way, bringing us to an abrupt halt. The boy swore loudly and struck the animal with a stick, and it snorted and groaned in protest. Even through the closed windows we could smell its stench. As he managed to push it out of our way, a herd of goats scattered across the street, but our driver kept his hand on the horn and slowly moved forward. It was in no way as busy as the last village, though - this was just a typical day in the life of the Iraqi.

Our vehicles negotiated the main street with horns blaring and some deft manoeuvring on the part of the drivers. For guys who had not been in-country very long, they were learning quickly, and the large bumper on the front of the SUVs certainly helped. Luckily this time we did not encounter a market, and although the place was total chaos we got through most of it pretty quickly. The lead vehicle approached the bad junction we had been told about, and although we could see some pretty unsavoury characters watching us from shop fronts and street corners, we managed to get the whole convoy through without incident. I think we were just lucky on this occasion. The Mahdi Army might not have recognised us, but they definitely knew we were coming.

After more potholed roads and a few more near misses with those red and white taxis, we finally reached the outskirts of Kabala. The dust-covered palm trees and brush gave way to the now familiar low, sand-coloured brick buildings that signalled the outskirts of the city. We had picked up quite a bit of intelligence on Kabala, with its rabbit warren of back streets, its twin mosques, their roofs clearly visible for miles around, and its many minarets. The football stadium, once used by enthusiastic football teams and their supporters, and more recently for public executions, was another landmark just off one of the main approaches to the city centre. The place was a thriving hubbub of Arab life, but underneath the usual chaos it was a hotbed of terrorist activity. There were daily attacks on the city and on its satellite towns such as El Hilla that were always in the News and the ferocity and regularity of killings and attacks was rivalled only by those in Baghdad.

As we pushed further in, the traffic became even heavier and more congested. Once or twice we had to resort to crossing the central divider, horns blaring and lights flashing, proceeding at speed towards on-coming traffic in order to gain a few hundred yards. To any civilised onlooker this might have seemed overly aggressive, but to stand still for even a few minutes was to invite a blast bomb, hand grenade, or worse still an

RPG launch into one or more of our vehicles. These people were experts at ambush, and well versed in manipulating traffic jams in order to set Coalition convoys up for attack. As long as they could kill even one Coalition soldier, they wouldn't hesitate for a moment to drive a suicide bomb into a stationary convoy, with absolutely no qualms about collateral damage. We had no intention of making it easy for them.

We were looking for Camp Juliet. It had been programmed into the GPS, but with many of the streets not on the map locating it was still a case of rough and ready reckoning. The landmark we had been told to look out for was a big green camouflaged water tower. "You can't miss it," they told us. Bloody right you couldn't! Suddenly there it was, rearing up in front of us at least 80 feet high, if not more, an enormous, hideous structure straddling one of the main city roads. Its bulbous head made it look like a rejected alien from the *War of the Worlds*. It would prove to be the ideal landmark for the team, though. Any time you were lost in the many city side streets, you just drove towards the centre until you picked up the sight of that huge monstrosity and you knew you were not far from safety.

Having identified the first reference point, we were now looking for the second. This was the old hotel and amusement park that had been built in Saddam's day. The hotel had been commandeered as the headquarters of the local Coalition Forces and the secondary offices and accommodations for our new principal and his staff. As we were to find out, it was protected by a mixed bag of soldiers, including many Poles. We drove at speed past the entrance to the park and from my side window I could clearly see a large sign declaring in English and Arabic that this was No Man's Land and deadly force would be used against anyone found in the area. It was strange, looking at the rusty amusement rides with their bright paint still visible but peeling, and the large models of giraffes and elephants, now buckled and bullet-riddled, to think of all the smiling faces and screams of delight that must have filled the place in happier times. It seemed obscene that it was now a free-fire zone - a killing ground that was the only means of keeping the bad guys off our walls.

We turned right and bumped over part of the central divider onto a side street that led to the main gate. The side street caused a bottleneck for any would-be suicide bombers trying to crash into the camp and prevented them from building up speed. As we negotiated the concrete block chicane in front of the camp entrance, I was aware of the four barrels of a Soviet Zeus anti-aircraft gun positioned in the back of a four-ton truck and placed in an over-watch position on the gate. The Poles meant to keep their camp safe, and God help anyone who was shot by that monstrosity of a weapon! The camp was the usual mixture of concrete T-walls and corrugated iron fencing topped by strands of razor wire. On all corners and at regular intervals, camouflaged net-covered machine-gun posts were positioned. To gain entry, we were first stopped by Iraqi soldiers who checked our ID cards before pulling a line of tyre-bursting caltrops out of the way. I got the impression that they didn't have a clue what they were looking for, but it was something that they had been taught to do. Next we were stopped by a Polish paratrooper, who did indeed check to make sure we were who we said we were. A large truck that had been parked across the entrance was then reversed out of the way, and we were finally allowed to pass through the two corrugated iron gates into the camp. The truck was another preventative measure against suicide bombers.

Camp Juliet was home to a large number of the Baltic Forces contingent from Estonia, Lithuania, Latvia and a few other small countries in that part of Europe. In addition to this group there was the usual smattering of American forces - U.S. Marine Corps Specialists, a small section of Force Protection troops, and a couple of guys we all thought were spooks. They kept trying to move around discreetly, which tended to get them noticed by the sharp-eyed troops, who rarely missed a trick. The bulk of the remainder were Polish paratroopers from the Sosabowski Brigade, a famous unit with a proud tradition dating back to the Second World War and named after the commander of the Polish paratroopers who jumped into Arnhem in support of the beleaguered British paras. Sosabowski was a much misunderstood commander, whom history proved right in his ideas and unfavourable comments about Montgomery's unfeasible plans for Market Garden. Time has a habit of proving things right or wrong, and I was glad I wouldn't be around when history eventually passed judgement on the war in which I now found myself.

In their own compound but attached to the one in the central complex by walkways, were approximately 200 Iraqi National Guard in a tented encampment. This was the main Iraqi garrison for the area, and had its own facilities and cookhouse. Last but not least was a mobile Special Forces unit who paid us visits during the day but at night went out with their sniper teams to have some fun. I thought these guys were worth their weight in gold, and I was to be proven right later in the tour. I still think more sniper teams should be deployed in hot spots. The Mahdi Militia hate them for obvious reasons - it's a beautiful deterrent.

We pulled up alongside some Bulgarian armoured cars and debussed to stretch our legs while K2 went into the hotel to find out where we were billeted. At this stage I think most of us could have slept on a bed of rusty nails. I looked around with considerable interest at the place I would be calling home for the next couple of months. Next to where we had parked were some small Portakabin-style huts housing the Poles and Baltic forces; next to them were three large tents used as transit accommodation, capable of sleeping forty soldiers at a push, and also the Polish cookhouse, which was home to most of the resident flies in Iraq at that time. Several concrete T walls acted as a barrier between the tents, leading up to two huts used as the company offices of the Polish paratroopers. Next to them were three rows of air-conditioned two-man rooms that would accommodate us, along with our principal and his staff. Behind these were more T walls, and next to them were a couple of cabins full of KBR workers who would man the new cookhouse that was in the process of being built.

At our end of the camp were the parking lot and fuel dump, all surrounded by concrete walls, and at the other end was the hotel, which must have been impressive in its heyday. Now sandbagged off at every window, it was one hell of a fortification. Inside were the offices of the politician we were to guard, as well as those of the force Commanding Officer, the Radio Room, Operations Room, Intelligence Cell, Medical Room, and all the other places you would expect to find in any military combat unit. Two upper floors, which gave access to the roof, had several manned machine-gun positions covering an interlocking fire arc. On the roof itself perched four Polish snipers who relished their work and were, as I found out later, experts in their chosen profession. At the rear of the building, where I assumed the servants' quarters must have been, some of the Bulgarian and Polish vehicle mechanics were billeted. This was the place to go to swap items or barter for services. You wanted to borrow tools, you came here. You wanted something built, you came here.

First impression: I had been in worse places. K2 came back with a list of hut numbers and in a sort of orderly gaggle we followed him round to the white-painted huts to identify our new homes. Each of them had two rooms, one for each operator, with a shower and washbasin in the middle and air conditioning. Blimey! This would be luxury compared with some of the places I'd been put in by the British Army. There was a number of rooms and one was designated our storeroom and armoury. It had been identified early that I snore for Britain and everyone was reluctant to share with me so I got the spare room, and I was more than happy with that arrangement. The guy in the other side of the hut was a KBR worker. I hoped he slept deeply, otherwise I was about to make an enemy!

The drivers were sent back to the vehicles to bring them as close to the huts as they could, to make unloading easier. It took about an hour to stack everything neatly in the storeroom, identify our personal kits, and make our sleeping bags ready for use at the earliest opportunity. Now that our drive was over and our supply of adrenalin had reached its limit, we were well and truly knackered. Sleep was going to be the first thing on the agenda.

K2 got us all together and told us nothing would be happening for a couple of weeks, so we would spend our time up-armouring our pickup truck and getting ourselves ready for the job in hand. Our principal was not due to take over the old Coalition Provisional Authority (CPA) building for at least another fortnight, so we had time for a route recce or two of the surrounding area. As part of our reconnaissance, the other team leaders and I were to identify our sentries' positions in the camp - that is as soon as they could transport us safely to the CPA building, which was about two miles away in the city centre. This would give us a chance to get to know the place and its weaknesses. Our Chileans were still undergoing training in Moyock, but were on schedule to join us within the expected timeframe. We still had no idea if they were bringing their M-4s with them or if they would be using the AK-47s. Either way, we would be getting more time to work on the AKs; they were serviceable, but we were still not happy with them.

We went for scoff in the Polish mess tent before falling out for the day. The food was badly overcooked and in most cases cold. It was prepared in the Thai Army Engineers' camp on the other side of the city and brought to us each day in a convoy of trucks and armoured vehicles: our own Meals on Wheels service. Despite the creaking, overworked air conditioners scattered around the tent, it was still infested with flies, which drove you mad by constantly attempting to land on the food you were just about to shovel into your mouth. The food was crap, but we were hungry. There was unlimited coffee, and as I had got used to the American way of drinking it black, I had several cups. We were all on a downer after the adrenalin rush of the trip had worn off, so the coffee helped bring us back to normal. The tent was packed with soldiers of all nations talking excitedly in their own languages, which came over as just one big noise. All of us had squeezed onto a long wooden bench at a table near the back of the tent when two characters pushed their way through the throng and introduced themselves as White Boy and Billy. We discovered that these two Americans had been the only bodyguards working in the area for a couple of months. They had no back up, little ammunition except for what they could scrounge, and very little cooperation from anyone. Initially they had been responsible for the safety of a couple of American officials, but then it was decided to put in place a full diplomatic mission and a full complement of bodyguards and support staff.

They were as happy to see us as if they had won the lottery. They were a mine of information too, giving us all the gen on both the area and its bad guys, and a complete run down on the CPA building and its weak points. They also had a network of contacts for acquiring extra equipment, but they would be working with us only briefly until they were reassigned. I never did find out their full background, although I was led to believe both were former United States Special Forces. Billy was the younger - late twenties, stocky, clean-shaven, round-faced and with a good sense of humour. White Boy, on the other hand, moustached and in his late thirties, was a total nut case. Nothing seemed to faze him. His favourite weapon was a Soviet-made combat shotgun that he'd acquired from somewhere. When it fired, the size of the flame protruding from the muzzle brake was big enough to scare anyone. He had used it successfully a number of times to stop hostile vehicles from approaching his principal's car. I don't think he hit anyone, just scared the shit out of them. It was my bet he was on someone's wanted list somewhere.

Billy tapped me on the shoulder. "Hi, Guy! I hear you're our token limey. Who were you with?"

"Para's mainly," I replied.

"Hey, no shit! I hear they're mean motherfuckers."

"Gentleman's Regiment, Mate! Next King of England's a Para." And I pretended to look offended, which brought laughter from those at the table who knew better on the 'gentleman' bit.

"Listen," Billy said, "I don't suppose you know where I can get some of that English white smoke?"

This set alarm bells ringing in the back of my head. The British Army didn't really have 'white smoke'. To my knowledge, somewhere in our history it had been decided that we wouldn't use white phosphorus - or

'Willy Pete' as it was affectionately known - anti-personnel grenades. I think we signed some sort of treaty. Rather than waste tons of the stuff, it was re designated 'white smoke' and placed in MOB stock to be issued only in time of war, which presumably didn't contravene whatever treaty the British government had signed. I guess it had been reissued in the war and Billy had somehow obtained some, not realizing what it was. In wartime lots of ammo gets passed around; even the enemies' ammunition and weapons get pressed into service.

"What do you want with that, Mate?" I asked.

"It's great stuff!" he replied. "Got into a spot of bother once with an armed crowd. They fired shots in the air and then tried to drag us and our principals out of the vehicle, but I managed to chuck one canister out either side. There was a fucking great WOOOF! and I couldn't see the bastards for the smoke. They were screamin' and yellin', but we got away. A couple of holes in our vehicle, but no injuries."

He laughed, and so did I! When I told him what I knew about white smoke he looked a little surprised, and everyone else was doubled over in fits of laughter. One of the Poles at the next table had obviously understood the story and translated it to his mates. They were seeing the funny side of it as well. "So you see, Billy," I finished explaining, "the reason they didn't chase you was because you'd just lit them up with two white phos anti-personnel grenades."

"Fuck!" he said. "I wondered where those scorch marks came from on the back of the car. Good stuff, though. Any chance of getting me some more?"

This started everyone off in fits of laughter again, which I thought was a good start to the tour.

After we had eaten, we made our way back to the 'hooches' as they were affectionately called in a slang throwback to Vietnam. K2 said that after the day's rushing about he didn't want to see anyone surface until 10:00 hours when we would sit down and work out our priorities. There were no complaints from the team about that and as night fell, heavy snoring could be heard resonating from our huts. It was so loud it would easily have drowned out the noise of incoming mortar rounds: for once I was not alone, and wouldn't get the blame for the noise.

I woke up with the sun beating down on my face. Shit! I'd left the curtain open and been woken by the heat. Six o'clock in the morning my watch told me. Bugger! So much for a lie-in! My arm and face hurt and when I got up and looked in the bathroom mirror my right forearm showed three white blisters and two more were growing over my right eye. Bugger again! That was the last time I was going to sleep without putting up my mosquito net. Next I tried my new shower for the first time and nearly burnt my skin off before I got the hang of the mixer tap. I managed to burn a sensitive part of my anatomy and the swearing woke up my neighbour. "Thanks for the early call!" he shouted through the wall. Turns out he was a distant member of the Gatling family of Gatling gun fame. A blond-haired Southern boy called Thomas. Smiling, he told me that he was from the poor part of the family. No good asking him for a loan then.

We went in to breakfast together and he told me a bit more about the place. He was working for KBR as part of their maintenance team. There were half a dozen of them in the camp, and he would introduce me to some of their more useful members, including John Wayne. "No, really, that's his name," he said. If we wanted anything, John was the man to see. Apparently he had contacts everywhere. It took several cups of coffee to get rid of the dust and the bad taste it had left in my mouth from the day before. I wasn't hungry, so I deliberately missed the overcooked culinary delights that had been brought in for the camp. The camp itself looked a bit more inviting than it had at first sight, though. It's amazing what a good night's sleep will do for you.

I had brought along a book about American infantry fighting in the Battle of the Bulge. It was a good read and would help me pass some of the time. Returning to my hut, I made a start on my book, and generally tried waste a bit more of the day. I remembered what Cory had said. "When you're bored or depressed, just count your money." He was right. I was sitting on my backside, but I was still getting paid, and that was the only way to look at it.

Later on K2 got us to gather round on the patio area between the huts. We only had one wooden bench, but camping seats, military cots and boxes appeared from nowhere and soon we were all perched around him waiting for the briefing. Our plan was to prepare our personal kit and vehicles, and we would also be helping with the defences of the camp. K2 had given the Camp Commander the benefit of his vast combat experience and the CO of the Polish paratroopers had accepted it. There were no defensive positions behind our huts, and anyone could get close during the night and lob a grenade over. Once our Chilean security guards got in-country, we were going to revamp the defences and use our people to man them during the night. The troops in the camp were a bit thin on the ground and needed our help.

It was about this time we were joined by Dingo, an Australian who had been working for another firm in the area. In Australia he was Police SWAT and had been in several sticky situations. Like everyone else, he had come out to Iraq to earn money to pay off bills back home, but he had ended up with a bit of a bad firm. Same old story - three bodyguards looking after four Iraqi businessmen. Seriously understaffed and underpaid, Dingo said he never felt he was protecting anyone. He always felt more like the duty target, and it was just lucky the bad guys didn't take the initiative.

Subsequently, K2 had approached him and offered him the opportunity to work for Blackwater. His employment had been cleared through Moyock, and his local knowledge would make him an invaluable member of the team. He was a good guy with a good sense of humour, and he certainly knew his way around Karbala. He was also inseparable from his digital camera, and had a gory collection of photos taken when a local Coalition Forces Bulgarian unit had been attacked by two truck bombs in their barracks. The sentries had killed the first driver, but his truck had exploded and set off the second car bomb. The resulting explosion blew the walls of the camp down and took out the front of a four-story building that was used as the Bulgarians' sleeping quarters. Over twenty soldiers were killed and many more wounded.

Dingo was on the scene and took photos to help with the later forensic investigation. They were very graphic and not for the faint-hearted. Looking at them reminded us all why we were here. He kindly made me a copy of them on DVD, as I wanted them for my own collection, which was steadily growing in size. I didn't think anyone back home would believe the chaos and human suffering I was seeing daily and I wanted a good record as proof. Who knew if one day I might get round to writing a book about it? For some, it was a wake-up call. The camp had been so badly damaged that it was uninhabitable and had to be bulldozed flat. Camp Juliet was now the nearest military presence to the scene of devastation. The Poles had learnt by making mistakes, and had designed the elaborate chicane we had to go through to gain entry to the camp. They were determined not to get caught the same way as their Bulgarian mates. Their security was white hot, and God help anyone who tried to crash their gate.

# Chapter 7

## The Team Takes Shape

Back in the States we had all been given call signs. Using your own name on the radio net was frowned upon and could cause a security breach, so we used nicknames instead. The Militia were not stupid. There had been cases where they had used a soldier's name to track him on the internet and threaten his family. The use of the Iraqi phone network was also one hell of a security breach if you were stupid enough to hire a phone in your own name.

The PSD team leader Rod Richardson, a decorated retired Lt Col USMC, call sign K2, was a legend in his own lifetime, although he would be embarrassed to be told this to his face. He was tall and bearded with his brown hair now showing signs of grey, and a Southern boy to boot. He had fought in every Mickey Mouse war since Vietnam. Attached at some stage to the British SBS, he was a born leader. Not one to suffer fools gladly, he tended to go off on one if you dropped a bollock, but he would immediately forget the incident and not hold it against you. He loved climbing mountains, and that's why he was christened K2.

Most of the other call signs were self-explanatory if

you knew the individual. 'Hollywood' was good-looking, with long blond hair and the sort of voice ladies like to listen to on the phone whispering dirty suggestions in their ear. Now in his mid-thirties, he was a retired SEAL. 'Stingray' alternated with Hollywood as unofficial Second in Command. Also a retired SEAL, dark-haired, thin-faced and slightly older than Hollywood, he loved diving, surfing, and parachuting. His call sign described him to a tee. 'Tank', a driver and shooter, was an ex-U.S. Marine with a shaved head and built like a bloody brick shit-house: he looked as if he was wearing American football padding under his t-shirt. 'Dallas' was a young, dark-haired retired SEAL and our team combat medical technician, a nice guy who knew his stuff. He spoke good Spanish and ended up as the translator and unofficial social worker for our Chileans, who of course all spoke Spanish. Next came 'Bullitt', with his dark unruly hair and a beard and moustache to match. He was a shorter version of 'Grizzly Adams' and you could imagine him in the woods and living off the land. Bullitt had spent some time in the US Army and 82$^{nd}$ Airborne Division, owned his own gun shop and was a weapons nut, so he had ended up as our armourer. 'Sparky', was our CAT car rear gunner, also an ex 82$^{nd}$ Airborne Paratrooper and another nice guy, with whom I got on well. He too had grown a moustache and beard, but unlike most of us he took the time and trouble to keep them trimmed. Nothing obviously remarkable about him - medium height, medium build - but could always be relied on in a tight spot. 'Mickey' was another SEAL team member, with slightly oriental features. Put a shemagh on him, and he looked more like a terrorist than the terrorists did. 'South Side' was another big guy, quiet but useful in a tight spot. 'Monkey' earned his name for being able to climb anything and fast. This leaves the site security team. 'Tango' was ex-U.S. Army and the designated team leader. Short, stocky, with dark hair and a round face, he was a friendly bloke, although he had a tendency to give long General Patton-style pep talks to his men. We all knew he meant well, though!

I was one of three section commanders for our team, and I was proud to call the other two my buddies. 'Zeppelin' was retired U.S. Navy, tall and slim with glasses and a ponytail. With the right clothing, he could easily be mistaken for a hippy. He loved heavy metal music and so he was named after the late 'sixties rock group, Led Zeppelin. His call sign fitted him like a glove. In the early days he always seemed a little unsure of himself but I, for one, never doubted his ability to do the job and do it well. 'Joker', my other mate and the third section commander, was also a little unsure at first. I think coming from a police background to an army orientated one was a bit of a strange planet for him at first. A detective sergeant, he had taken leave of absence from the police so that he could serve in Iraq. He was a quiet guy and could keep a straight face no matter what was going down. However, as we all found out at some time or other, he was a keen practical joker and so his nickname had been born.

Two additional members of our team were our dog handler 'K9' and his dog Roy. Roy was a German Shepherd purchased by the Company in the former Czech Republic. He was both a search dog and an attack dog, and was well worth the $20,000 reportedly spent on him. As for me, as the oldest of the bunch I got the call sign 'Pops'. It was a unanimous vote and it could have been something worse, so I guess I got off lightly.

The PSD team had over-all responsibility for the principal. My own team's job was to take care of his security in the base camp, clear the route to the CPA building each day, clear the buildings daily, and then 'stag on' until the principal had left the building. We got paid a bit less than the PSD team. What's wrong with that picture? Each section commander had up to fifteen Chileans under his command control. We were responsible for working out guard rosters and the general well-being of our guards.

We had been in-country a few days and were getting used to camp routine when we received a message telling us our Chileans were en-route. The further good news was that they were bringing their issued equipment, including their M-4s. The staff at Company Headquarters had managed at the last minute to sort the paperwork needed to clear Customs and bring the weapons into Iraq. I had only just finished varnishing the furniture on the last AK assault rifles the night before, trying to make them look a bit more presentable for our Chileans, but we could now put them back in the store only to be used in an emergency. All the AK magazines had been filled, so they were ready for instant use as well.

Escorted by Regular Army military vehicles, the dust coated coach carrying the Chileans pulled into the camp compound at about 1300. They were hot and weary after God knows how many hours of travel, and as they stepped down from the coach and stretched their aching limbs you could see how tired they all looked. I guess the strain of taking the same route as us through the same villages and in a large coach, knowing that had the shit hit the fan they would have been a sitting duck, had taken its toll on their nerves. I was greeted by Ramon and Eduardo and a few others I had got to know by name, and I think they were glad to see a friendly face. Like us they had been encouraged to grow their facial hair, and they seemed to have made it into a bit of a competition. Being dark skinned and from a country which has such a diversity of extreme weather, the long moustaches and increased hair growth made them look like a bunch of bandits. All that was missing were Sombreros and Ponchos. If photos of this lot got back to Chile they would never believe they were just ordinary security teams. Someone in Blackwater had christened them the Black Penguins because of their short stature and dark skin. I didn't think that was very complimentary but I could see why! I don't know about scaring the Mahdi Militia, but they certainly scared me. They looked around them and were not too impressed with the large tent that was to be their home for the duration of their stay in Kabala. It was air-conditioned, but to call it Spartan would be an understatement. Anyway, after the initial moaning and groaning and a hot meal, they settled down and accepted their situation.

As team leaders, we were introduced to the Chileans first. I was surprised to find that although they had all been taken on as security guards and were supposedly equal, they had in fact already developed a rank structure. They had been hired through Grupo Tactico, and as ex-Chilean military they were fiercely nationalistic and still respectful towards their former officers and senior NCOs. One retired major, the senior-ranking officer Eduardo, went by the call sign 'Ghurkha' and was automatically in charge with another major whom I nicknamed 'Poncho Via', as second in command. Pez and Johnny had both been sergeant majors and they in turn had already split the Chileans into teams ready to be deployed. This made our lives extremely easy and eliminated many of the initial problems we expected. In my short time with the Chileans I found them good soldiers: extremely well-disciplined, extremely friendly, and all very professional. They were also fiercely loyal, and I wouldn't hesitate to work with them again if I got the chance.

Once they had got over the shock of their accommodation, they began asking for tools and timber to improve their living conditions. I went begging to the various sections of the camp and managed to scrounge a few large sheets of plywood from the Polish workshops, and then I got a couple of the Chileans to help me carry them back to the tent. When I got there I discovered I needn't have bothered - they had already raided KBR's stock of building materials, all of it earmarked for other projects. It was too late to give them a bollocking or get it returned, as half of it was already cut up into different shapes and was being assembled into what ever they had their in their minds to turn it in to. They were all feverishly working away, determined to customise their living accommodation with

176

their stolen wood before anyone realised it was missing. It was too late for me to do anything about it so I just shrugged and tried to work out how we were going to hide all these 'modifications' from plain sight. I urged the two sergeant majors, Johnny and Pez, to make sure it was well hidden because KBR were sure to come looking for their lost material and their tent was going to be the obvious place to start.

They had already decided that the best way to hide their improvements was to turn them into something less recognizable. It wasn't until some hours later that KBR realised they were missing a lot of building materials, but by then the Chileans had been hard at work. The tent now had a large plywood partition in the middle that helped keep the heat in at night. It boasted several individual plywood partitions around bed spaces, and suspiciously new-looking plywood shelves and plywood tables were dotted around the tent. An attempt had been made - not very successfully, I might add - to make some of the furniture look older by rubbing dirt and tea bags into it and staining it with brown streaks. Unfortunately the newness of the wood was still pretty obvious. The ultimate achievement was the internal plywood office built at one end of the tent for the officers and NCOs to use for briefings, with an internet café opposite for all Chileans to use, even though they didn't yet have a computer set up, let alone an internet connection. Now that's what I call preparation and planning!

The search for the missing timber came and went, with the KBR foreman looking suspiciously at the Chilean handiwork but unable to prove anything. It did wonders for their morale knowing they put one over on KBR and had improved their lot at the same time. I knew I was going to have to watch these guys. No telling what they would want to build next. Over the next few days they managed to get an internet connection put in by the U.S. Force Protection soldiers in the next-door tent. They produced a laptop and made up a roster so they could take it in turns contacting their loved ones. Their morale went up 200%.

When our Principal arrived back in-country I discovered this guy was big. Obesity does not adequately describe it. He didn't walk, he waddled. I first met him accidentally outside our quarters when he heard my accent and asked what an English subject was doing with an American team. He spoke several languages and had been appointed by Paul Bremer to bring peace between the warring factions in Karbala. At first I thought he seemed a nice bloke, but as time went on I was to find him manipulative, rude, and a definite control freak. Anywhere we went we always knew he would finish the meetings in time to get back for his dinner. This endangered the PSD team by establishing a routine - a routine that K2 went out of his way to break on every occasion he could. Our principal got angry if he missed a meal, but didn't realise that K2 was saving his life and keeping him from being ambushed. We would soon be guarding this guy in the CPA. This would be a difficult job, but would end up being made harder by his meddling.

Internal training was taking place with the Chileans, and briefings on the local operations run by the Poles were a daily occurrence. At night we would sit on the patio outside the hooches and get a daily sit rep (situation report) from K2. The situation outside our world was deteriorating fast, with talk of an uprising by followers of the Shiite cleric Muqtada al-Sadr, and the number of insurgents moving over the border from Iran to join al-Sadr's Mahdi Militia was growing every day. There was a warrant out for Al Sadr's arrest for ordering the death of another cleric. He was seen as an upstart by many of his peers, but more than that he was a nasty, dangerous individual who was being sadly underestimated, as history was soon to show. My own personal opinion is that he should have been taken out immediately by any means possible before he got any more powerful. It didn't happen, and the Coalition Forces were already suffering more and more casualties because of him and his followers. Over on the far side of the compound, work was progressing at a fast pace on our new cookhouse, or DFAC (Dining Facility) as our American friends refer to it. At least in the camp things were starting to look up.

While the Chileans were building their internet café, we were setting up our own. We'd been having problems with communications and had very little contact back home. Originally we had been given the use of a couple of spare office computers, but our principal decided he didn't want us to use them in case we sent sensitive information back home, or downloaded a virus. This was the first time we experienced his meddling. One night a few of us were sitting in the cabin that housed the spares waiting our turn to contact our families back home. K9 and Dallas were on the machines available, with a third at the back of the room reserved - or so we thought at the time - for the US ser-vicemen attached to us. A couple of us were sitting on hard backed office chairs waiting our turn and a cou-ple more sat outside smoking. A young American sol-dier came in and sat at the rear computer, and by rapid way he tapped the keyboard he obviously knew what he was doing. He looked the computer geek type: John Lennon glasses and the 'I've just got out of school look' completed the picture. I chatted and made small talk with Zeppelin while we waited, and then our principal suddenly stuck his head in the door and gave us all a dirty look before disappearing just as quickly.

"What the fuck was that all about?" Tank asked.

"Haven't got a clue, Mate, but he looked pissed off about something." I said.

I stood up to stretch my legs and noticed our computer geek friend had the same screen up as Dallas had. In fact it was Dallas's screen and he was reading his pri-vate conversation home and getting some kind of kick out of it, as he had a big smile on his face.

"What the fuck you doing?" I asked, leaning over him. He quickly flicked the screen off. Apart from that he didn't look worried but just leaned back in his chair.

"This shithead has hacked into your computer, Dallas!" By now our friend had about six angry contractors surrounding him. "Hey, Man, I'm just doing my job," the geek said nonchalantly.

"So what is your fucking job?" one of the guys asked. "You some kind of pervert?"

"Hey no, Man! Your boss was afraid you might be sending out sensitive information and could be a secu-rity breach, so I have to monitor your conversations."

"Fuck you, Motherfucker!" Tank said. "You read my mails and I'll put your head through that fucking screen."

I was as angry as the rest. "Spying on us from the same fucking room! You've got some neck, Mate, and it's going to get you fucking killed." I said.

It was bad enough that our own principal had no faith in us, but that this dickhead had the nerve to sit in the same room and spy on us was too much. As for sensitive information, it was us that briefed the principle each day to keep him out of trouble, so we were the last people he had to worry about. Our geek didn't realise how much trouble he could be in and had happily boasted that there was not a computer in the place he couldn't hack into. With so many pissed off contractors in the room it suddenly dawned on the idiot that now might be a good time to leave, so he switched off his machine and hurriedly left the hut.

"What a shithead!" said Zeppelin, "if I see him near these computers again I'll shoot him!" And I suddenly thought of several places on the camp where we could bury the body.

We reported the incident to K9, who had a private word with the principal. I don't know what was said but he came away from that meeting in one hell of a foul mood. The following day a padlock and hasp on the hut door told us we would not be using the computers again. That had been our one lifeline home and it had been cut off by a manipulative, nasty piece of work of a politician. He had been caught out spying on us and out of sheer spite he cut off our one link to home. The excuse we were given was that the computer room was being turned into another office, but in the weeks I was there it was never used again. I was sure this guy had a screw loose, so what he was going to achieve in Karbala was anyone's guess. What the hell was Bremer thinking of when he put this useless dickhead in one of the most dangerous hot spots in the country! - unless that was the very reason they had sent him there, to get rid of him. At this rate his bodyguard team would be doing the job for them. He now had a pissed off security team as well as the local Militia after his blood. This just went to show what a tosser our principal was, and yet still we were duty bound to protect him with our lives. Life's full of surprises! It was about that time, though, that K2 was able to make a Thuraya satellite phone available for a call home now and again, so that helped a little.

Soon after all this we built a cubicle outside the hooches and installed a laptop, which now made us completely independent of our principal and his office. If we wanted to use the computer, we signed a book and were limited to about an hour at a time. Due to the time difference between Iraq and the UK it had to be late at night when I contacted Carol, but being late also meant that most of the other guys were in bed already and I could have more time: it was just me and the nine million camp mosquitoes. We built a wooden box around the lap top to protect it from the dust and to give whoever was using it a bit of privacy. On the side of the box some joker scrawled KARBALA INTERNET CAFÉ in black marker pen.

As I got into the camp routine, so I began to meet the key players. I got in with the KBR (catering suppliers) crew, which usually meant a quiet beer in 'Mr Fixit' John Wayne's cabin with Ken, Thomas, Derek and a couple of the other KBR workers. John was a strange bloke. He was another Southern boy, about six feet tall, with blond shoulder length hair, and in the right get up he would definitely be classed as a cowboy. He had his own 20 foot Corimec cabin which was more like a passion palace than a place of work. One end was his electrician's work shop and at the other end was his bed space. Anything electrical thrown away in the bigger camps John had scrounged and repaired. He had an electrical mosquito killer than made loud cracking noises every time some poor unfortunate insect got lured into its purple light and was rapidly incinerated. He had subdued lighting, a sound system that was second to none and all the comforts of home, including a well-stocked fridge and a large flat screen TV set. Several members of different units joined us, and it became a regular haunt. Wheeling and dealing I'm not going to specify went on in that hut, but it was all good for the morale of the troops. Thanks for everything, John! The only thing that worried me was the 24-hour non-stop fashion programmes he used to have on. That was until he explained it was the only way the guys could watch scantily clad females on Arab television. Mind you, the group that went in to watch these programmes in their free time became experts on hemlines and stitching. They even recognised the different models from different shows. It's worrying what combat does to some people!

On the camp we had a hajji shop situated in one room tucked into the corner of the hotel, 'hajji' being the name given to anything run by local Arabs. Cheap electrical goods could be bought there, as well the usual gifts, shemaghs, traditional Arab clothing, and carpets. Our shopkeeper was a plump little Iraqi, always ready to please the troops - a true wheeler and dealer. If he didn't already have it in the shop, give him time and he could get it. I don't think I would have bought a used camel from him but I'm sure he could have got me one if I'd asked. Having a bit of colour in your room by way of an Arab wall carpet brightened up your accommodation; otherwise it was a bit austere and you could get easily depressed. It was very important to stamp your identity on your bed space, personalise it a bit with photos of your family and such. Sounds a bit soft, but it worked: it helped take your mind off what was a very dangerous job. In his own way, by making his cheap and cheerful Arab wares available to us, our wheeler-dealer gave the guys the opportunity to do just that.

Also in camp were a couple of Iraqi interpreters. We would have to work alongside them a lot in the future. They were nice guys and very pro-Coalition troops, although they still had all the old Muslim standards, such as the idea that a woman had no rights and was classed as a man's possession. They couldn't yet grasp the full meaning of freedom, giving me the distinct impression that Iraq was not ready to be a democratic state.

We would be sharing the CPA building with Polish paratroopers, who had an out-building in the front of the main compound as a PR office. They and the Bulgarians also manned armoured personnel carriers at the front and rear of the main building, giving us a bit of much-needed heavy metal support. They were a good deterrent. The over-all security of the main building would be down to us, but we did have some military support on the roof in the shape of two Bulgarian snipers and a couple of recoilless rifles with Bulgarian crews, and we would develop a good working relationship with these guys. Once a week there was a doctor on the premises, who ran a clinic for the locals. At times this could be a heart-breaking job, as he had only limited medical supplies and could not help everyone.

In the main camp we didn't have much to do with the Iraqi soldiers billeted outside in their own compound. They mounted local foot and mobile patrols, carried out vehicle check point and search details, and guarded the outer perimeter of the camp. They hadn't proved themselves reliable though, and we were all wary of trusting them. In the main block were also a dozen or so U.S. Marines. They were friendly enough, but I got the impression they didn't see us as fellow soldiers, just as armed civilians. Sergeant 'Gonzo' Gonzales was the exception. He went out of his way to help us, which proved invaluable on more than one occasion. We were making new friends, but in some cases it was slow going.

Our team leader was invited to sit in on the Polish commander's daily debrief, so at least he saw us as fellow combatants. It was during one of the early meetings that K2 brought up the subject of the weak defences at the back of our accommodation. The Polish commander agreed with him, but said he didn't have enough men to man all the positions. K2 offered our services, and within a couple of days we had built several machine gun posts and fall-back positions around the camp. It was decided that our Chileans would have the job of manning the positions to the rear at night only, so a roster was made up - no hardship with the numbers at our disposal.

For the section commanders it was a sleeping duty once our guards were mounted, and we were only called out of bed in the case of a 'stand to', or other emergency. We began working a day on, a day off; so that when we started manning the CPA we would be on guard one night and guard the CPA building a day later. Day on, day off - not bad in my book, and there were no complaints from Ghurkha or his men. Sandbagged emplacements were constructed on the roof for our 240 machine-gun so that it could give covering fire to the gate. It got cold after dark, and it was decided to have a cook on all-night duty supplying coffee to the guard.

The grand opening of the DFAC was a day we had all been looking forward to. It was a clean, well-lit establishment and with the KBR Pakistanis cooking fresh food things were definitely improving. I think the Poles were pleased they'd been relieved of this duty and could now concentrate on soldiering. It also meant fewer convoys per day from the Thai camp, and so fewer ambushes and less risk to their soldiers.

As a section leader I could go where I wanted to within the camp, and I spent a lot of time on the roof of the hotel with the Polish snipers, tuning in to their perception of the surrounding area. It seemed surreal overlooking the old fun fair and knowing that it was a killing zone when it should have been full of kids enjoying themselves. Large signs planted at intervals informed the locals that approaching the camp would result in certain death, and in one or two cases these warnings had been followed up with bullets. The local Mahdi Militia occasionally tried to sneak through, one or two terrorists at a time. Through their night vision goggles the snipers watched them coming, and then quite calmly took them out. This didn't mean they could afford to be complacent, though. The bad guys subsequently tried using strong lights to blind the snipers' NVGs. The term for this was 'flaring', but in all cases the snipers turned off their goggles until the light was extinguished. The end result for the Militia was the same: a dead Militia man.

I don't think anyone actually gave us an order, but we all decided at about the same time that the pickup truck had to be up-armoured. It was a white 4X4 hired through KBR with no added protection for the driver, no machine gun mount and no protection for the gunner. In other words it was a sitting duck, but its job was to be the third vehicle in the principal's security convoy to provide fire support and somehow protect the rest of the PSD team. The principal's vehicle was armoured and the second vehicle was a kit car with partial body protection. The Gun Truck had nothing: its crew was on a suicide mission if they ever got into trouble. We were prepared to accept that risk, but we all wanted a fighting chance of survival. K2 told us there was nothing we could do to the actual body of the truck; it had been hired from KBR and the hire contract stated it had to go back to them in the same condition we had received it. I guess even if we'd got blown up, the bits would've had to be accounted for in a waste disposal bag. Bullitt, Zep, Sparky and I all got stuck into the problem. If we couldn't weld anything onto the body then the next best thing was to build a wooden frame inside and sandbag the vehicle. It looked good on paper, but not when we started to build. The frame came along nicely but when we started to put in filled sandbags we met problems. The vehicle could just about take the load until we started to go above the body sides, and then it got lower on its springs and just couldn't take the weight. If we'd tried to go any higher the truck wouldn't have been able to maintain a decent speed, and with all that added armour probably wouldn't stop that easily either. We tried taking out the sandbags and dropping in some armoured plate we had scrounged, but decided that if the vehicle did hit an IED the plates would become just so much more shrapnel, as they were not securely welded. In the end we sandbagged the bottom of the vehicle and the sides of the cargo area. The gunner was only protected from an explosion below the vehicle and from any direct small arms hits below the waist. The rest of him was exposed and he was just reliant on his personal body armour and a lot of luck.

We were still waiting for the promised Kevlar helmets to arrive. The driver's compartment had a few Kevlar body armour assemblies hung on the inside of the doors, but no protection against mines and not much against small arms fire. In all the time I was there we never received an armoured gun truck, and our skill, situation awareness, aggressive driving and a lot of luck were all that saved us from injury or death

For the target reconnaissance we had prepared our so called up-armoured pick-up truck and loaded the two Suburban's with emergency equipment. K2 wanted us to do an on-site visit to the CPA building; it had been a couple of months since anyone had occupied it, and the Iraqi Police had been guarding the place. All the computers had disappeared along with every stick of furniture, yet the only people in the building were police. This proved they hadn't changed their thieving ways and still couldn't be trusted. We needed to check things out at the earliest opportunity to make sure there were no nasty surprises awaiting us, as only a short time ago a serious incident there had resulted in seventeen deaths. The target had been General Abbas, the local police chief. In accordance with his daily routine, he had pulled into the outer perimeter gate with his escorts. These consisted of several pick-up trucks full of policemen, several police cars full of his own Iraqi bodyguards, and also his own police car and driver. Abbas was waved through as his escorts parked up in the outer streets, only a chase vehicle with his driver and personal bodyguard being allowed in with him. As the two vehicles entered the outer car park a third police car showed official ID and was waved through by the Iraqi guard. As Abbas's driver turned into the inner compound and passed the Hesco barriers protecting the building from blasts, the police officer travelling behind him realised they had another car in the compound that shouldn't be there. He stopped his car and walked back to the unknown vehicle to check its identity. The bomber realised he wouldn't get any further and blew himself up, also killing the bodyguard and driver and fifteen policemen. The general's bodyguard had done his job and protected him at the cost of his own life - a sobering thought, and a stark reminder to all of us that this was what we were paid for. The government immediately moved all their officials inside the Polish airborne camp and had hardly budged outside while they waited for us to arrive. Our job would be to escort and protect the principal and his straphangers, retake the government buildings, and mount a 24/7 guard.

K2 decided to kill two birds with one stone. We would be checking the routes to and from the CPA building; once on the target, we needed to check for booby traps and possible weak spots in security. We would not alert the Iraqi Police to our impending visit, and we would carry out the mission early in the morning before they were fully awake; we hoped this strategy would reduce the likelihood of an ambush on the way to the site. The site security team and section leaders would be going along to have a look at our new real estate, so this would be an interesting trip, and one I was looking forward to: our first chance to do something useful. I was getting fed up with filling sandbags - if I never saw another one in my life, it would be too soon - but this brought back memories of the basic bodyguard courses I used to teach, when I had to bring home to the hopefuls in the most brutal possible detail exactly what their job entailed. Too many wannabes had seen Kevin Costner in *The Bodyguard* and believed the Hollywood hype. It was nothing like that. I used to walk into the classroom, hold up a sand-bag and then ask the students to tell me what it was. Of course, they all laughed and gave the correct answer. "That's what *you* replace, Guys! This is what you are - a sand bag, a bullet catcher. That's all! You're there to get in harm's way to protect your principal, and the sooner you switch on to that, the sooner we can get into the serious training."

Faces fell, but it was true. That's what they were there for, and that's what they got the big bucks for. We had more in common with these sandbags than many of our people knew.

# Chapter 8

## The Recce

The full team minus the Chileans packed into our three vehicles. We were stowing as much ammo as we could carry in every pocket and every pouch on our body armour. I rode rear left shooter, with Sparky in the well and Bill (K9) rear right; Tank drove with Stingray, map reading. We had the limo, K2 had the lead vehicle, and everyone who was left crammed into the 'Follow' or CAT car. Our three car convoy pulled out of the camp, negotiated both Polish checkpoints and accelerated into the side street, bumping and bouncing over the potholes until we turned onto the main road. It was 0600 hours, just getting light, and the Iraqi Police would still be sleeping.

Our lead vehicle drove by the big picture of Ayatollah al-Sistani, the Head Cleric, that dominated the road junction. Just past that picture we turned about and did a U-turn down the other side of the road, accelerated past a few battered local vehicles and got up to a decent speed. A few cars stuttered down the road ahead of us and Tank hammered the horn to get them out of the way. That would be bound to lose us the element of surprise because we were only just over a mile away from the target and they had to hear us coming! We followed the lead car in a wild zigzag through the traffic towards the roundabout that marked the outside of the government building entrance. The lead suddenly swerved left and bounced across a patch of waste ground, and we followed.

"Shit!" yelled Sparky as he ricocheted off the roof of the limo. "Warn me about the damn bumps, Tank!"

"Watch out for the bumps!" Bill shouted back.

"Funny bastard!" was the immediate response.

The lead car pulled into the CPA outer compound as the Iraqi Policeman on guard pulled the tyre busters away from the razor wire on a piece of string. Once this was done, we proceeded to negotiate the chicane and then the Polish armoured personnel carrier moved back to allow us to enter the car park where the suicide bomber had blown himself up a few weeks before.

It was 0630 hours as we slowly rolled past the unmanned inner gate and pulled up outside the main entrance of the CPA building. The Iraqi Police were rubbing their eyes as they staggered out of their sleeping quarters; it was still too early for them, but they wanted to see what the commotion was. Hardly any of them were carrying their personal weapons. If this had been the bad guys, they would have been caught napping - literally.

By the time the three vehicles had halted and started to reverse into a position that would allow them a speedy exit, we had already debussed. Charging through the main doors at speed we occupied the ground floors of all three buildings and started to work our way up to the next level in three teams. Human excrement, rubbish and the remains of some of the furniture littered the stairs. It was obvious the Iraqi Police had looted and then trashed the very place they were supposed to be protecting. Slowly we checked each room in turn. Some of the doors hung from their hinges where they had been kicked in; nothing of value was left anywhere. The entire building would have to be refurbished and repainted before anyone could think of moving back in. It would not do for the local seat of government to be situated in a derelict building, but it would cost a bloody fortune just to replace all the computers.

Finally we gained access to the roof and had our first clear look at the surrounding town of Karbala. Both of the other teams had also got to the roofs and came up on their radios giving the all clear. Meanwhile the Iraqi Police had just about dressed themselves, and their captain came in search of our boss to find out what was going on. K2 was just about polite, but wouldn't tell the Iraqis anything about why we were here, other than that we were checking the place over for our principal. After a few minutes of recceing fire positions and ascertaining which buildings overlooked us and would be potential sniper positions, K2 gave the word to 'collapse', which meant withdraw to the vehicles at speed. It had been a successful 'look see', and we'd let the locals know there was a new group of bad asses in town. As quickly as we had arrived, so we departed, leaving a few Iraqi policemen scratching their heads and wondering what all that was about.

Over the next couple of days, in preparation for the eventual take-over of the CPA buildings, we drove the local routes and identified possible choke points. Most of the locals were indifferent and just wanted to get on with their lives. Their problem was the Iranians. The people of Karbala hated the Iranians, but they liked their money and the Iranians had plenty of it. Iran was doing its utmost to destabilise the area, and was feeding as many Iranians into the city and its surrounding countryside as it could get away with.

We finally got the green light to occupy the CPA building. My team would be on the first shift, but all three section commanders would be on site to identify any problems. We loaded up our vehicles and put all the extra equipment in the back of the pick-up truck. Tango drove the first vehicle, Joker the second and I brought up the rear with the CAT car pick-up. It was a cold, dusty morning, just starting to get light as we pulled out of the camp at 0600 hours and pushed at speed through the slowly building traffic. Tango took an indirect route, switching from one main road into a few side streets, and then onto another main road into the centre of the city. This was designed to throw off any ambushers, but our choice of routes in and out was seriously limited, so all we could do was keep our fingers crossed and stay alert.

We reached the roundabout outside the CPA building where a couple of Iraqi policemen were attempting to control the traffic. The policeman on the gate was in no hurry to open up but the longer we sat at the entrance, the more chance we had of being hit. I gave the order to debus and my Chilean guards in the back jumped out and took over the junction at gunpoint. This galvanised the Iraqi guard into action and he pulled back the razor wire and tyre busters so our vehicles could proceed. By now everyone was out of the vehicles but the drivers, and covering all angles. He could see we were not in the mood to play games, so he decided to let us in without any further delay.

We rolled slowly through into the compound, the guys on foot using the vehicles for cover. With the vehicles parked, two sentries were nominated to guard the front of the building and I took a small team up the left-side staircase, clearing the stairwell and landings. Zeppelin and Joker took a team apiece, with Tango going up via the centre stairs. We surprised a few police who were casually walking through the building, but other than that they didn't show a lot of interest in our presence. As soon as I'd gained the roof with my team, they automatically took up position on all four walls, as per our briefing. Looking up, I could see Tango already on centre roof, so I waved and then gave him the all clear over the radio. Once everyone had reported in and we were happy with our situation, we called Base Camp and reported to K2 that the building had been secured. After that I radioed Tango and told him I was beginning a foot patrol through the building.

Walking back down to the top floor, I could see that the building had been redecorated; workers were still painting and plastering, but it was a big improvement. It even smelt clean - or maybe the paint just masked the smell of the place. Some of the office staff were already at their duty stations and said good morning. They knew we were there to protect them from attack while they were at their workplace, and most seemed grateful. They were not getting paid while they sat at home on their arses, and they were all just happy to be back at work and earning. I was to learn that most of these people were sincere in their efforts to make Iraq a better place: they were as sick of the fighting as anyone. Unfortunately, I think they were in a minority.

While we were doing our thing K9 was using Roy to sniff for anything nasty that might ruin our day, and once he had reported all clear the team leaders met in the foyer on the ground floor. Most of the doors that I had seen wrecked on our last trip had been fixed, so at least it looked like a working government building. I reckon that due to our presence the Iraqi Police guards were intent on doing their job and checking the IDs of people entering the building. They'd had their holiday and now wanted to be seen working - they wanted to keep their jobs.

Behind the main staircase we found a small room with a large glass front. We could use this as our chief storeroom and a place to rest but still observe the entrance. A couple of chairs were procured from somewhere and we worked out a system by which everyone could have a quick five minutes rest in the room and take the weight off their feet for a short break. We also rotated the guards so they didn't get bored with being in one position all day. All the team leaders were starting to see the Chileans as their boys, and close bonds were beginning to build between us. This wasn't like the Military where you keep your soldiers at arm's length. If we didn't trust each other, then we wouldn't be able to work together. I knew I had a good team.

About an hour after we had gained control of the place we heard the PSD team coming. They had told us they were on their way, but we heard them honking their car horns to clear the way five minutes before they arrived. It was a Catch 22 situation: if we heard them coming, so did the bad guys. The choice was to be stuck in heavy traffic and be a target, or to broadcast where they were and maybe get ambushed. Either way, they would have to rely on their own skill and expertise to get them out of any sticky situation - after all, that's what they were getting paid for.

I was on the centre roof when the PSD convoy swept into the inner compound. Tango covered the main stair-well and everyone was on Alert. If the bad guys wanted the advantage, this would be the time to hit us. Our principal was escorted from his vehicle into the foyer, where he was met by one or two minor officials. The building had not yet fully opened, and so all the grand gestures were reserved for later. Hollywood and Stingray flanked the principal, with K2 immediately behind him ready to steer him back to the vehicles if anything went wrong. Dallas had made a point: it took just seconds to get him up the stairs and into his office. We had already checked out the area with the dog before his arrival, so all that was left to do was to secure the front door of the office to make sure no one got in without being thoroughly checked by the team.

The PSD rotated within themselves, a couple of them resting in the cars while the others stood to their duty posts. We, on the other hand, stayed alert and on patrol the entire time the principal was on the premises. Everyone was determined the day would go smoothly. Throughout the next few hours many officials reported to our principal to present their credentials, cleaning ladies in black hijab bustled through the building and Iraqi Police went about their day-to-day routine. It was becoming a busy place.

At the back of the building was a small prison for local offenders. This was a real eye-opener to me. If our prisoners back home think they have a bad deal, they should try staying in that jail for a day and I don't think they would ever consider re-offending. It stank, it was over crowded, and I'm pretty sure there was no TV in the cells. To one side of the CPA buildings were the law courts, and on the other side was an infants' school. To the front was a large open parking lot, overlooked on two sides by residential buildings. To the right was a wall with a sandbagged gun position manned by Iraqi Police. This had a small foot gate for certain personnel, but the main entrance on the opposite wall was the only way in and out for government and military vehicles.

Outside the right-hand wall were the town centre and market place. If we were going to be attacked by shooters it would be from that direction, where they had the most cover. Overlooking us was a large mosque and minaret. There was some rule that no building could be higher than the mosque, which meant that most buildings in the area were the same height as the roof on which we stood. It was a sniper's paradise. We would have to improve the roof protection, or we were going to take casualties, and I for one didn't fancy being the duty target. It was getting near lunchtime and we heard K2 on the radio telling his team to "stand by to move!" Once again everyone stood to and covered the PSD team's withdrawal from the premises. To the sound of their car horns blaring into the distance, we stayed at our posts for another hour. To leave immediately after them would make us a duty target. We also had to hold the building to assure there was a firm base for them to fall back to, in case they came under attack.

When we had been in position for a while and heard over the radio that they had arrived safely back at Camp Juliet, Tango gave the order for us to withdraw. Each section leader checked in the wake of his team to make sure nothing had been left behind and then cleared the building. Our drive back was just as precarious as the drive in, even more so because of the heavy traffic. Tango took us a different route back and despite the local drivers we arrived safely at base camp. That night at Orders Group we compared notes. It was decided that each morning we would take a quantity of sandbags with us and use them to build defences on the roof. It was our most exposed position and we had to do something to counteract sniping. Other than that, the day had been a success and everyone was pleased. Our site security teams had shown how professional they could be, so that was one less worry and took some of the weight off the team leaders' shoulders. The Chileans had carried out their part of the operation like clockwork, and that night we gave them a pat on the back and said it had been a job well done. In fact everyone was starting to work as a cohesive team.

# Chapter 9

## Ashura Massacre

For Muslims Karbala is the most venerable of cities. At the Battle of Karbala, fought on the site of the modern city in 680 AD, Imam Ali ibn al Husayn and his brother Abbas ibn Ali were killed by Ubayd Allah ibn Ziyad. In the course of time shrines were erected to commemorate their martyrdom, and it was around these shrines that today's city was born.

In 2004 on one of the holiest of days in the Muslim calendar, the Ashura Festival of March 2nd when Karbala city centre was packed with pilgrims, nine Iranian suicide bombers belonging to al-Qaeda blew themselves up. This was followed by rocket and machine-gun attacks. One hundred and seventy law-abiding Shiite Muslim citizens were instantly vapourised and hundreds of others maimed, wounded and blown to pieces. As the day wore on the death toll continued to rise, and the gutters of the streets ran red with blood. Three more explosions near the Kazimiyah Shrine in Baghdad killed another 58 Iraqis. Khalid, one of our Iraqi translators, confirmed the bombers had been Iranian. Two other potential bombers had been captured with their explosives intact and one bomb harness found at the side of the road, perhaps indicating what we would call a 'resignation'. There had definitely been at least nine separate suicide bombers, and they had caused devastating carnage.

The Koran forbids one Muslim to kill another. However, if the same words are interpreted by the wrong people they can be twisted to suggest that it is acceptable to do so if they are the 'wrong type of Muslim'. The Iranians who carried out this attack didn't see the Iraqi Shiites in Karbala as true Muslims, so in their eyes the killings were justifiable. As for the terrorists, they would still go to Paradise of course, and be waited on by 74 virgins. Brigadier General Mark Kimmit, the American commander in Baghdad, originally blamed Abu Musab al Zarqawi for the attacks, but it was later proven that they were directed by his field commander in Iraq, Abu Abdallah al Hassan Ben Mahmoud.

When the attack took place we were on a routine administration run to Lima, the Thai Army camp. It was patently obvious that our vehicles were not manned by Iraqi terrorists, but the Thai Army Gate Commander had his orders and so he shut the gates and no one was let in or out. This typically knee-jerk response left us in their open parking lot with no cover other than our vehicles, and with thousands of pissed-off pilgrims filing past on the road outside. All we could do was put the vehicles in an all-round defence position and hold our ground until we could get into the main camp. It gave us a few hairy moments: at any second the thousands of pilgrims passing by might take it into their heads that we were to blame for their troubles and turn on us.

Army ambulances screamed down the road towards the city centre to try to evacuate the wounded because the local civilian services just could not cope. Somehow they had to make their way through the one and a half million pilgrims estimated to be in the city centre. Overhead, chopper medevacs brought in the first casualties to the Polish field hospital located within the Thai camp. They came in fast over the top of us, banked and were down in one slick manoeuvre. They were that low and fast I could smell the burnt aviation fuel and hot exhaust as they went by. Even though it was carrying injured pilgrims, a helicopter would still be too good a target to let by without someone firing at it. The wounded on board would be just so many more martyrs to the cause, so the pilots were not taking any chances. This was a real nightmare. Soviet built Hip and Hind helicopters were stacking up to land on the small helipad, and they couldn't unload the wounded quick enough. A helicopter gunship circled the camp, daring any would-be terrorist to try his luck. They had no takers, though: the enemy wasn't that brave. Meanwhile, we sat there in the car park like a bloody wagon train waiting for the Indians to attack.

"Fuck this!" K2 said to no one in particular. "Let's get the fuck out of here before it gets dark. These dickheads are never going to let us in." There was a bit of a scramble as we all jumped into our allotted firing positions. "Ok, let's roll!" K2's Southern drawl came over the radio. "Keep closed up and watch for sudden movement. These bastards are gonna be all around us so look out for grenades."

We managed to push through the chaos and drove back towards our base camp as night fell. It was so dangerous after dark that usually no one travelled, but in this instance, we had no choice in the matter. Everyone was pretty wound up as we negotiated an Iraqi Police checkpoint. A single report rang out, and my heart missed a beat. As left rear shooter, I craned my neck trying to locate a muzzle flash so I could return fire. "Go! Go! Go!" Billy shouted as our driver pushed a battered red and white saloon car out of the way to the crunch and ripping noise of cheap Iraqi bodywork, and cleared the checkpoint for the vehicle behind. It took seconds for the three vehicles to break contact and speed away from the X, but I caught a glimpse of an Iraqi policeman walking casually out of his Sanger, looking puzzled as we sped past. His rifle stood against the outer Sanger wall. So much for our alert, well trained Iraqi comrades!

The drive back was fast and furious with everyone on the alert for further attacks. We finally got back to Camp Juliet without further incident. When we had the team debrief later it was decided that what we'd had heard was either an Iraqi negligent discharge, or a car backfiring. No one had seen a muzzle flash and there were no holes in the vehicles, but the boss wasn't unhappy about a possible over-kill. Everyone had reacted well to what we thought was a genuine shot being fired. Our job was to get the principal to safety, not stand and fight, and our drills had stood us in excellent stead.

That night we received a contact report. There was more bad news; three of the American civilian administrators had been killed in an ambush. There was one American male, Robert Zangas; one American female, Fern Holland, and one Iraqi female, Salwar Ourmashi. Holland was a women's rights activist and lawyer working for the CPA. Zangas, the driver of the vehicle, was a retired U.S. Marine now working as a civilian administrator and advisor for the CPA. He had been driving Holland back from the El Hilla camp to their living quarters. Why they didn't wait for their escort no one knows. The Iraqi woman killed in the attack was Holland's translator.

Fern Holland was a pretty blonde 23 year old who ran the Karbala Women's Centre. The Centre looked after and advised women who had been raped or beaten by their husbands, a very common occurrence in that part of the world. In order for a woman to prove rape in Iraq, or any Muslim country for that matter, she must have four male witnesses to the act. Not a very likely scenario and definitely one that is legally stacked against the lady in question. Holland was actively campaigning for women's rights in Iraq and was the driving force behind the Centre. Most Iraqi men have a macho mentality. As far as they are concerned a woman has no rights, but is just another possession; if women's rights caught on, the whole of society would be undermined. Holland was therefore public enemy No.1 in the eyes of the local male population. She was told many times that she was putting herself and others in serious danger, but she still insisted on travelling without armed protection, believing a bodyguard would only hinder her work. I would like to use the word 'naïve', but just plain bloody 'stupid' comes to mind. The old saying that seems to fit the bill in this case is 'the road to Hell is paved with good intentions'. Holland's intentions may have been good, but she just got herself and two colleagues killed. They had just passed through an Iraqi Police checkpoint when a police pick-up truck pulled alongside. The occupants of the American vehicle were not unduly worried because this was a familiar sight, so they didn't attempt any evasive action. When the police opened up at point blank range with their AK-47s, all three were killed instantly. The police vehicle turned around and fired into the car again. The police from the checkpoint ran forward and managed to arrest the killers, who turned out to be bona fide police, and they were handed over to the Polish Army. This incident proved beyond a shadow of a doubt that the security forces had been infiltrated by the Militia.

It was two days before our PSD team took our principal and one of his female advisors down to the CPA. The Women's Centre was on the corner of the same block, and they stopped by to break the bad news of their director's death. The Iraqi women were devastated, and I think it was possibly this episode that at last galvanised the CPA staff into action. The CPA building and the Governor's office would be guarded 24 hours a day. This was the bright idea of our principal, and the reason he gave was that he wanted to protect the furniture from being stolen. Guess who were the nominated duty targets for this job? We had nicknamed the CPA building 'the Alamo', though I think Camp Juliet might have proved to be more like the Alamo if we ever got surrounded. If it came to it, I hoped our side would win this time.

As a matter of course we all started putting together escape packs. If it turned bad in the CPA and we were overrun, it would be a long two miles through a hostile city to get back to the base camp. Rations, spare ammo, a Union Jack to signal aircraft, compass, water and a shemagh - that would have to do for an emergency kit. It should be enough, but I hoped I wouldn't have to use it. For the next couple of days each team took as many sandbags as they could in the pickup truck and slowly built defensive positions. The roof was starting to look safer. We now had plenty of places to fire from and, more importantly, take cover behind. Our Chileans had built wooden frames and stacked sandbags around them, shaped not only to protect from the front, but also the rear in case of overshoots. They were clever people with their hands. Give them a saw and some wood and you'd have a suite of furniture built in five minutes.

Back at base camp, K2 was doing his best to talk our Principal out of the dumb idea of looking after his furniture 24 hours a day. It would be a stupid man who risked even one team member's life for a chair. Stupidity did, unfortunately, just about sum up the guy we were protecting. I sometimes wondered if it was really worth looking after this bloke for the money - as they say, "money isn't everything." I'd also heard the old saying, 'money can't buy you happiness', but then some clever sod had come back with, "No, but at least you can be miserable in comfort." Oh well, another day another dollar!

Directly to the front of the CPA building and about a quarter of a mile away lay one of the mosques. In the past, this and the minaret beside it had been perfect vantage points for snipers. Of course, being a place of worship, the Coalition Forces were not allowed to return fire. It's okay for Muslims to desecrate their own mosques, but it's not something we are allowed to do. The general consensus within modern political circles is that we would not stoop to the same level as the terrorists. Well, I'm sorry if I hurt anyone's feelings, but I believe that if bombing the shit out of the place and killing the terrorists saves one innocent life, then go for it! The team had been on the government buildings for a couple of days and already we had the lie of the land. There was a limited number of routes in and out of the place, but we had worked out a system for moving from one to the other, creating a multitude of confusing routes designed to baffle a waiting ambush party. We hoped this would make it harder, even if not impossible, for us to be ambushed. The place was starting to take shape and I think we had the confidence of most of the Iraqi people working there. We were polite to them, and they in turn were polite to us. Identity cards were a problem, as the Iraqis carried their own national ID card written in Arabic, which we had no chance of deciphering - not to mention the fact that most of their photos were about ten years out of date. In addition, they carried another ID card for their place of work. Unfortunately, every official who took over a part of the government also changed the ID card to his own system, meaning that there were several different cards in existence at the same time, and without an Arabic reader among us we couldn't tell a forgery from an original. As a result, we had to bring in yet another ID card that *we* could understand, and then educate people into wearing it where it could be seen at all times.

March 14th started out like any other day, and the local cleric had just finished calling the faithful to prayer. Everyone mounted up and the vehicles moved out at 06:20 hours. We had got used to staggering the timings for security reasons. The three-vehicle convoy manoeuvred through the streets at speed. "In at six, out at nine," Tango's voice came over the radio, giving us the route of travel through a roundabout. The lead vehicle negotiated the obstacle at breakneck speed and Pez, one of the Chilean sergeant majors, leant out of the passenger side, raised his hand, and made the thumb and fingers, hand-upturned signal that Iraqi drivers understood as the signal for "Wait, be patient." Sometimes it worked, as this time it did, though the number of weapons bristling from every one of our vehicles might have had a little bit to do with it. Other vehicles saw us coming and pulled over out of the way. We were now very confident in our way of driving and our way of handling impatient Iraqi drivers. They in turn were getting used to seeing us about and conditioned by years of Saddam's convoys, they mostly got the fuck out the way - those that didn't got politely 'nudged' out of the way. We turned right off the last roundabout into the chicane that led to the government building. The guard recognised us and moved the barrier as quickly as possible for us to get through. Not all the guards were hostile towards us, and some went out of their way to help. Today we had a friendly one on duty.

I was driving the Hate Wagon, the name that had been given to the rear gun truck. It carried two Soviet made machine-guns, one mounted and the other as back-up; I'd also loaded on thirty extra sandbags for the roof emplacements. We were third and last in the convoy, with five of the Chileans perched precariously on the back. As we manoeuvred through the main entrance and turned right past the Hesco barrier into the inner courtyard, the two Iraqi policemen on gate duty sprang to life and had it open seconds before we got there. Our three vehicles screeched to a halt, with everyone jumping out into an all-round defensive position and staying there for a few minutes to make sure we were not being followed, or targeted by the neighbourhood sniper. The PSD were up early today and arrived close behind us, dismounting quickly and making their way into the building as we got on with our job.

When Tango was satisfied that we didn't have a follow-up, he detailed off a couple of the Chileans to stand guard while we unloaded the sand bags onto the forecourt. Each man grabbed a sandbag and made his way to the roof. We stacked them neatly in the centre of the roof and everyone then went back for another one. A couple of trips each, and all the bags were where we wanted them.

When everything had been unloaded, including personal kit, I realised I was missing my Camelback. I walked back out to the Hate Wagon, M-4 in hand and asked one of the two Chilean guards in the back to throw it down to me; then I grabbed it by the top carrying handle and turned to walk back to the foyer.

The loud report to my right was close enough to sound like a small explosion. There was a ringing in my ears and I saw spots before my eyes. I instinctively knew I'd been hit and for a brief second panic surged through me, but at almost the same moment I felt I had it under control. I didn't immediately feel any pain, but I knew that would come later. I was still on my feet and thinking clearly, so that was a good sign at least. The first thing that crossed my mind was that a sniper had hit us. It was not loud enough to have been a bomb but was close enough and loud enough to have been a round strike. I felt dizzy, but as my senses cleared a little, I found myself running towards the main entrance giving orders for everyone to take cover and look for the sniper. I could see most of the Chileans had taken cover and were already looking around.

Everyone who has ever been in a contact will tell you that at times things seem to move in slow motion, when in fact it's quite the reverse. In the split seconds it took for this to happen, I felt a burning sensation across the top of my right leg. On looking down to find out why the fuck my leg was on fire, I saw the side of my right hand burst open and spraying blood over the concrete forecourt. My brain had still not registered that I'd been hit - I think I was too busy swearing! Then the pain in my hand kicked in and brought me back to reality. Fuck! Now that did hurt! I managed to run the last few feet to the main entrance with Dallas, our medic, running after me, shouting for me to stop and sit down so he could check me over. I had no intention of stopping for any bastard until I was under cover; there was no way I was going to get hit a second time, but by now everyone else was trying to find something to shoot at.

Once inside the building, Joker and Dallas almost rugby tackled me to get me to sit down, but all I could think of was getting to a fire position and returning fire. I was dragged out of the line of sight of any sniper and propped behind one of the supporting pillars of the building. Now that I was sitting down and taking stock I was beginning to feel a bit sick. I also felt embarrassed! I'd been in-country five minutes and had already been shot, and to make matters worse I was the only Brit in the team. Why couldn't it have been someone else! Dallas told me to shut up, take a deep breath, and look at him. I didn't. He wasn't that good looking. I glanced up at Joker who was wiping smears of blood from his face. Now I was concerned.

"You okay, Tony?" I asked, completely forgetting about my injuries.

Joker was bleeding from a few tiny shrapnel wounds to his arm and face. "Yeah! I'm okay, how about you?"

As he sat me down, Dallas was pulling out the contents of my blow-out bag, my personal first aid kit. You always use the casualty's kit, not your own, as you never know when you might need yours. I had a nice big slice through the meat of the palm of my right hand, from the outer left side of my wrist right through to the centre of the palm. It was bleeding heavily and by now hurt like hell. I had dropped my Camelback, probably from the shock of the impact, but I'd had the presence of mind to hold onto my rifle. Dallas started groping me. We weren't that close, so I asked him what the fuck he was doing. "Looking for exit wounds, you stupid bastard!" came the reply. Finally he was satisfied I had not been hit anywhere else and proceeded to clean my wound. It was then that I felt a funny sensation in my right leg and looking down I realised that not all the blood on my trousers had come from my hand. I brought a small hole in the top of my trousers to Dallas's attention. Fuck! This was turning into a bad day after all. One of the Iraqi security guards raised my arm to slow down the blood while our medic worked on my leg, and one of the hijab-clad little old ladies came across with some paper towels to see if she could help stop the bleeding. I wondered if she was worried about - me bleeding, or the fact that I was bleeding all over the recently laid carpet.

As Dallas went to work on me, I realised one of our young Chileans was hovering nearby looking a bit lost. I told him to get to a firing position and look for the gunman. He looked at the ground all embarrassed and then blurted out that he was sorry, but he was the one who'd shot me. Everyone froze and looked at him. "I'm sorry! It was an accident - I didn't mean to!" He looked as if he was going to burst into tears, and I instantly felt sorry for him. Apparently he had jumped out of the truck behind me with his thumb on the safety catch and his finger on the trigger and smacked his barrel on the tailgate of the truck. The armour-piercing round in his rifle had gone through the vehicle and splintered. Five large pieces of shrapnel had gone through my Camelback, missing the canteen but destroying in its travels my two cans of lemonade, my toilet roll and my insect repellent. There were going to be some very confused flies in the area. On top of that, it's hard to have a good shit when you have to watch out for the bullet hole in the centre of your bog paper.

When the shrapnel sliced through the top of the ruck-sack, one large piece went through the palm of my hand, passing through my clenched fist and slightly nicking one finger on the way out. It hit the road and came back penetrating the top of my right leg. The doctor later said that the round must have been spent by the time it hit my leg because it entered and then bounced out, leaving me with a small hole and the brightest multi-coloured bruise you have ever seen, from the top of my leg to the knee and all the way around. Joker had taken some of the shrapnel in his arm, most likely from the tailgate of the vehicle. So this was what they called friendly fire. It wasn't feeling very friendly right now. I knew I would have a very stiff leg for about a week, but at this stage it hadn't sunk in how lucky I'd been.

Dallas was dressing my hand wound when I got the shakes. It only lasted a few seconds but it's a really em-barrassing moment for any soldier who thinks he has everything under control. I felt calm under the cir-cumstances, but shock has a way of making a liar out of you.

"Shit! Sorry, Mate!" I apologised. It was the only thing I could think of saying at the time.

"You're doing fine, Pops," Dallas reassured me. "It's nothing too serious."

"Sorry Dallas, I don't make a habit of getting shot!" I said taking deep breaths as he had suggested.

Under the circumstances I felt pretty good, and both wounds had subsided to a dull ache. My fingers and wrist still moved okay, so I guessed nothing vital had been hit, and I figured it looked a lot worse than it felt. After Dallas had cleaned and dressed the hand wound, and I was as comfortable as I was going to get under the circumstances, he started probing in the leg wound with a pair of forceps.

"Ouch! What the fuck are you doing?" I blurted out as I recoiled from the pain.

"I'm looking for a bullet. There's no exit wound, so it's got to be there."

"Dig any bloody deeper and you'll make one!" I snapped back.

Dallas couldn't find an exit wound in my leg and was worried the shrapnel might still be lodged in there somewhere. Tango had already radioed back to base to say we had a man down, and after asking me how I felt and whether I could still walk, Dallas made a judgment call to get me back to Camp Juliet and have me looked at by the Polish doctor.

Leaving most of the Chileans on location, I was transported in a two-vehicle convoy back to camp. Things were starting to hurt now and my mouth was very dry. Although I couldn't use my rifle, I had my pistol in my left hand so I could at least put some rounds down in an emergency. I was still in the 'golden hour' - the medical term given to the first hour after being wounded when the adrenalin is still pumping and a medic has the best chance of stabilising the casualty. I knew I wasn't seriously injured but my body didn't know that, and so I was suffering the shock and pain the body goes through if anything nasty and out of the ordinary happens to it. My hand was hurting, but surprisingly my leg wasn't. I could still move it and had even walked to the vehicle unaided.

We were trying to keep the incident in-house, and I had no objections to that. It wouldn't be good for the principal to know his team were shooting each other. Dallas and K2 agreed it would be best for me to go to the Polish field hospital in Camp Lima, the Thai base, as they had an x-ray machine there. Thomas from KBR walked in as Dallas finished taping up my hand and leg.

"What the hell have you done?" he asked.

"Stuck my hand in a broken bottle." It was the first thing that came into my head. "Must have been a big bottle!" he said, giving me a strange look as he shut the door to his room.

Stingray, Hollywood and Dallas volunteered to take me to the hospital in the armoured limo. It was a bit of a drive and risky in one vehicle, and I didn't want to endanger anyone else on my account, but they insisted and so I was overruled. It was another hectic ride to the hospital, and I felt a bit of a fraud when we got there, as it didn't hurt any more. I hobbled into Casualty Reception and Dallas explained what had happened. The Polish medic told me to get on the table, and then sent for their surgeon. He was a nice bloke, a paratrooper major, and like most surgeons he had a wicked sense of humour. One of his medical staff removed the dressings and started to probe the wounds, with Dallas looking over his shoulder and muttering out loud to himself, "I've done that!" As the doctor started a different angle of attack on my hand, Dallas said, "I've done that as well!" He seemed disappointed the Polish medical staff were doing the same things he had already done, and so he'd learnt nothing new.

While the surgeon was probing the hand wound, he looked at me and told me with a thick Polish accent that his English was not so good. He turned my hand over as he reached to one side for a small plastic bottle. I swear he smiled as he asked, "How do you say in English, this will hurt a lot?"

Before I could register his joke, he poured the contents of the bottle into the wound. "Fucking hell, that hurts!" I said, instantly feeling like the big baby I must have looked.

I wanted to shake my hand to put the fire out, but the doctor held it in a firm, vice-like grip. Almost as soon as I registered the intense pain it subsided. My hand bubbled and frothed and felt as if it was on fire. The pain lasted a couple of seconds and then ebbed away. The stained and discoloured skin now took on a healthy pink glow around the wound. I later learnt he had used peroxide, but it had worked and got rid of all the shit that could have caused infection. As I wiped the tears from my eyes, I actually thanked him.

Dallas and Hollywood were busy taking pictures of my wounds as this was happening. That's while the two bastards were trying unsuccessfully not to laugh at my pain and subsequent antics. Both being trained medics, they wanted anything they could use for later lessons. The doctor obliged them and explained what he was doing, but I told them both to fuck off - they were my injuries and they hurt, so fuck off trying to take photos. They just laughed all the more. Bastards!

My wrist and leg were then x-rayed. The chunk of metal that went through my wrist had missed everything vital, but had caused an unusual V shaped hole that was going to take some stitching. There was only one hole in my leg, no exit wound. I had been moving forward when hit and the leg muscle was tight, which is why the spent bullet hit and bounced out. It left me with a bit of black carbon under the skin. The hole was too small to waste stitches on, and the x-ray showed a ring of iron filings that later came out as little septic blisters, but nothing to worry about.

The hand wound had to be internally stitched to help close the v-shaped hole before the rest of the wound could be closed. Sixteen stitches later and it felt good. The needle the doctor used to kill the pain hurt more than the bullet wound, and it didn't help when he came out with comments like, "I'm sorry I have forgotten my glasses. It will have to be big stitches." I'm convinced he had seen every episode of *MASH* on TV. He used the same script. Eventually the doc was finished. I flexed my hand and straightened my leg. Considering I'd just been shot twice by the same bullet I felt pretty good. To be honest they were just scratches and I had been extremely lucky. I wouldn't even have big enough scars to be able to squeeze a pint out of the veterans whilst recounting my war stories at the local British Legion. You could have got a worse injury putting your hand on a broken bottle, just as I'd lied to Thomas earlier. My two team mates had got all the photos they needed, as well as the telephone number of one of the Polish nurses, so we decided to leave and get back while we still had daylight.

When we got back to camp everyone came over to see if I was okay. The boss told me to stand down for a few days to recover, but I declined the offer. Sitting in my hut brooding about it wouldn't have been good, and so I went back with the rest of the guys to finish the day's duty on the CPA building. I knew I'd had a lucky escape, but I didn't want to think about it too much. I just wanted to keep busy. Plus if the shit hit the fan, I didn't want to miss anything!

Arriving back with the afternoon shift, I came face to face with the young Chilean who had shot me. Immediately after the incident he had been disarmed and his weapon unloaded, but he still stood at his post with an unloaded weapon. He had actually requested this, as he was ashamed of what he'd done and knew he had let down his fellow Chileans. If he'd done a better job and badly wounded me, I'm sure I would have felt differently, but he hadn't and so I really felt sorry for him. I had sustained two flesh wounds and bore him no ill feelings. Shit happens. I knew he would suffer for what he had done by losing his job and a good wage. Back in Chile he had nothing. He had a young wife and child and had come to Iraq for the same reason as the rest of us, to pay his bills. Now he would be sent home in disgrace, and already the other Chileans were ignoring him. I asked him if he was okay, and he nodded ruefully. He was relieved to see I was not badly hurt and kept telling me how sorry he was. I told him to forget it, not to bother. I wasn't angry with him, just disappointed. He was one of my own team and I liked the bloke, but it was out of my hands now, and he would have to suffer the consequences of his actions. One by one as the afternoon shift progressed the Chileans came over to tell me how sorry they were for what had happened and that they hoped I didn't blame them all for it. They were a good bunch, and I had always liked them.

Just before the end of the shift both the little old lady in the hijab and the Iraqi security guard came up to me and asked in broken English if I was all right. I was a bit embarrassed, because up until then I had not met many Iraqis I liked. These two people seemed genuinely concerned for my welfare. Maybe there was a good reason for being in this shit-hole of a country after all.

The following day I was back on duty and standing at the front entrance to the building; we were still doubling up on duties to get the place sorted out. My hand now sported a nice, tight white bandage. It had stopped hurting, but had started to itch like mad. On duty in front were the two Chilean majors, Ghurkha and Pancho. Both spoke good English, and wouldn't take shit from anyone. They were the first contact the Iraqi people would have with us and so it needed to be an impressive one. We had been standing there for a couple of minutes when we were joined by two of General Abbas's bodyguards. Both spoke passable English and were related to him. That's how most jobs in Iraq are secured, by family members. Families are the only people you can trust - although that doesn't always follow, as Saddam killed members of his own family in order to rise to power. Both of these lads were in their mid-twenties and had been partially educated in America. They introduced themselves and shook hands, and were immediately on the scrounge! I didn't blame them. Both were after low-slung holster rigs similar to ours and were prepared to pay for them. I said that I would look in the PX next time we got to Lima and see what the prices were. I'm not stupid: I wanted to see their money up front.

Suddenly there was a resounding whack from behind us and we all turned round. Our little old lady in the black hijab was chasing two Iraqi guards down the corridor and laying into them with a broom. Both guards were howling in protest, but retreating from the onslaught.

"What was that all about?" I asked one of the young bodyguards.

"Oh," one of them answered casually, "they were laughing about your injuries, so she hit them with her broom." We did have friends in this country after all.

For two reasons I opted not to tell Carol I had been wounded. One, I thought it would worry her unduly; two, it was only a scratch. My big mistake - never lie to the wife!

When I got back I quickly got on the computer to check my email. The roster system had long since broken down and it was now first come, first served. I had worked closely with some of the female admin staff back in the Company's U.S. base when we put together all the manifests and Customs forms after building the team boxes, so we'd got to know them and their husbands fairly well. When they received the casualty report from our incident, they recognised my name and sent me an email hoping I was all right. Unfortunately Carol was monitoring my mail because she was running the parachute club while I was away. The very next message was from her. It simply said, 'What's this about??' It took a week of grovelling before she would speak to me properly again. She wasn't mad at me for getting shot, just mad because I didn't think to tell her, and she had to get it from someone else. There's me trying not to worry her and all I get is bollocking for not telling her. I will never understand women as long as I live.

# Chapter 10

## Prison Unrest

On March 18th, IslamOnline.net and News Agency announced that a 1,000 pound car bomb had been detonated next to the Mount Lebanon Hotel in Baghdad; the PE-4 explosives used were Russian-made. At first it was claimed that 27 people had been killed and 45 wounded, but subsequent and more reliable reports lowered the casualty figures. Security was only light for the hotel and surrounding area, a popular destination for Britons, Jordanians and Egyptians. The blast flattened one building and damaged two others, smashing windows, scattering glass shards over a wide area and scorching the front of the Mount Lebanon. Blood was splattered on the walls and ceilings, with dozens of stray dogs feasting on the widely strewn body parts. Two Britons were among the wounded.

A few days later we were about two hours into our duty when the prisoners in the jail started to make an unholy racket. One of the landings in the CPA building had a window that looked out over the prison yard and the outside exercise cage. It was visiting day at the prison and for some reason this had caused a problem. The black hijab-clad women waiting outside were very animated and although we couldn't hear what was being said, we could see that they were protesting vigorously over something. There were lots of raised arms and raised voices. The prison guards, armed with a mixture of pistols and AKs, were trying to clear the compound of visitors forcibly, which only had the prisoners shouting and waving their arms through the bars of the cage, while a few guys in business suits were arguing with the guards. This was exactly the sort of minor incident that had a habit of escalating into a full scale riot if it wasn't nipped in the bud early enough.

As I found out later, the guys standing around in suits were defence lawyers. The ruckus was nothing to do with us, unless any prisoners tried to make an escape, so we went about our business. However, after about an hour it was obvious that the noise was getting worse and things were not calming down. A crowd had gathered outside the west wall by the market area and was joining in with the protest, and another group of people had reinforced the families at the back gate. It wouldn't take much to turn this really ugly. It turned out that the commotion was an impromptu protest about prison conditions. The Iraqi police and prison guards were holding the protestors back, but they were in serious danger of being overwhelmed by sheer numbers. If the rioters got into the prison there would be bloodshed and if they gained the CPA building we would be next on the list.

We felt we needed to do something before things got really out of hand. I called up Ghurkha on the radio and told them to position the machine-gunners and some riflemen on the roof overlooking the prison yard where the crowd could see them. Then Joker and I went to see the Polish and Bulgarian CIMIC personnel in their front office. The crowd had scared away their queue of customers, and they were getting ready to lock the doors. They could see this was turning ugly. Accompanied by our trusty guard dog Roy, Joker, K9 and I walked down the path to the inside gate like something out of *The Good, the Bad and the Ugly*. We all pulled our pistols. This was a society brought up carrying an AK-47 assault rifle but they didn't like a pistol: we were using their mind set against them. In Saddam's day, if a pistol was pulled someone got executed. Our rules of engagement wouldn't let us open fire unless we were in real danger, but I hoped the Iraqi protestors didn't know that.

We stepped clear of the gate and the Iraqi security guards and then, keeping ten feet apart, we moved towards the west wall in full view of the crowd. I felt a tightening in my stomach but it wasn't fear: it was the adrenalin rush that I always got when I went into an incident. You could almost hear several hundred heads whip around in unison to face our way, and they all went quiet at the same time. It wasn't us they didn't like, it was the dog. The Iraqis called our dogs 'devil dogs', mainly because they acted like puppies until the handler put the lead on in a certain way, and then they knew they were expected to work. This unnerved the locals, who were used to treating their Heinz 57 mutts as something to kick if they got bored.

As we walked towards the group they rapidly began to disperse. They were followed-up and separated by the local Iraqi Police, who up until our arrival had pulled back and just stood by doing nothing. Satisfied that we had sorted one problem, we decided to see if we could be equally successful in the prison yard. We took the left hand path, which led through the police guard-room and into the part of the building next to the Law Courts. Going straight ahead past surprised police-men who wondered why we were there, we negotiated the lower hall and made our way into the prison yard. One or two prisoners shouted at us from their cage, which was a metal cage structure attached to the out-side of the main prison wall. It was used as a prisoner's exercise yard and I had seen up to fifty men jammed into it getting a bit of fresh air during the day. Its di-mensions couldn't have been more than thirty feet by fifteen and they would get a bit of fresh air, but with so many prisoners there was no room for any exercise. I didn't need to understand Arabic to know from their tone that we were being insulted and sneered at by the inmates. One of them even spat in my direction, but his aim was crap and he only succeeded in dribbling green saliva down the front of his shirt.

K9 took Roy close enough to the cage for the dog to bite any outstretched hands, and the prisoners pulled back and went very quiet. I was growing to love that dog. What family members were still in the yard de-cided to leave, shouting and moaning in their native tongue. With a bit of pushing and shoving the pris-on guards helped them on their way and shut the steel door behind them. Within minutes the entire situa-tion had been defused, and we all felt very pleased with ourselves: we had stamped our authority on the place. I waved to Ghurkha on the roof and gave him the thumbs up. Joker came through on the radio and told Pez to go back to our daily routine and thanked him for a job well done.

After carrying out a last check on the west wall we went back to the Poles' CIMIC office in the front of the building. The senior officer was introduced to us as Captain Victor, a bald-headed Polish paratrooper in his late thirties who turned out to be a very friendly bloke. He asked us if we wanted a coffee, which seemed like a good idea. Unfortunately, the Poles like their coffee like mud. Talk about 'ground coffee' - I think they used real ground! In time I came to like it, or maybe I just got used to it, but this time it took some swallowing. This we did, as it would have been rude not to. Most of the Poles and Bulgarians spoke some English, but Captain Victor's English was near perfect. We were invited back any time for a coffee, and they had plenty of rations and a small kitchen they offered to share with us. Things were starting to improve considerably. We finished our drinks, thanked our new Polish and Bulgarian friends and went back to the main building to check on the other guys.

As I reached the first landing Poncho called up on the radio to tell me the Polish EOD was asking for us. I hurried back down to ground level, but they were just asking if we could use anything they came across that might be considered serviceable. We thanked them and said yes, if it goes pop, bang, or farts loudly, we can use it. They thought it was a shame to destroy any ammunition that we could put to good use, as they knew that in a defensive position like ours we could never have too much ammo if attacked. A few fragmentation grenades and a couple of RPGs (Rocket Propelled Grenades) wouldn't go amiss, but there was not much chance of getting them.

We had been trained to be very wary indeed of grenades. There were a lot of Russian ammo and weapons lying around in this country, and one nasty bit of kit were a Soviet-made grenade designed to explode instantly. It was to be used in booby traps and especially in ambush trip wires. Trouble was, it was the exact same shape as the normal infantry hand grenade. In time, the warning markings rubbed off, leaving a grenade with no visible signs of identification at all. Iraqis on both sides had lost limbs or been blinded when they tried to throw this grenade, only to have it blow up in their faces.

The following day I received a radio message from Minotaur, one of the Chileans on duty on the roof. An unidentified four-ton truck had suddenly been allowed to enter the rear street and reverse into the prison yard. By the time I got there with Joker it was being unloaded. There were hundreds of boxes of black shoes - a new issue of footwear to the police and prison guards. As we watched, for every box of shoes unloaded onto the yard, two were passed over the wall to waiting family members. These people had thieving down to a fine art. Once again we walked into the yard with K9 and the dog, and the yard emptied, except for the few guards who carried on unloading.

K9 decided now was as good a time as any to use the dog to search the truck for explosives. Using its rubber toy as an incentive, he took the hound around and through the load and truck until he was satisfied they were clean. By now the Iraqis had relaxed. The dog was on a lead: they were safe, and they stopped to watch, so we thought that now might also be a good time to show the locals how good the dog was. I borrowed a fragmentation grenade from one of the Bulgarian soldiers and hid it, without the dog seeing it, inside an old generator in the yard. K9 then spread a few of the boxes of shoes around the yard to act as a distraction. He made a fuss over the dog, and then changed his lead over. It was like switching on a robot. The dog's ears went up and you could see him take an interest in his surroundings. K9 led him all over the yard. The Iraqis pulled back whenever the dog got near them, but their curiosity was getting the better of them. We could see them wondering if the dog would get it right and find the grenade - I swear one or two of them seemed to have a side bet going. As if he was working to a script, Roy trotted past the grenade, stopped, sniffed the air, turned around and walked past it again. He then stopped, walked out in front of the hiding place, and sat down looking straight at it.

K9 made a fuss over him while the Iraqis smiled and nodded their heads in approval. They may not have liked our dog, but they certainly respected him. The guards and prisoners seemed to be impressed too. K9 explained that the dog had first gone past until the scent petered out and then back the other way and done the same thing. Then it picked the middle of the cone of scent and pointed to where it figured the explosives were. Clever bloody animal! You can keep your mechanical explosive sniffer; give me a dog every time.

As the morning wore on, Joker began complaining of stomach pains and was sweating heavily. He was using the toilet a lot, and despite drinking a lot of bottled water he began dehydrating badly. He was starting to look very pale too, so we called it in and it was decided to send him back to camp to be checked out by the doctor. Zeppelin would come out to relieve him and I agreed to do a double shift to balance things out. Zeppelin's team came on shift early, so my team all went *back* early, so that we wouldn't have to do double trips. No one complained: there was nothing to do back at camp anyway, and working made the time go quickly. Joker apologised for screwing up the shift but we told him not to be stupid, it could have happened to any of us.

Within 40 minutes we had changed the teams and settled down. Zep told me he had problems with the Iraqi Police taking shortcuts over the barbed wire to get to work. The trouble was, if they could get over easily, so could anyone else. You could buy a policeman's uniform anywhere, so we wouldn't know we had an impostor in the compound until it was too late. It was like talking to little children trying to educate the police not to do this. We decided to bring it up at the nightly debrief; K2 needed to know about any potential security breaches, no matter how small.

The rest of the day finished without further incident, but as we began to pull out of the building a burst of automatic fire echoed around the place. It was close but there was no impact or thump, so it was not incoming. It could have been anything - Iraqis think nothing of firing into the air to celebrate weddings, deaths, basically anything they feel is worth celebrating. Trouble is, what goes up must come down and so we had the occasional accidental death. It also meant we had to positively identify targets before we opened fire. Nothing is simple in Iraq. Anyway, since no rounds had come in our direction and we had no identified targets, we kept going.

It was the usual push through traffic to get back to camp, but despite the shots fired earlier, the journey was uneventful. When we got there Zep and I went to check on Joker and found him in his pit. He had dehydrated so badly that Dallas had wired him up to a saline drip, but he'd already taken most of the litre and still looked no better. The Polish doctor would check on him when he got back from the Thai camp. When we left to let him rest, Dallas was just slinging another litre of fluids into him. That didn't look good.

After the evening meal we had our nightly meeting. The main topic of the day was another bomb attack. A massive bomb had exploded in a Baghdad hotel, completely destroying it, and this was followed up with a drive-by shooting. About 21 people had been killed, mostly English and Americans. Zeppelin brought up our concern about Iraqi police climbing over the wire, which now seemed pretty trivial compared with the bomb attack. K2 said he would bring it up with General Abbas and try to impress on him the seriousness of the problem: if he was not careful, he was going to have a suicide bomber in his office.

There was a big meeting scheduled at the CPA complex, with a lot of VIPs expected, as well as a few of the local opposition leaders. Zeppelin, Tango and I had agreed to share Joker's duties until he was well enough to come back on shift. He was losing weight from both ends and the poor sod could hardly lift his head off the pillow. The doc had given him something to help and all he could do was rest, drink lots of fluids, and wait for the bug to work its way out of his system. There was a good chance we would all catch it, whatever it was. I just hoped I didn't get it as badly as poor old Joker.

By now we had managed to educate most of the locals working in the building into wearing clearly displayed identity cards, and we had tightened up security in other ways too. The Iraqi Police on our gates were seen to turn away people who had no ID with them - now that was a turn up for the books! - and some of them were doing a good job of stopping, searching and turning back people who didn't have good reason to be there. The other guards had to be reminded constantly. It was a case of 'every day is a Monday'; you had to keep starting from scratch to re-educate them, which could be very frustrating. Considering the large number of policemen they'd already lost on the site, I was surprised it took them so long to switch on.

After our visit to Joker, two U.S. Military Police Humvees pulled into the outer car park, so I went down to have a chat. I wanted to see if they had anything interesting to tell us about what was happening in the surrounding area, and of course see what I could scrounge. Their unit was attached to the 82nd Airborne and they were a good bunch of people. One of the top gunners told me they had actually been in their first contact within an hour of arriving in-country. That had been about a month ago and they'd been in several contacts since, although luckily without any fatalities. As we chatted I found that Intel had no hard information to make them expect trouble that day, but of course with so many different factions in one room anything could happen. This was Iraq, where things could kick off big-time within minutes. The MPs had been told to look in throughout the day in case we needed backup and the patrol commander was more than happy to do that. Karbala was a potential powder keg. With us now manning the high ground in the area, our compound was about as safe a place as any for them to pull into to take a break.

I told them about our current ammo state and they said they would have a word with their boss. They came across Iraqi 7.62 ammo all the time and if they could get permission to hand it over to us, we would be in better shape. Although we had M-4 Bushmasters, our heavy weapons were all Soviet-made and a different calibre. It was up to us to get ammo from anywhere we could. I would've liked one of their grenade launchers on the roof, but for some reason they wouldn't part with one. Some people have no sense of humour!

It was time to patrol the street to the rear of the buildings. It was a wide street with a Hesco barrier and barbed wire running down the centre, cutting it off from the rest of the population and giving us a small slice of No Man's Land. The right-hand side had a vehicle chicane and foot gate to allow people in. The left-hand side was blocked off with Hescos and earth mounds topped with razor wire. All this was at the rear of the Law Courts, giving them a secure back door. Behind the main building were the Iraqi Passport

Office and a couple of civilian administration offices, which meant a constant stream of unknown civilians entering and leaving by this route every day.

To act as a deterrent and to give the Iraqi Police a bit of backup, we had set up a machine gun post overlooking their position, and another defensive Sanger overlooked a side street that came down to join ours. We had also reinforced the Hescos two blocks deep at that point to prevent, or at least slow down any VBIED that tried to hit us. Several shops dotted the street, amongst them a butcher's with some dubious looking meat hanging outside on hooks and attracting the local fly population. Its sanitary conditions would definitely give Health and Safety back home a heart attack. There was also a store selling everything from car parts and electrical goods to household cleaning items, and a carpentry shop with its owner's wares spilling out onto the street. The goods ranged from finely carved furniture that could happily adorn a stately home to objects at the lower end of the scale that resembled padded tea chests. He had obviously cornered the complete market in this area.

All day long the prison security guards shouted their orders across to the shops, and the shopkeepers sent boys back with plastic bags to be passed through the wire. Family members of the prisoners also handed through packages of food, asking the security guards to pass them on to their loved ones. I did see some of these being searched prior to disappearing into the prison, but I wondered how many of them got to the prisoner and how many were spirited away by the guards. Security was bad - anything could find its way through - and it was a hard job trying to educate the guards on security when they only saw it as an inconvenience. Their whole philosophy was, well, if it's Allah's will that today I die, so be it! Myself, I'd rather not leave it all up to Allah.

The Poles had named the row of shops "Sesame Street" after the children's TV series, in honour of the character called Oscar who lives in a dustbin. The entire street had tons of shit and rubbish piled up in mounds all along it, and the place stank to such an extent that you couldn't help but gag if the wind blew the fumes your way. This rubbish had been reported as a serious health hazard, and the local council officials had promised it would be removed because it was a real problem. Just walking the inside strip of the street had a calming effect on the locals. Some smiled and waved, and we waved back. Some tried out the little English they knew, and we answered them back politely, but we never stood and engaged in long conversations. No reason to give the snipers an easy target. We noticed that our gate guards seemed to take a new and serious interest in their jobs as we patrolled by. They thought they were being checked up on.

When we took Roy with us the children called out asking his name. The adults were scared of the dog but the children seemed to have no fear, just the innocent curiosity of any young child in any country around the world. Roy developed quite a fan club. Every day children coming back from the adjoining school called out to ask where he was. Even the guards wanted to have their photographs taken with Roy, though they were reluctant to stand next to him and always insisted that one of us be in between them and the dog. I reckon he must have ended up the most photographed dog in Iraq. Our Roy became a celebrity.

As we passed the back of the prison we noticed a battered minibus parked underneath an overhead canopy. I hadn't seen it drive in and no one had reported it. K9 put the dog around it and it reacted. Shit! That's all we needed with the meeting about to kick off. Zep went inside to ask who it belonged to, and within seconds a large, well-dressed Iraqi came running out, claiming ownership of the van. He showed his ID card, which identified him as a policeman. No problem, but in future he should let us know when he was parking in the compound. It was obvious we needed a list of vehicles and owners, and to have some sort of vehicle pass for easy identification.

The meeting was about to begin. On the agenda was a brave attempt to get security in the area tightened up. Clearly some sort of cooperation was needed between the different factions, but to get them to pull together on anything was near impossible. One of the biggest events in the Muslim calendar, the religious festival of Muharram was fast approaching, and if security was not improved we could have another bloodbath. This at least was something they all agreed on. Five million pilgrims were expected to travel to the city of Karbala to visit the two mosques, and movement would be impossible for us and the security forces during this period. One idea being bandied around was for us to stay on site for the duration of the festival, but five million pilgrims really could turn this into the Alamo if they kicked off. Captain Victor told us there were no plans to leave him or any of his guys on site during this time, so we wouldn't have the 'luxury' of military support, or the comforting presence of their armoured vehicles. He was going to express his concerns to his commanding officer and see if he could put pressure on the powers that be to scrub this idea. He could see the stupidity of us staying: it would be like a red rag to a bull, and might even cause an incident.

Our PSD team delivered the principal to his office and took up their positions. After the usual hand shaking, cheek kissing and introductions, the meeting commenced. It lasted about two hours, and the only thing that was decided after much tutting, teeth sucking, and tea drinking was to hold another security meeting the following week. We waited for a while after everyone had left, as was our usual practice. The Poles and Bulgarians started their engines, and with clouds of black smoke belching from their armoured vehicle exhausts they trundled out in convoy back to their base at the Thai camp. Anyone who fired at that convoy was going to be in what our American friends called a 'world of hurt', of this I had no doubt.

"OK, Guys!" I said over the radio, "Bug out!" I received an acknowledgement from Johnny, and saw our guards on the roof gathering their rucksacks. It's amazing how quickly soldiers can clear a position when they know they're going back for a rest. We did a head count in the lobby and made sure nothing and no one had been left behind. Once satisfied that everything was accounted for, we very quickly mounted our vehicles. With everyone covering their arcs we pulled out of the location, waved to our now friendly security guards, and pulled out into the street for the journey back to camp. Yet another day and another dollar earned. We were getting used to the routine.

# Chapter 11

## Defence and Security

A couple of days later we had a three vehicle admin run to Camp Lima where the Polish Hospital and Thai engineers were based. I was using this trip to visit the hospital and have my leg X-rayed. The chicane at their camp was a long one, with a Hesco and concrete T wall lined corridor designed to trap any unsuspecting terrorists within its confines. With nowhere to go, they could quite happily blow themselves up without hurting anyone else. There was a machine-gun post at either end of the chicane, which could make life very difficult for any would be bad guys. All in all, it was a very formidable defensive position.

The Thais were friendly enough but spoke very little English. Unfortunately their defences meant it took ten minutes minimum to penetrate the bloody place, but after what seemed like ages we finally got into the main camp. Just inside was a hajji market where you could get cheap DVDs and other electrical goods. I was dropped off at the hospital tent, identified by the big Red Cross on the roof, and the rest of the team went off to the market while the three drivers filled up the vehicles at the KBR-run refuelling point. Our dirty clothing was delivered to the laundry and I had my leg seen to by a very attractive blonde Polish lady.

The Polish medics were quick and thorough in their examination of the wounds, which were starting to heal nicely, and I had my hand redressed. It was still a bit stiff, but other than that I felt a bit of a fraud. The X-ray showed lots of tiny metal fragments around the leg wound, but the surgeon reckoned they weren't worth digging out. I was extremely glad about that: it had hurt enough having them put in there. Thanks to the pot-holed roads our journey back to Camp was the usual bumpy ride, but once again there were no dramas. Any visitor to this country could be forgiven for thinking that the war was over and things were normal, but this was Iraq and nothing stayed quiet or normal for long.

At the briefing that night we were informed that the plan to guard the CPA building 24 hours a day was back on the cards for the religious festival on April 10th. "I hope that's Queen Anne furniture in there," I said. "I'd hate to die for Ikea flat pack muck!" Joker and Zep standing nearest to me tried to muffle their laughter, but K2 just looked over and glared at me. Okay, so I guess it wasn't that funny a situation.

Everyone went to bed that night hoping that someone would see sense and cancel the mission again, then at about 01:00 hours all hell broke loose outside the camp. Gunfire erupted a few hundred yards away from the amusement park area. There was no need for any orders to be given; everyone paraded outside the huts with body armour and weapons ready for a fire fight, but it was soon apparent that we were not the target. Mickey gave an exaggerated stretch and yawned. "Another wedding party?" he asked quizzically. K2 went to the Polish Operations Room to see what was happening; by the time he came back the shooting had quietened down to just one or two rounds being fired and then nothing. Stillness settled over the area once more. As it turned out, an Iraqi Army patrol claimed to have bumped into an enemy target on the outskirts of the camp and a running battle had ensued. There were no blood trails or bodies, and chances were we would never know what the hell they'd been shooting at. We were stood down, but just as we'd settled back in our beds a long burst of machine-gun fire echoed across the compound. One of the Polish BRDMs could be heard patrolling the Death Zone looking for something to shoot at, but by this time the bad guys had decided to go home to their beds as well, so we finally got our heads down.

The following day we woke up to the usual hustle and bustle of the camp. After breakfast we got the off-duty personnel together to reinforce Camp defences, which meant a couple of hours of filling sandbags and then transporting them to whatever positions needed them. Our teams were doing a good job and the defences were pretty formidable. With the rest of the day off, some of the blokes started building an outdoor gymnasium, and K9 had said he'd like to have a kennel so that Roy would have somewhere to stretch his legs during the day. A stack of wire bed frames was piled outside the Polish workshop, and we managed to spirit away four of these and assemble them in a square behind our living quarters. Wire and some corrugated tin sheets were acquired from elsewhere and within a couple of hours our dog was the proud owner of a large, well-ventilated kennel and run. When K9 put him in there to see if he would take to it he made a couple of circuits of his new home, then plonked himself down and went to sleep. We all felt that was a stamp of approval.

Everyone chilled out for the rest of the day or got on with personal admin. Roy's fan club increased daily with a queue of Polish and Bulgarian soldiers asking if they could take him for a walk around the camp. K9 didn't mind: it gave him a break, and Roy got all the exercise he could use. He was gentle as a lamb with his friends, but the same animal could be a ruthless killing machine at just one word of command from his handler.

The main topic for the orders group that night was our pay. Moyock had still not got it right and only a couple of the guys had been paid. Also on the agenda were telephone privileges. K2 was trying to sort out something for the Chileans and us, but reception was terrible and trying to find a reliable phone system was proving a major problem. Our principal had turned out to be a real mean bastard who liked nothing better than interfering with our lives. This was the sort of principal you were warned about when you did your course and hoped you never get. He had already cut down on our Internet access and then stopped it completely on a whim. Luckily, our team leader had acquired a laptop for us and the Karbala Internet Café on our patio was working well. It was our only link with our families back home. Dingo had been busy taking photos of the team working and of our surroundings, so we were all building up our own private photo libraries. It would be a good souvenir to show the grandkids - well, not all the photos, as I few of them would definitely put the poor little blighters off their dinners and give them nightmares.

Our principal's personal assistant was as bad as he was: a real hard-nosed female with long dark hair and a stern face. She was dubbed the Wicked Witch, not just by us but by everyone in the camp. We didn't think she would be capable of doing a good turn for anyone, even if she'd been paid to. The PA really needs to be nice to the team. Our job was to protect the principal, not his staff, so the PA was classed as a strap-hanger. If it came down to it, she was expendable. The principal and the Witch were both scared of their own shadows and yet they didn't have a good word to say about any of us, even though we risked our lives every day to protect them. If the firm sorted my pay out and put it in my bank, I could put up with this crap; otherwise the incentive to put my neck on the line for these people was definitely waning. We would do everything in our power to save everyone, but if it came to a choice the Witch could find herself on her own: it wasn't wise to piss off the PSD team. Mind you, if she *was* captured by the Militia it would only take a few hours of her moaning and complaints for them to hand her back and apologise.

In spite of everything, my morale had gone up quite a bit since I got a phone call from Carol. I was missing her more each day, and of course she didn't want me out in Iraq, but we needed the money. I had done this sort of work with less equipment for so many years as a serving soldier that I didn't really feel particularly threatened, and as a soldier's wife Carol was more than familiar with it all, but the separation didn't get any easier.

Intelligence had informed us of a possible three-man suicide squad attempting to bomb our position. One would be dressed as a woman in a black one-piece hijab. We called the senior Iraqi police officers on duty in the CPA building and explained the situation; we told them they had to be extra vigilant, and keep checking on their subordinates to make sure they stayed on their toes. Today we had to be even tighter on security. Lives depended on it. At first the day went by without incident, and then at about noon when everyone was starting to look forward to the end of the shift, one of the guards approached me and said there was a lady at the gate who wanted to talk to an English speaker. I started to walk towards the left-hand foot gate next to the Polish CIMIC office, and as I approached the gate and the IPs guarding it I noticed a woman in a black hijab standing to one side of the other civilians. The hair on my neck stood up. Shit! Why me? Trouble was, all the women wore the hijab. Then I could see that her face was uncovered and that she was a woman in her late fifties. I breathed a sigh of relief.

"Do you speak English?" she asked, waving a sheet of paper at me. I replied that I was English and she thrust the piece of paper through the fence for me to read. It was a letter on U.S. Department of Defence stationery informing the reader of the holder's identity. She had been a political prisoner of Saddam's regime. Her husband had spoken out against Saddam and been put to death for his bravery. Not content with that, Saddam had killed every member of the man's family he could get his hands on and then imprisoned the wife. To be the only survivor after having witnessed your whole family, including children, put to death must have been unbearable for the poor woman. Allied forces had released her during the Gulf War, and she had become a friend to the Allies and a source of local intelligence. I read the letter and handed it back to her, wondering why she wanted me to read this heart-breaking story. She then handed me a second piece of paper, written by a patrol commander somewhere in the area. It gave the officer's contact telephone number and name to prove its authenticity.

The word 'grenade' leapt off the page at me. It turned out that she had confiscated a number of grenades from some local youths, and then tried to hand them in discreetly to a patrol. The patrol didn't want to carry this problem around with them either, so they gave her a letter of introduction and told her to hand in the grenades at a government location. She didn't trust the Iraqi security forces, so she had come to us. She couldn't have security officials knocking on her door to collect the grenades because that would have endangered her own life. All the poor woman wanted was for someone to arrange a pick-up point. I called across to one of the Polish soldiers, explained the situation and told him to take her to Captain Victor. I must admit that I too was very glad to hand that one over.

A little while later there was a really tragic incident at the same gate. I had just walked down to check on the long line of Iraqi civilians waiting to see the Polish CIMIC people or the doctor when I was approached by K9, who was on a roving patrol. He pointed to the pitiful sight of a young mother standing in the queue of civilians and carrying a baby. The child was a few months old and hanging limp in its mother's arms, its eyes tightly shut. At first glance it looked dead. I at once brought the child to the attention of the doctor, who said he already knew the woman. Apparently she had been in looking for help only a few days before. Some time previously the Poles had managed to send a baby back to Poland for a life-saving and ultimately successful operation. What could have been a good public relations exercise had backfired: now every mother in the country was trying to get her seriously sick children seen to. Understandable though this was, there was no way all these children could be helped - there were just too many of them. The baby at the gate had been turned away from Baghdad's Children's Hospital as a hopeless case and sent home to die. Now the desperate mother had brought it to us to see if we could help.

The doctor was really upset when he had to explain that it was too late for this little one. It had a hole in its heart and only a few days to live; all he could do was give the mother some powdered milk and some medicine for herself. K9 gave her a couple of bottles of water and managed to explain that she was to use it for the baby's milk, as it was cleaner than the water from her well back home. She was heart-breakingly grateful for this small kindness as she left with the child, and we all felt completely helpless. I thought the doctor was doing brilliant work, but he was visibly shaken. I wouldn't have wanted his job for anything.

"You can't save them all, Doc," I told him - as if that would cheer him up.

"I know," he said, "but in this country the innocents deserve to be saved, and there are so many fucking bastards that don't."

\*\*\*

The Polish Civil Office had to deal with all sorts of problems, but was handling them very well. I had become friendly with one called Hendrick, who worked hard liaising between the Polish soldiers and the local Iraqis. He was frustrated by the slowness of the Iraqis and their reluctance to make a command decision. Every one of them wanted to be the boss, but no one wanted to be seen to be in charge. As well as the tragic problems, the Polish Civil Office got some ludicrous cases. One such came from a large, well-dressed Iraqi gentleman who wanted compensation for his damaged house. A suicide bomber had tried to attack the front gate of one of the camps; he had been challenged and shot, but managed to blow up his vehicle. There was no damage to the gate, but the blast did damage a few private Iraqi residences in the vicinity. This guy wanted compensation that was totally unrealistic: his house must have been the size of a small palace. He was quite adamant that even though the damage had been caused by one of his own countrymen trying to kill Coalition Forces, it was the Poles' fault, and they should pay him for his house. Captain Victor and his translator really enjoyed showing him an Iraqi insurance document clearly stating that they were not liable for this kind of damage. They suggested maybe he should try getting the compensation off the insurgents. They could give him the telephone number of the Iranian embassy if he wanted it. He stormed off in a huff.

***

We had just settled in for what we hoped would be a quiet afternoon shift. It had been a boring day so far. The mornings were usually the more hectic period, as the Iraqis generally finished work by 14:00 hours, which left the afternoon shift with very little to do. Suddenly we heard the PSD team over the radio, informing us they were about to enter the CPA compound. Captain Victor had just made me a cup of coffee and was about to give me his daily intelligence report, but as soon as we received the message I dived out the back door of the CIMIC office and gave our two sentries in the front foyer the heads up.

Joker came out as advance, and I positioned myself on the first landing. From this vantage point I could keep an eye on the Iraqi Police guards milling around outside General Abbas's office, and also see the front entrance. Our two armoured limos with the Hate Wagon in the rear swept up to the front of the building followed by a cavalcade of other security teams. At least a dozen 4x4s and pick-up trucks followed behind. Unfortunately the front of the building only had room for about four vehicles, let alone several trying to turn around. The other teams had clearly not done their homework. They hadn't sent in an advance to check out the building, nor had they taken the obvious and easy option of contacting us as the team on the ground to ask for advice. Consequently, they now found themselves in a bottleneck, and the only way out was to reverse into the outside compound. The PSD teams and their principals had to unload in a disorganised fashion in the driveway, even though they were still in a protected area, and it was not exactly the professional, orderly exit usually expected by our principals. 'Cluster fuck' to use an American term, would be an understatement. Five different principals and their escorts were all jockeying for position and getting under each other's feet as they made their way towards the ground lobby.

Our principal, who by now was known as 'Mr. Fat Dollar' by the Iraqis, sweated and strained under the weight of his bullet-proof vest as he led the group into the building. The bodyguard teams had at last got their act together and now an orderly procession advanced up the stairs to the first floor. By the time our principal reached the top landing he looked as if he was about to have a heart attack. His breathing was coming in short gasps and he didn't look at all well. Good! Nice to see him suffer for a change! Meanwhile K2 signalled that he wanted Joker and me to cover the two corridors that ran off the first floor to the right and left, connecting the main building with the adjoining two. While we were doing this our dear principal leant against the stair rail, visibly sweating badly and trying to get his breath back.

We found out later that the CPA representative from El Hilla had paid him a surprise visit with a couple of other VIPs. On the spur of the moment Mr. Fat Dollar decided to impress his guests by bringing them to see his offices, accompanied by all his strap-hangers. Our PSD team had only about five minutes to get their act together, but they got an extra hundred dollars a day more than we did to take this sort of shit, so they didn't get much sympathy from me. The visit lasted no more than 40 minutes. They wandered from office to office, speaking to Iraqi officials who only wanted to go home for the day and were not really interested in meeting VIPs. General Abbas was particularly pleased to see them (I don't think!) as he had just asked for his car to be brought round to the front and was about to go home for the afternoon. Eventually the entourage filtered back down the stairs to the ground floor lobby and gained the safety of their vehicles under the control of their individual teams. Horns blaring, they charged out onto our roundabout and down Charlie Route back to Camp Juliet.

By now the Poles had had enough. Once they saw what was happening they closed their office and drove off in a two-vehicle convoy, leaving behind just a few paratroopers to lend support. They were in no mood to meet with politicians. Our own team followed the others out of the area, and silence once again settled on the CPA. The glaring heat of the day was replaced by a warm breeze as the temperature rapidly dropped, and the daily hubbub of the Iraqi government building died away as they shut up shop and drifted home. As they passed, many of the workers would say 'Alaikum Salaam!' or even 'Good Afternoon!' to us and the sentries; one or two would even shake hands. The people that worked in the CPA building, the ordinary people, were beginning to accept us. Most now realised that we were there to protect them as well as the principal, and were not simply messing them about with tiresome personnel and bag searches.

A couple of days later we were waiting for the PSD team to arrive when we heard shots fired. We took a compass bearing on the area from which we estimated the shots had come - north east, the opposite from the team's direction of travel. Tango called up the lead vehicle, and just as he was informing them what had happened another burst of automatic fire came from the same area. By now the team was only seconds out from the compound, so they decided to keep coming.

There was an important security meeting on the agenda for that day. As usual, a lot was expected and hoped for. By now, though, we were used to the Iraqi way of doing business: they would promise you everything they thought you wanted to hear and then do absolutely nothing - too much effort! This meeting was no different from any other, and as usual, after much cheek kissing, tea drinking and hand shaking the participants left with nothing decided. Meanwhile, things seemed to be getting hot in the area, with the guards being regularly sniped at after dark: nothing too accurate so far, but it was becoming more frequent. The local bad guys were getting much too confident.

A few days later, we had just been relieved by Zeppelin and his crew after passing another quiet morning at the location. As we left the CPA and started to manoeuvre through the chicane, the IP guard pulled back the razor wire barrier. Being lazy, he had tied a set of tyre busters to the bottom of the wire with string. It's not called razor wire for nothing: a couple of the tyre busters had been cut loose, and they bounced under Tango's vehicle as he pulled forward. Of course he didn't see them and ran right over them. I was driving the second vehicle and didn't know there was a problem until there was a loud bang and his vehicle disappeared in a cloud of dust.

From where I sat it looked like a grenade explosion, so I hit the brakes and shouted for my crew to debus and take up all-round defence. By now Joker had realised what had happened and debussed from his vehicle to help, while Tango pulled forward on two flat tyres so as not to block the chicane. We sat there like sitting ducks until he cleared the obstacle. I pulled my vehicle in front of his though, to give him a bit of cover while he changed the tyres. Pulling my pistol and leaving my long gun in the vehicle, I did the rounds of the team, checking their arcs of fire and making sure they were using all the cover available. Joker's team would have made a good Formula One pit crew - they changed the tyres within ten minutes. All the team were back in the vehicles and rolling just as General Abbas and his cavalcade steamed out of the building on his way home. We had cleared the chicane just in the nick of time.

All the same, our brief halt in the entrance had obviously been noticed and reported. No sooner had we got onto Delta Route than we picked up a tail. K9 in the rear vehicle was the first to spot it. A grey van dropped in behind us and took all the same turns we executed. We put in a couple of extra turns to check, but there it was, still a few cars back, trying to be inconspicuous. As we hit a straight stretch our rear vehicle dropped back suddenly and slowed, forcing the grey van to swerve and pull alongside so as not to collide with us. K9 showed the driver his Glock. The man's eyes went wide when he realised he had been compromised; he hit his brakes, dropped back into the traffic, and was gone.

This was getting interesting, as we had been followed earlier that day when we left Camp Juliet on our way to work. That time it had been an Iraqi Police car, which had continued to tail us even when we doubled back on ourselves. Either he was so intent on following us that he didn't catch on, or he was just too stupid to realise we had spotted him. Either way, when the rear gunner in the Hate Wagon brought his PK up into the aim and took a bead on the IP vehicle, the driver suddenly decided to take a different route.

By now shooting incidents were become a nightly occurrence around our camp as well as the CPA building; they had become more frequent and were getting closer. It seemed our defences were being tested, so the following morning we went into work an hour earlier to prevent establishing a routine. We caught the Iraqi Police asleep on the job as usual, with the same guard on the barrier as the night before. The razor wire roll was pulled back and Joker accelerated forward. Suddenly there was a loud bang, and the back of his vehicle disappeared in a huge cloud of dust. Who would believe it! The guard had once again left tyre busters on the ground, and once again we had blown a tyre. No way, not twice in two days! My guys started to tumble off the back of the truck and take up their now familiar fire positions in defence of the stationary vehicles. As I dismounted Joker dived out of his seat, drawing his pistol as he exited. He was fuming. I swear steam was coming out of his ears. Up until that moment I didn't think Joker was capable of losing his temper, but lose it he did. With his pistol drawn he stormed towards the guard, who by now had gone white. "You stupid bastard! Are you fucking thick? Look what you've done *AGAIN!*" he shouted at the now terrified guard.

"Don't shoot him, Joker!" I called, knowing full well he wouldn't. However, the guard didn't know it, and he was shitting himself. As Joker continued to shout at the guard, his crew pulled out the jack and tyre levers and got on with the job of changing the wheel. It was an hysterically funny scene, but I was not about to give Joker my impressions just at that moment, as I didn't think he would see the funny side! The wheel change finished, all of us including Joker climbed back into our vehicles and drove into the compound. The Bulgarians on the BRDM parked in the front car park had tearstains streaming down their faces; they had been laughing so much. I hoped Joker hadn't seen them. He was having a bit of a sense of humour failure. We took post and carried on with the morning routine. Zeppelin had reported that we still had Iraqi Police climbing over the barriers and wall, despite General Abbas telling them that the security of the compounds would be imposed by use of deadly force. Today everyone was keeping a watchful eye out to try to identify persistent offenders. Our mates the MPs drove into the outer compound at around 11:00 hours. K9 and I were just finishing a tour of the ground floor and went out to meet them.

As we stood there talking and getting the latest word, I spotted a man wearing an Iraqi Police uniform and carrying a bag climb over the Hescos at the far end of the outer compound. It was a slight blind spot in that it was covered by only one of our guns, and a person could be over the wall very quickly if there was something on the other side of the wall to step up on. Under normal circumstances an intruder would then have to walk across 200 yards of open area before he could do any damage, but with military and police vehicles around, the view was partially blocked.

I excused myself from the conversation and walked towards the intruder. He hadn't seen me, and to be honest I don't think anyone else realised what was going on. The guy just approached as if he hadn't a care in the world, which at that precise moment in his life he didn't have, but I was about to change that. I brought my rifle into the aim and shouted "Qif!" the Arabic word for "Halt." He duly halted, looking extremely worried, and so he should be: I had every intention of shooting him if he didn't obey. I motioned to him to put his hands on his head, and as he did this, he glanced left and right as if looking for help. The compound had gone quiet and you could have heard a pin drop; all eyes were on the drama unfolding in the courtyard. I was determined that these people were going to learn about security one way or another, even if I had to shoot someone to prove it. Two of the Chileans came running up and covered the guy from opposite sides, and I told him by hand signals to put the bag down. This he did, and one of the Chileans searched him and the bag. He had ID on him that clearly identified him as a policeman and at this point one of the IPs from the law courts came running across shouting in broken English, "He policeman!" indicating that he knew the offender.

By now Captain Victor had come out with one of the interpreters. I was pretty angry at this policeman's stupidity, and the interpreter explained in no uncertain terms that he had nearly been killed, and that there was now zero tolerance on taking short cuts: if he could do it, so could a suicide bomber. I turned back to the MP vehicles as the policeman was ushered away by one of his colleagues. All the MPs had their weapons at the ready and their gunners sat behind the top guns. "These idiots have no fucking common sense!" I said to their patrol commander. "And they wonder why we get fucking angry at them!" I was slowly calming down, though.

"Thought you might need a hand," he responded with a smile on his face. "We're not allowed to fire first, but if you had, then of course we would have joined in to assist you."

I wondered if that Iraqi policeman realised how much shit he could have been in and what he had nearly started. The rest of the shift went quietly, and once again we had an uneventful drive (by Iraqi standards) back to base.

\*\*\*

Blackwater's Iraq Projects Manager Dave Jackson had come out from the United States to pay us a visit. In the short time he was with us he explained the problems we and the Company were facing, what was being done about them, what new kit was on its way, and other such matters. It was mostly good news. Our pay problems were being sorted and should be okay by now. I was going to check with my wife that night on the Internet and hoped the money would be there. Not many project managers would come all that way to sort out the guys' problems personally, so he had my vote. Sure enough, that night Carol confirmed that my wages had finally hit the bank. At last we could pay some bills and keep the bank manager happy.

A couple of days later I was on the roof of the CPA building with Joker and Tango when we noticed about 30 police cars, shiny and new without a scratch or dent, being delivered to the police compound at the end of Sesame Street. That wouldn't last long! Tango laughed, pointed to the police compound and mimicked a well-known TV advert - Your tax dollars working for you!

"Yes, I can definitely see my tax dollars being well spent." said Joker.

The next minute, car horns were going and lights flashing as the policemen played with their new toys. "Bloody hell!" I tried to shout over the din. "What a racket!"

For weeks afterwards you could hear sirens going off at all times of the night until finally they seemed to get tired of that game. Thank God!

The same day the cars were delivered we heard a shot from the alleyway at the bottom right of the outer compound and policeman went running in that direction, carrying assault rifles and with handguns drawn. Joker and I couldn't leave the compound to go pro-active, as our job was to guard the place. We could only go to the bottom wall and observe. Several hundred yards down the alleyway I could see one of the new police cars and lots of police and other people milling around. When they finally came back one of the policemen told me that the 'Ali Baba's', their nickname for bad guys, had attacked a policeman in his new car but they had been beaten off. We learnt later from one of the translators that a policeman had gone to a local shop for a cup of coffee; when he got back into his new car he caught his pistol in the seatbelt and as he tried to untangle it he managed to shoot the dashboard. So an idiot police-man had shot his own car - now that would look good on a charge sheet! But after all I reminded myself, this *was* Iraq.

New razor wire had been ordered and delivered, and we'd already used it to reinforce the entire back wall and most of the front compound. The police and, so we hoped, the bad guys were going to find it harder to climb over. We had identified other weak points, and once we got more wire we would stop up those holes as well. For the moment, what we had would have to do.

As the religious festival got closer there were subtle dif-ferences in the police on the checkpoints. They tried to stop us on at least two occasions, which they had no right to do; of course we smiled, waved, and barrelled on through. We also noticed the occasional bloke in black pyjamas with a green waist sash standing to one side of the checkpoint. These people always glared at us as if they wished looks could kill. Sometimes they were making collections, supposedly for the local mosque. Other times we saw some of them carrying weapons. They held them muzzle down, for they knew that if we felt threatened we were entitled to shoot to kill, and would do so without hesitation.

The green sashes they wore identified them as followers of Muqtada al-sadyr, a rising star in 2004 among the evil elements in Iraq. His supporters were acting as 'religious police', pulling people out of their cars at checkpoints on a whim and beating them up. Women were punished for wearing make-up, men for smoking, or whatever else that week's insulting behaviour towards Allah was deemed to be. They made it up as they went along, and they would often fine people on trumped up charges. They had the run of the place and the real Police did nothing to stop them. I had even heard of them shooting people at the side of the road, although I'd never seen this for myself. A bad atmosphere was building: you could sense it all around you. On our day off we took three of the vehicles on an admin run to the Thai camp. We needed clean laundry. The first thing we noticed was the growing number of hajji vehicles cluttering the road. Old minibuses overloaded with passengers trundled past, with bundles of belongings strapped to their roofs and cages of livestock and furniture tied to the sides. Many had bright but badly painted colour schemes, and were festooned with religious pennants and icons hanging in the windows. They reminded me of "I've Been to Brighton" stickers. Other vehicles carried pictures of their favourite clerics, and they all sported flags of black, green or red that showed their allegiance to the various clerics and mosques. It could only get worse as the date of the festival loomed.

As we tried to negotiate the roundabout and enter the chicane at our place of work, we found the Iraqi Police hadn't opened the barrier. The sentry was not at his post and a pick-up gun truck had been placed in front of the chicane, completely blocking our entry: the gun truck was unmanned. We could see a couple of policemen near the inner gate, but no one seemed in a hurry to open the barrier. We were left with a three-vehicle convoy hung out to dry on the roundabout with very little cover, playing duty target once again. I was in the gun truck at the back and had drawn my pistol to cover the traffic passing to my left. The two Chileans in the back were trying to cover a big area with their M4s, as every passing vehicle was a potential bad guy. One of our Chileans jumped out and pulled the razor wire from our path, and then Tango put the front car's nudge bar up against the Iraqi gun truck's bumper and revved. There was a wire-snapping twang, which I assumed was the hand brake on the Iraqi Police truck giving up the battle; it rolled back, giving us enough room to drive past. Two Iraqi policemen came running from their barracks block yelling at us, but it was too late. They should have been at their posts. We picked up the Chilean who had pulled the barrier across, and drove into the main compound.

Later on that morning things started to heat up once again. There was a crowd of religious nuts protesting outside the barrier on the market side, and Joker and I decided to go outside with the dog and K9. The dog and a show of pistols had broken up a few minor groups before, and we had no reason to think we wouldn't have the same effect this time. I was advised by Uday, a nephew to the general and one of his body-guards, not to go outside. He told us these people were total fanatics who carried knives under their robes and would not hesitate to use them. If they could get close enough to us, we could be in trouble. They didn't worry about being killed, as they all wanted to be Martyrs. I believed him, so for once we left it completely to the Iraqi Police and just watched from a vantage point on the roof. The police reinforced the wall and for about two hours there was a lot of shouting, and banner and fist waving. As the sun rose higher in the sky and it got hotter and hotter, the protesters started to wilt and the group got smaller. Finally they gave up and went back to wherever they'd come came from.

As I was walking back downstairs to the first landing I heard a message on the radio. It was Ghurkha reporting an intruder climbing the back Hescos. I ran back up the stairs and made the roof in seconds, arriving just in time to hear Ghurkha shouting "Qif! Qif!" He held his rifle above his head, so whoever he was shouting at could see the weapon and know he was about to use it. He glanced over his shoulder, saw me, and I swear I saw him grin. He turned back, looked down the iron sight of his rifle, and squeezed off an aimed round down into the street at a target I had yet to see. Bastard! He knew I intended firing a warning shot at some stage to wake these people up. We had talked about it at great length - he had beaten me to it.

I walked slowly to his side of the roof and looked over the wall; if there turned out to be a body, we might have a lot of reports to write out. In the street below were two Iraqi policemen frantically climbing back over the hescos. They had been warned not to climb over, and now they we finding out why. I patted Ghurkha on the shoulder: he had done it by the book, so at least I wouldn't be writing a report that night trying to explain a shooting. "You bastard!" I whispered in his ear. "You were determined to shoot at someone, weren't you?" He looked over his shoulder and grinned again.

An hour later one of the Chileans reported his wallet missing from his rucksack. He had put it in his fire position and then walked over to the opposite wall to check the area. When he turned round again he was just in time to see an Iraqi policeman put the rucksack down and walk quickly away to the nearby stairwell. He checked his gear and found his wallet missing. Racing down the stairs, he reported the theft to Johnny and they quickly caught the guy trying to leave by the front gate. He denied the theft, but we took him up to the roof with the translator and searched the area. As luck would have it, another one of our guys checked the Sanger over and found the wallet outside the Sanger on the weapon's ledge. It was out of sight, deliberately placed where it couldn't be seen but could be picked up later when the position wasn't manned.

The Iraqi went white when he was shown the hiding place. Our Chileans wanted to throw him off the roof, but I talked them out of that idea: it would only have added to the mess in Sesame Street. He was dragged unceremoniously downstairs and handed over to the police. They were equally baffled about what he was doing there because he came from a different station somewhere over on the other side of the city. Visibly shaken, he was taken away for interrogation, and that was the last we saw of him: he was no longer our responsibility. After this incident though, everyone was told to put their personal gear under the main stairwell in our little office where we could keep an eye on it at all times.

Later on I went downstairs to the ground floor to find K9 examining the dog. "What's up, Mate?"

"I don't know," said K9. "He's had scar tissue on his head since I got him, but it seems to be getting bigger. He's a bit listless and not really himself."

I had a look at the spot he was talking about. It was just above Roy's eye, and definitely looked a bit puffy. "Could be an insect bite - but I don't know what would've left him with a lump that big," I said. Trouble was, we had no vet or anyone else qualified to treat the dog.

Our doctor had a look at him when we got back to camp. He said he needed to slice open the skin and look into the scar tissue, but wasn't sure if he had enough drugs to knock Roy out. Anyway, the doctor agreed to try to carry out surgery on him and he made up a concoction from the drugs he had available. He couldn't guarantee knocking him out completely, but hoped to anaesthetise him enough to allow the wound to be opened and explored. Several hours later Roy was groggy, but despite four of us holding him down he wouldn't go to sleep. He fought to stay awake, stopping the doc from opening him up. That was one hell of a tough dog.

The following day, our German shepherd was back at work as if nothing had happened. The doc phoned back to Poland and spoke to a friend of his who was a vet. It seems a dog's constitution is much tougher than a human's, and he had been given enough drugs to kill a couple of people. The vet then called Camp Lima and spoke to the surgeons there. They agreed to operate, but would have to set up an open-air operating theatre for him because of health risks, and would also have to mix another concoction to knock him out. There was nothing in their drug lists strong enough to do the job on its own.

The PSD team took Roy and K9 to Lima on an admin run and waited around for him. Everyone left behind kept their fingers crossed: Roy was a well-loved dog and a member of our team, and we all looked out for him as much as he looked out for us. They still didn't manage to knock Roy out, but they made him groggy enough to open him up. Inside the old scar tissue they found a large wad of in-growing hair. The surgeon reckoned he had broken the skin when scratching an itch, and managed to push hair into the wound; it had then continued growing under the skin until it started to be noticed. A wad of hair was removed, and the wound cleaned and stitched back up. The hospital staff made a collar for the dog to stop him scratching, and the PSD team brought him back the same day. He jumped out of the vehicle under his own steam and ran around everyone, waiting to be patted. The following morning he was excused from his usual search duties, but when he did wake up he walked around with his head down showing all the symptoms of a drunk with a bad hangover. He'd had enough drugs pumped into him to kill four humans, and all he had was a hangover! Within a few days he made a full recovery and carried on as if nothing had happened. Roy was easily the toughest member of the team.

It was a short while after this that we proved to our Iraqi guards on the CPA building that Roy was not 'just' a dog. Joker and I, and K9 with the dog on a lead walked out of the inner gate into the outer car park to talk to our Military Police friends who had just pulled up to take a break. From across the waste ground to the left of the parking lot about 20 wild dogs came running. All were mixed breeds, and all but one was smaller than Roy. The largest one was obviously the leader of the pack and out to prove he was the area alpha male and bully by squaring up to our dog. As they got closer the whole pack suddenly stopped, as if realising they'd bitten off more than they could chew, but the leader still came on until he was about ten feet away. His hackles went up and he bared his teeth, growling as he approached.

Roy didn't make a sound, but you could see he was wound up and ready to strike. One of the Iraqi policemen standing behind us on the gate sneered. "They will kill your pretty dog."

"They won't get the chance," K9 said, and as if we all knew what the others were thinking, the three of us together pulled our pistols in a single movement and levelled them at the pack. They must have been close to pistols before because as we drew, the entire pack ran away back over the waste ground and around the corner out of sight.

"You will do that just to protect a dog?" asked the policeman, surprised.

K9 looked at him. "That's not 'just' a dog. He's one of our team, and we always protect our team mates."

The Iraqis thought we were strange, but anyone who has been brought up around dogs will tell you that they repay your kindness. You look after them, and they will look after you. As well as that, our dog was an expensive piece of necessary equipment and if he had been bitten, even if he had won the fight - which I don't think was in doubt - cross-infection, or even rabies might have been the unhealthy outcome.

On at least one occasion the Insurgents had tried strapping a bomb to a dog. The dog had died in the explosion, but failed to kill any humans. In Northern Ireland we had used these trusty animals as sniffer and guard dogs. On a couple of patrols in Iraq, the dogs had warned their handlers of hidden explosive devices designed to cause severe casualties. Dogs indeed had saved many lives, and we hoped that Roy would continue looking after us.

*Our back wall fire positions.*

*Fall back positions inside the cam.*

*Blackwater Chilean crew.*

*'Sparky' Sadly KIA at a later date.*

*A Belgian camp destroyed by a VBIED.*

*Blast victim.*

*After a hard night Standing-too on the roof 'Joker' slumps back in the accommodation tent in need of a strong cup of coffee.*

*Dog handler 'Tiny (centre) with a few of the Chilean Security team.*

*South Side and bullets in a fire post. The return fire from this weapon surprised a few snipers.*

*The duty Chilean Team get their nightly briefing.*

*Local arms haul.*

*Bill 'K9 and 'Pops' with Roy the dog outside the Hooches at camp Juliett.*

*Waiting to go to 'Downtown Karbala'. 'Dallas the team medic and Chilean 'Agony Aunt' and 'Tank' the teams rear gunner chill out.*

*An aggressive looking Chilean team.*

*Side of the Bulgarian Barracks.*

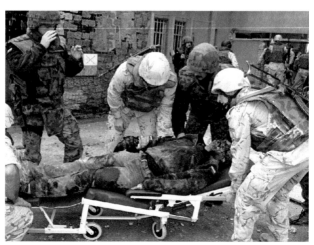

*Lost fingers.*

# Chapter 12

## Fallujah Ambush

On the night of March 31$^{st}$ we received some seriously bad news during the evening briefing. Blackwater had lost four PSD guys in Fallujah: Scott Helveston, Jerry Zovko, Wes Batalona and Mike Teague. They had been ambushed while escorting two flatbed trucks carrying plastic kitchen ware for the American Army. The trucks under escort were being driven by Iraqi nationals, so there was a potential security leak straight away. CNN were playing grisly scenes of the locals dancing up and down in the street while the vehicles burned in the background. One of the bodies was dragged through the streets behind a car, all were burnt beyond recognition and three of the corpses were then strung up from a bridge. All the while the local Iraqis could be seen working themselves up into a screaming, wild-eyed frenzy, all semblance of civilisation stripped away: they were just a horde of crazed savages. At that moment I felt so much hatred for these people that I would gladly have dropped napalm on them for the pleasure of watching them burn. If you're thinking, 'so he's no better than them', I can only say you needed to be there to witness it, and then you might feel differently. We all knew of course that if we were wounded and captured we would all suffer a similar fate - and maybe ours wouldn't be so quick. The team killed were good guys, but they had been set up by a mixture of bad intelligence, bad decisions, and allegedly the Iraqi Police.

Yes, we all wanted an excuse to kill a few of the bastards in return and we hoped we would get the opportunity. The story we heard at the time was that they'd asked for directions from an Iraqi Police checkpoint, which promptly sent them down a road towards an area controlled by Insurgents. New in-country, the team naively believed that the Iraqi police were on our side and could be trusted. Once they had gone through, the police closed the road behind them. Realising there was a blockade ahead of them, the first vehicle warned the rest of their team at the back of the convoy. As they did so, the last vehicle was hit by a rocket-propelled grenade and small arms fire and both operators were killed instantly, but the other vehicle didn't know that and turned around to try to rescue them. They in turn were hit by an RPG and also killed outright, but the vehicles they were escorting crashed the barricade and got away. This was the story we heard on the day of the killings, although a lot more details came out later. They had been hit by RPG's, poor bastards, but there was some comfort in the thought that at least they had been killed outright: we could accept that as an occupational hazard. But as were to find out later, nothing could have been further from the truth.

At the same time as we were watching these scenes on television we were all loading our magazines, checking our 'burst out' bags and generally getting ready for war. K2 was already in the Polish Operations Room telling the Operations Officer we were about to go to Falluja to recover our team mates, and the Poles made no attempt to stop him. Unfortunately at this stage our principal came on the scene red faced and angry and informed us that should we get in our vehicles and attempt to leave the camp, he would have us arrested as mercenaries. Now an outsider might think he was reminding us of a point of law. Deserting our principal and going out on a limb like that would change our position from one of a defensive PSD team to that of a proactive mercenary unit. He was right of course, but personally I think he was shitting himself at the thought of being left without the protection of his PSD team and their support group. Reluctantly we stood down and put our equipment back in our hootches. As time was to tell, if we *had* gone to Falluja we might have caused a little less damage than the US Marine Corps eventually did. If ever a town deserved to get hammered, Falluja did. Tasked with recovering their countrymen, it was three days before the U.S. Marines could fight their way into the place and recover the bodies. To begin with one body was missing, but some imaginative interrogation of one of the local known villains led them to a spot on the riverbank where it had been buried.

The story that came out later painted a completely different picture of events, and one that got many of us doubting our own security and protection. Blackwater was putting into place new contracts. Some - like ours - were fairly well planned but others were a bit hasty, the company overstretching itself by trying to keep all its new customers happy at the same time. We had additional equipment in our team boxes to enable us to improve our living conditions if we needed it and we had plenty of weapons and ammunition, but some of the other locations had been put into place in a hurry and Blackwater relied on its teams there to use their experience and imagination to make the job happen. Additional equipment was on order, but as in the disastrous case of the Fallujah team, it hadn't caught up with them yet. In training we had been told that if we didn't like the look of a situation, it was our job to make a decision not to get into it in the first place. We could refuse to go out, and anyone in the team had the right to air his views on a potentially bad situation. In reality that was not the case. Rock the boat, and there'd be a black mark against you which might be taken into consideration if you wanted future work. You could well find yourself out in the cold without a job; also no one wanted to be branded a scaremonger or, even worse, a coward. The same went for some of the team leaders and in-country contract managers. They were keen to get promotion and a few had accepted the role because they had been senior NCO's or officers in the military, and so quite naturally thought they could plan and lead these types of mission; unfortunately that was not always the case. I have seen some team leaders though, ex private soldiers in the military, who had taken on the leadership role in Iraq and had a natural flair for it. For instance, our old friend Shrek from the Moyock training course and some of the guys I'd trained on the ranges from the second batch of FNG were on this mission. Their team had been hurriedly thrown in to a contract Blackwater were taking over from Control Risks Group.

Shrek and the rest of the management team were ambitious and keen to show they could do their job, and with the minimum of fuss. Unfortunately they found themselves thrown into accepting the mission before they were ready for it. The armoured vehicles promised in the original contract Blackwater had signed with Eurest Support Services, a subsidiary of KBR had not arrived and like us they had been forced to use soft-skinned vehicles. Unlike us, they didn't have the luxury of even one armoured vehicle but instead drove Pajero SUVs without protection, which stuck out like sore thumbs in the middle of local traffic. Iraqi vehicles all look like rejects from the local Destruction Derby, sporting dents, holes and rust, so a new SUV had 'America' painted all over it. I heard later that there had been a personality clash between Helveston and Shrek and that he had ordered the guy to go on the mission or be fired. Helveston had been a 'Pretty Boy' pin up for the SEALs and had his own keep fit video company for a while. He had even appeared in movies, including GI Jane, and it's just possible his over the top image hadn't gone down too well with some of his team mates. They should have been professional enough to get over it, but unfortunately with all that testosterone flowing this is not always the case. Somehow he had definitely rubbed Shrek up the wrong way. Shrek and Helveston had had a big argument the night before the mission resulting in Helveston e-mailing Blackwater with a written complaint about his actions and his doubts on the mission.

No one likes being called a coward so Helveston still went out on the mission even though he had misgivings. Later big things were made in the media over the fact that the four guys had never worked together as a team. In my book that should not have mattered: the refresher training they had received in Moyock should have got them all working off the same page. As professionals they should have been able to have slotted into any team, and with a detailed briefing for 'Actions On', should have been able to carry out the detail safely. The later story to come out said they had no maps and very little intelligence, but I find it hard to believe that anyone would have gone on a mission in a known hostile environment with so little knowledge. The only guys who knew the truth on that can never tell us - they're dead.

Where the story turns really bad for me is that they were sent out with only four escorts, instead of the six needed and required by the contract. Two of them were in the front Pajero and two in the rear vehicle. There were no rear gunners - critical to any team's survival, as anyone can drive up behind you. Watching your rear mirror is no substitute for a good rear gunner with an aggressive attitude and plenty of ammunition. He is the most important man in any convoy and the difference between life and death in an ambush, as this team unfortunately found out. This was total negligence on the part of someone; the convoy should never have been sent out undermanned and with no gunners. The team then got lost and asked for help from an Iraqi police unit, which escorted them part of the way into Fallujah before melting into the traffic and leaving them to their fate. Thanks to a security leak, the local Militia knew they were moving through the area and had also been wrongly told that they were CIA. Not that it mattered, as any infidel killed would bolster their reputation. They weren't worried who they killed. That this was an easy 'soft' target for the bad guys was in no doubt, and they were quick to seize the opportunity.

The convoy became stuck in heavy traffic and had almost come to a standstill. It was at this moment that the Militia chose to strike - it wasn't the well prepared ambush the Militia would like the world to think. A group of murdering rabble armed with AK-47s and hiding their faces behind shemaghs skulked in the coffee shops and alleyways either side of the gridlocked Main Street. The Blackwater convoy then got stuck in the usual traffic jam that anyone in the area could not only have predicted, but set their watch by. This showed a serious lack of local intelligence. When the rabble in the side streets were satisfied that both vehicles were stuck and separated and couldn't give each other mutual fire support they pounced. Charging from the shadows, they sprayed Helvenston and Teague's vehicle with full automatic fire from their AK-47s. At such close range and in soft-skinned vehicles neither man had any chance to defend himself. They might as well have been unarmed. An AK magazine holds 30 rounds of 7.62 comfortably and on full automatic fire from several weapons at the same time, the onslaught was unstoppable. Within a blink of an eye both men were dead. On the video I later saw the Militia make hesitant grabs for the dead men's weapons and equipment, as if they were afraid it was a trick and they would suddenly get up and fire back. I don't think they could believe they had killed them so easily. After all they had thought they were CIA. Once they realised both men really were dead they gave it large for the camera, jumping up and down and shouting "Allahu Akbar!" Meanwhile the second vehicle with Zovko and Batalona inside tried to turn around by driving over the meridian. Not to get away, as had been reported by the Militia, but to try to rescue their friends. No bodyguard team leaves its mates behind and certainly not in a situation like this. In a fire fight a soldier looks after his own, and these guys were former soldiers. Their training kicked in and they tried to help their colleagues by going back. As they made to turn around they met the same fate as the other two. Their soft-skinned Pajero was peppered with rounds and within an instant both Zovko and Batalona were dead as well. Both vehicles were set on fire and then finally all the bodies were dragged out and kicked around by a crowd of locals.

They were not there anymore. The inner spark that makes a man - his soul if you like - had left the body. This was just so much cooked meat. The corpses of these poor bastards just fell apart, or were pulled apart by the crowd. Finally, with no respect for the dead, their body parts were hung from a bridge. If only they'd had armour fitted to their vehicles, I have no doubt they could have survived the initial onslaught. They would certainly have been able to return fire, and even if they hadn't been able to escape the ambush, at least they'd have sent a few of the bastards to Hell first.

Meanwhile, for us in Karbala nothing had changed. We still drove a soft-skinned gun truck.

***

A few days later I had gone to bed early after leaving a message for Carol on the internet. At 00:30 hours all hell erupted near Position Five at Camp Juliet when the Poles and Iraqi Police exchanged automatic fire with a car. It took seconds for me to put on my gear, grab my weapon and move to the assembly point on our patio. I was expecting to find the guys stood to, but I was the only one there. Gun battles at night had become the norm and everyone seemed to be sleeping through them.

This one was different. Rounds from an AK-47 were flowing in bursts and could be heard impacting our outer wall. I ran down to the Polish duty room to see what was happening and found them in a bit of a state. Their checkpoint outside the main gate was not answering the radio. I legged it back to my hut to get my night vision gear and ran into Zeppelin, who was now fully dressed and looking for a gunfight. Dallas and Mike were just emerging from their trailer. Mike was dressed in Hawaiian shorts, T-shirt, and running shoes, carrying his rifle. Dallas was in similar attire, except he had his NVG on his head. The firing was already dying down, so I walked to the main gate to get a sit rep from the Polish sentries. Zeppelin checked the rear of the compound. Dallas and Mike checked out position five. The Poles told me that a taxi had moved towards the main gate without its lights on. The driver had tried to negotiate the chicane slowly and quietly, and found his way blocked. An Iraqi soldier had walked towards the car with his rifle at the ready position, and realising they were not going to get any further the occupants reversed out at speed, firing AKs at the same time but had not hit anyone. The Poles had the advantage of night vision goggles and opened up on the car. Although it was hit several times it still managed to get away. Why the Poles didn't open up with their Zeus anti-aircraft gun, I will never know.

As I stood at the gate with the Polish Guard Commander, an Iraqi Army twelve-man fighting patrol was making its way out to check the area forward of the main gate. They would be lucky if they found anything. Dallas came up on the radio to say he had them in sight from the fire position he was now occupying, but he lost them as they entered the alleyways on the other side of the road. About 20 minutes later, we heard a single shot ring out and there was no doubt the Iraq patrol had sustained yet another negligent discharge. Anti-climax! And everyone took a slow stroll back to their beds.

***

With the military now backing K2's suggestion to scale down our operations at the CPA building, we had spent less time there each day as the religious festival got closer. Our principal was becoming more nervous, and so the PSD made fewer movements. By now there were in excess of five million pilgrims in the city, and a bed space (not a room, but just enough space for a bedroll) was selling for 30 U.S. dollars. These people couldn't afford to feed their families half the time, but they could find the money for pilgrimages while their children went hungry back home. This country had its priorities all arse about face. It was going to be wall-to-wall hajjis. We wouldn't be able to drive in or out of the CPA and if the Mahdi Army chose this time to attack, no one would be able to pull us out. The Iraqi Police who guarded the place when we left for the day had one full magazine of ammo for their AKs and a magazine for their Glocks. As one policeman told me, "I fire my magazines and then I go home." I couldn't blame him. You can't defend a place without ammunition.

During the build-up to the festival you could feel the tension rising in the city and so we decided to spend our time fortifying our fighting positions on the roof and improving perimeter security, just in case it did kick off. Our bosses continually had meetings with General Abbas who, like everyone else in authority in this country, agreed to everything we said and then did the minimum. And he was one of the better administrators. We decided to solve the problem ourselves.

Early the following morning we rolled into the location and woke the Iraqi police, including the gate guard. We unloaded sandbags, timber and several rolls of barbed wire. Our first job was to reinforce Sesame Street, and so we ran a mixture of Dannert wire and razor wire three rolls high from the Passport Office to the side gate Hescos. This successfully cut off the back alley as an easy route to the building. Willy, one of the Chileans, and I wired the rolls together while Joker covered us. A shifty looking group of locals on the corner were eyeballing us, and we couldn't take any chances. One of our machine-gunners on the north roof shifted his position and brought his Russian made PKM GPMG to bear, and one of the Bulgarian Army snipers joined him with a Dragunov, its long barrel and scope easily identified from the street. Surprisingly, the group of locals dispersed rapidly.

Our next task was to put more wire on the back Hescos so no one could jump over. The IPs were getting pretty disgruntled now that we were cutting off their short-cuts to work; it meant they had a long walk around the location, with only one entrance available to them. Why couldn't these people realise it was for their own good? Did they want to lose another seventeen colleagues? How many more would die before they switched on to their personal security? Children are more easily educated!

We spent the rest of the day carrying sandbags up the three flights of stairs to the roofs. All three buildings needed more work. The Poles and the Bulgarian Military had confirmed once again that they had no intention of manning their positions in an empty building. They considered it suicide, and liable to cause an incident rather than prevent one. Meanwhile our principal was still worried that the Iraqi guards would steal his furniture!

The rooftop fighting positions were about as good as they would ever be. They were not perfect, but gave some cover from snipers, shrapnel, RPG and direct fire, and we could at least return fire from relative safety. We no longer considered ourselves duty targets and were looking for the opportunity for some payback. That day more United States soldiers died as a result of a roadside bomb. Someone must see these devices being planted, and if only they were not so scared of the Insurgents and reported them more often, we could win this war and Iraq would get the peace it pretended to want. I had been so bored with my first day off with nothing to do but sleep that I decided to go to the CPA building with Zep and Tango to give them an extra gun. The three-vehicle convoy left at 06:30 hours; Pajero in the lead, White Suburban behind, and Chevy pick-up bringing up the rear as usual. I hitched a lift in the pick-up truck. On our arrival at the government building, the two Iraqi policemen in the gun truck were asleep at their stations.

I dismounted with five of our Chilean guards and posted security on the roundabout, covering every vehicle that approached. Two half-asleep Iraqi policemen dragged the razor wire away from the road and another then reversed their gun truck out of the way. One of our guys checked the road to make sure there were no tyre busters left behind and then waved the convoy through. The convoy did a slow roll and we ran the fenders using the vehicles as cover. Once inside, we covered the rest of our guard force as they unloaded the vehicles of personal kit and crew-served weapons. With all of our escape packs secured in the office under the stairs, we now broke into teams to carry out once again the daily chore of clearing the buildings at speed.

When we had been in place for a while and were satisfied all was clear, I tracked down Tango to the ground floor lobby where he was talking to K9 and told him of my concerns from a few days ago. I wasn't happy that the IPs still had ways of getting over the wire, and Zep had reported a couple of new cases. There was obviously something up against the walls on the outside where we couldn't see it. Apart from the local Iraqi Army and Police who did the occasional patrol, there was no real effort to patrol the immediate area. The British Army operates a clear wall policy. Nothing is allowed to touch the outside walls of their camps: if anything is found up against the wall, it should not be there and is treated as hostile. This is also prevented by regular patrolling at irregular intervals.

I told Tango I wanted to go outside the wire to identify these points for the Poles, who had engineers with them. Maybe then they could do something about these crossing points. He agreed, but we were to have every gun on high points to cover our movement; I was to take only one guard with me, and it had to be a volunteer, as I was asking him to do something outside his job spec. There was only one blind spot - a short stretch down by the law court - but this was an especially dangerous place because it was also along the main road into town and packed with pilgrims' vehicles. We would be out of line of site for about ten seconds, although we would still be in radio contact. This was outside our job spec, but sometimes you had to use your initiative. I remembered the words 'airborne initiative' from my days in the Parachute Regiment. A Sgt once explained to me the airborne initiative is something you get a bollocking for if you don't use it and when you do use it you get a bollocking for not doing as you were told. It was a no-win scenario, so you might as well accept it and get on with the job in hand. We decided to use our initiative.

Ghurkha left and came back with Spike. There had been no shortage of volunteers, but he had chosen Spike because he looked like one of the meanest - bald head, no neck, short and stocky; a young Telly Savalas look-alike and a refugee from a Clint Eastwood film. He spoke only one or two words of English and was really a very nice guy. We just didn't want the locals to know that yet. I asked Ghurkha to explain to him that I would be checking the outer defences and I needed someone to watch my back. Spike grinned in reply and said "no problem," which just about exhausted his English vocabulary.

Tango and Zep positioned themselves on the north and central roofs respectively to watch our progress. I would raise my arm in the air to signal a possible breach point and the other team leaders would note it. When I got back, we would look at what we could do to reposition our machine guns to cover these weak spots. If our police knew the weaknesses in our defences, then we could guarantee the bad guys knew them as well. For our personal protection, we would have at any one time an RPK machine-gun, an 84mm light anti-tank weapon, and at least six riflemen armed with Bushmasters covering our every move.

Spike and I came up on the net for a radio check and confirmed with everyone that we were ready to move. We got several reassuring replies from the roof. Checking our weapons were locked and loaded, we exited the back compound through the rear gate of the CPA building, and turning right took a slow deliberate walk towards the rear foot gate. The stench of Sesame Street hit us as soon as we started our patrol, a smell of pure human shit and decay mixed with rotting vegetation. It made us both gag, but we gritted our teeth and continued to walk towards the Iraqi gate guard, who had their backs to us. This was a nice way to wake up your lungs first thing in the day! The guards were doing their job for once and stopping and searching visitors to the building. It was nice to see them working as they should without our having to prompt them, and I made a mental note to give them a pat on the back when I returned. They looked surprised when both of us greeted them in Arabic and walked through the gate. This was not normally done.

We turned left, with me on point and Spike about 20 feet behind me and to one side. This way, our staggered formation made us a harder target. Both of us wore sunglasses against the glare of the Iraqi sun, but this had the added advantage of hiding our eyes. It makes people nervous if they don't know whether you're staring at them, so they tend to look away and avoid eye contact. The local shopkeepers were starting to open up and put their wares out as we started our long walk down the wrong side of the barbed wire. Just like the Iraqi guards, they were totally surprised, and must have wondered why these two strange looking, heavily armed infidels were walking down their street. This is the sort of reaction I was hoping for - catch them unawares and keep them guessing!

We worked our way slowly down the street, covering each other as we went. Locals walking towards us gave us a wide berth, some stepping to one side to let us pass. One or two wished us a good morning, but not many were brave enough to be seen to be friendly to us in public. We of course returned the compliment. Looking into the shops as we went by, I could see where Wal-Mart got its ideas. You could buy everything from a new suit to a chest of drawers, all in the one shop. I stepped around the tables and other pieces of Arab furniture littering the pavement outside the carpenter's shop. It had a nice smell of fresh sawdust, which made a change from the usual smells in the street. Both of us, while being polite, were watching hands. If we could see their hands, it was not a problem, but people with hands in pockets or hidden under robes got a second look as we went by. Spike turned around at intervals to check our six riflemen. A couple of times we stopped and moved into doorways. This gave us a chance to have a look around and check for anything out of place. A few feet from me on the concrete pavement sat an old woman. She was dressed in a black hijab which covered her face and head completely. She was muttering the same phrases over and over again while holding out a begging bowl. Children in dirty clothes ran past her, laughing and shouting. The woman went completely unnoticed, a product of modern Arab society. At the end of the street on our right was the police compound where we had seen the delivery of new police cars some nights before. Past this, and running left to right, was the main street, filled with the chaos of Iraqi drivers and pilgrims' cars and minibuses. Many of the occupants gave us dirty looks as they drove by in vehicles festooned with pennants and stickers that boasted of pilgrimages previously undertaken. The 'Religious Police' pounced on anyone not displaying this sort of paraphernalia.

Intelligence had told us that the Iranian-backed Insurgents would use the masses as cover to infiltrate the city. It was believed that arms had been smuggled in, probably by coffin, and stockpiled in readiness for the festival. An increase in coffins had been observed on the roads, but there was no significant rise in burials, so the coffins had to be going somewhere. Coalition Forces would not check coffins in case they were accused of violating the religious rights of the local inhabitants. Yet again, the Muslim extremists were using our sense of decency against us. Staring directly at one scruffy bugger driving a beaten-up van I had the satisfaction of watching him look nervously away as if he had something to hide, and almost crash into the back of the vehicle in front of him. It's the little things that give you pleasure.

Around the corner was a market or 'souq', to use the local term. I nodded to Spike, and he came up on the radio in Spanish to inform Ghurkha that we were about to go down the blind side of the Law Courts. Approaching the market stalls we got the usual glares from the locals, our walk taking us between the Market and the outside Hescos in full view of the Iraqi guards on that side of the wall. Once again, we got looks of disbelief. The glares from the locals resulted from the fact that we had closed the compound entrance on the north side of the wall, causing them to lose trade from the Police Station, Law Courts and Government Building. Signs on the wall declaring our readiness to use deadly force had certainly upset them as well.

Moving past the stalls, we watched for unusual hand movements or a sudden display of weapons. Luckily there were not that many people out shopping, and up on the roof I could see the outlines of our shooters covering us, which was reassuring under the circumstances. Seeing we were obviously ready for trouble, the locals ignored us, and went about their usual business in the market. I gave Zep a radio check and got a five by five in return. He was receiving me loud and clear. I hoped our short foot patrol showed the contempt we all felt for the Insurgents. I'm sure there are many good and honest folk in Karbala, but as long as they refused to inform on, or continued to protect the bad guys, they were also to blame for all the bad shit coming down.

Satisfied we had made our presence felt, I told Tango over the radio that we were returning. Our route took us back over the way we had come, and as we went I pointed out at least three easy access points. Two were caused by rubble piled up against the Hescos, and the other was a pile of paving slabs stacked as a big step. They were well trodden, so they had obviously been used for quite a while. Our boys would now watch over these spots as a priority, and at the earliest opportunity Polish Army engineers would remove them. Our return was a bit quicker than the walk out. I remembered to give the Iraqi guards on the gate a few encouraging words on their searching, though I was sure they would sit down and have a cup of tea as usual once we were back inside. Past their position, a few minutes later we gained the security of the CPA building without incident.

\*\*\*

Later on I was discussing the patrol with Tango and K9 downstairs in the lobby when a single shot rang out. Over the radio came, "Shot fired! Wait! Wait out!" After a few seconds Ramon, one of our Chileans, came up on the air.

"Pops, Zep fired a warning shot!"

"What's his twenty?" I asked.

"Centre roof!"

"Okay, we're on our way!"

Tango and I had reached the first landing at a steady run when Ramon came back on the radio. He told me that Zep had fired the warning shot at an Iraqi policeman climbing over the Hescos at the back of the building and carrying a black plastic bag. Of course our guards shouted to him to stop, but the IP had calmly climbed back down, walked to the South Checkpoint, gone through without being checked, and was now making his way towards the prison entrance. The street was packed with prison visitors, people trying to apply for passports, and duty guards coming and going. He seemed to be trying to blend in with the crowd, but our guys on the roof were doing their best to keep an eye on him and at the same time radio his position to us. We were getting a continuous running commentary on the radio in Spanish, and Pancho was doing his best to translate it into English for us as we moved in on the bloke.

K9 and I raced back downstairs to the ground floor, out the back door and towards the prison entrance. Meanwhile, Tango ran up the stairs to see if he could pinpoint the guy from the roof. A large crowd was forming at the entrance and we pushed into it with pistols drawn. We couldn't see him.

"To your left, Pops!" came Tango's voice over the radio. "You're ten feet from him. Left! Left! In front of you - the IP with the black bag!"

I almost collided with the big bastard. My pistol was up and in the aim "Qif! Down on the fucking floor!"

My Arabic deserted me and I fell back on good old Anglo-Saxon. He turned and could tell from the sound of my voice and the look on my face that he was in a world of hurt.

"Fucking *now!*" I thrust my pistol towards his face and he dropped the bag and got down on his knees. K9 searched the bag as I covered the bloke.

The IP was doing his best to laugh the situation off, but we weren't laughing. He tried to speak to some of the Arabs around us, who were pressing ominously closer, and then Tango joined us with his pistol out. The crowd drew back as we pushed our captive into the prison compound.

In the bag were a spare uniform and boots. He had been pretty keen to get to the prison entrance - strange, when his job was in the main building and he had nothing to do with the prison, which held thieves, rapists, terrorists, and all sorts of other scum. For all we knew, he could have been planning to help one of them escape. Tango decided to take him to General Abbas; he needed to know how bad the situation was getting. At this point the guy produced an ID card showing he was a warrant officer. Tough shit, Mate! I had already relieved him of his Glock pistol and now I took his extra belt ammunition. Tango made him put his hands on his head and we rough-handled him up the stairs to the general's office. By now some of the other police were gathering on the landing, and we could tell by their attitude that they weren't happy about the arrest, no matter what the man might be guilty of. After all he was a Muslim and we were Infidels. An aide stopped us at the office door, announcing that the general was in a high level conference with some tribal leaders and couldn't be disturbed. Tango was in no mood to wait though, and he knocked on the door and walked straight in. K9 frog marched the IP into the office and I stood at the door with my pistol still drawn in case any of the other police milling around on the landing got any stupid ideas. I felt a little out-numbered until two of the Chileans appeared on the scene and casually covered the police with their rifles. I liked the Chileans. They were good at reading a situation and using their initiative. They had used it now, just in case we needed back-up.

Meanwhile, Tango apologised for his abrupt entrance and explained to the General what had happened and that one of his policemen had nearly been killed for disobeying warnings, despite everything we had told them. I guess Abbas lost a bit of face by being spoken to in this way in front of his tribal leaders. He looked at the now terrified policeman with a total look of disgust on his face. The leaders had gone very quiet while they waited for the general's reply. "Ok, take him out and shoot him," Abbas said casually, and then turned back to his meeting as if this was an everyday occurrence.

Without a moment's hesitation Tango and K9 turned and marched the guy out of the office. They had no intention of shooting him, but he didn't know that - and nor for that matter did any of the other Iraqis. The now grey-faced IP was visibly shaken, and I almost felt sorry for the bloke, but you have to realise what could have happened if he had been a suicide bomber. In that densely packed area, none of us would have stood a chance. Iraqis and contractors alike would have been wiped out, and many innocent Iraqi family members along with us.

As we walked away from the general's office one of his aides rushed out after us. "General Abbas has decided to jail this man instead!" he blurted out. "Please hand him over to me, and I will see that he is punished." Tango looked as if he was giving it careful thought and then somewhat reluctantly agreed. The aide bundled the IP into an adjoining office and gave him one hell of a bollocking. I cleared his weapon and handed it over with his ammunition to another policeman who had marched in as the aide's escort. Of course, General Abbas had only given the order in the first place to regain any 'face' he had lost when we disturbed his meeting. He was just trying to look tough in front of the tribal leaders.

A little later I saw the guy being escorted down the stairs to the prison. If they did jail him, I didn't fancy his chances of survival in there. After that no one actually saw him in the prison, so they more than likely let him go. After all, he was a Muslim and we were Unbelievers. That's how things worked in this screwed up country. At the very least, we had pressed home the point that where security was concerned there would be no compromises.

About an hour later I checked the IP gun post at the north entrance. About 100 yards away yet another IP was climbing over the Hescos! This was in full view of the gun position and they did nothing. I was really getting pissed off with these people, so I walked out in plain sight of everyone present, shouted "Qif!" and simultaneously brought my rifle up to fire. The IP fell forward off the Hescos in fright, so I covered him and told him to walk towards me with his hands up.

In perfect English he said, "I'm sorry! I thought we could still take a short cut." "Fucking walk around, you stupid bastard! You nearly got shot!" I growled.

"Yes!" "Yes! I'm sorry!" he replied.

I left him showing his ID and being searched by the Iraqi gunners, who had now decided they'd better be seen to be doing their job. I needed a coffee - or something a lot stronger. How many times did we have to tell these idiots before someone got killed? It was definitely a frustrating job at times.

The next day we got word that the principals had no intention of leaving Camp Juliet and we were all stood down. The team had a leisurely breakfast and had just started to get their day's admin sorted out when we were told, "Ten minutes, ready to move!" There had been change of plan yet again, but by now we were now used to it. Everyone scrambled to get their body armour and chest webbing on and grabbed their weapons ready to move.

"Ok Guys, slow time!" Tango informed everyone. "They've decided to move at 12:00 hours."

This gave everyone a bit of breathing space to get personal admin done and enjoy an early scoff at 11:30 hours in the DFAC. Then it was a steady roll out the gate and into the now streaming black mass of pilgrims who packed the city roads.

It was slow going and we dismounted several times to clear a way at gunpoint for the vehicles. New roadblocks were springing up all over the place. The local mosques had built temporary wickerwork roadside temples and sleeping shelters, where - for a price - a weary pilgrim could grab a few hours' sleep, or a drink of water. These were guarded by IPs or civilian security: all armed, although they were very careful not to point their guns in our direction. Once again our now familiar 'Religious Police' in their black robes and green sashes, and carrying AK-47 assault rifles, could be seen in large numbers 'assisting' the police. It was all very reminiscent of the Nazis in wartime Germany. Twice we got held up at roadblocks, forcing our people to dismount and provide security while we attempted to force our way towards the CPA compound. Even the drivers had their pistols drawn as we slowly rolled forward, with every vehicle approaching having to be treated as a potential suicide bomber. Finally we gained the relative safety of the compound and by now the sweat was pouring off me. I could never have imagined I'd be so pleased to see the inside of that shit hole! As was now the norm, the guys dismounted and took the high ground at speed, positioning machine-guns and shooters on our usual vantage points. Meanwhile, Tango informed K2 of the traffic problems. We had expected our principals to arrive behind us, but there had been yet another change of plan and they had decided to visit the Women's Centre. This was a stone's throw from the CPA block and we were standing to, defending the government building in case they had a problem. We could keep them in sight from here, and in the case of an attack they could fall back to us where we could protect them and give a good account of ourselves from our defensive positions.

Monitoring their channel on the radio, I heard K2 telling Tango they were now aborting the trip because of the large number of people and vehicles blocking the road. Tango gave the order to bug out and we did so in record time. With all the team equipment and personnel loaded in the vehicles, we waved to our Iraqi guards and pulled out into the traffic. There was no way we could get through on the main roads, so Tango used his GPS to get us through to some of the side streets. These were not quite as bad as the main roads, and were mostly filled with people on foot who moved out of the way when they heard us coming.

We were forced to manoeuvre around burnt-out vehicles, mounds of rubble and rubbish, a dead and bloated fly-ridden goat, and the other detritus usually to be seen festering in an Arab back street. Four times on the way back we had to dismount to clear the route. We were expecting to be attacked at any moment, and tension mounted within the team, but the bad guys must have had as much trouble negotiating the traffic as we had. It took almost an hour and a half to travel the couple of miles back to Camp. Everyone was physically and mentally exhausted by the time we got in, and that was certainly not a trip I wanted to make too often. We still hadn't finished for the day though: K2 had yet another task for us. He'd got KBR to release a pile of sheet hardwood, and we were to put the sheets on the tops of all the huts with a layer of sandbags. This was not because of enemy fire, but to protect us when the religious festival finished and everyone in the area fired their weapons in the air in celebration. What goes up must come down, and it would be embarrassing to get killed this way.

That night I got an email off to Carol letting her know I'd had my dressings removed, and that my hand and leg had healed nicely. I sneaked a six-pack of beer to the Polish medics as a thank you: it was the least I could do. It was hard enough to get beer around there, so I knew they would appreciate it. The treatment and stitching had been so good I didn't even have a decent scar. No free beer in the bar for me, telling the veterans my war stories!

# Chapter 13

## Gun Fight at the Alamo

The reports was coming in that Najaf was in deep shit, and we knew that Bill and White Boy were down there on a mission at the Salvadorian Army Camp. Intelligence coming in via the Polish Operations Room informed us that somewhere in excess of 3,000 Mahdi Militia were attacking their area. They also managed to get a message out via mobile phone that they were low on ammunition, and the last sit rep said the commander in the Spanish camp 500 metres from their location was considering withdrawing to prevent casualties. He intended to leave his camp to the Militia, and that was about as cowardly an act as I had ever heard of. So far not a shot had been fired at his camp.

We then received our own intelligence, reporting a Mahdi Militia group at least a thousand strong. It seemed they were only three kilometres away and advancing in our direction. The local police could do one of two things - go home, or join them - and so far we hadn't heard of any police units in the path of the advancing Militia putting up a fight. Within 30 minutes of receiving this information at Camp Juliet, the 150 Iraqi soldiers stationed in the adjoining compound stacked their weapons, folded their uniforms and equipment into neat piles, and quickly disappeared in the direction of their homes. Three of their senior officers stayed behind only because they had nowhere else to go.

As for us, we began to prepare for war. There was no panic, no sweaty palms, and no quivering lips. This was what we had trained for in the army, and it wasn't the sort of thing you were taught on a civilian bodyguard course. Slowly and methodically we broke open liners of belted ammo for the guns, reloaded the Russian made PKM belts, filled magazines and generally got all our shit together. If we were overrun it would be a case of every man for himself. We would try to stay in groups for mutual fire support, but wouldn't be getting any back up because we were 'only' contractors and too far down the food chain to be given a lift out of the shit by any Military means. We wouldn't be crying about it: it was just part of the job, and what we got well paid for.

The site teams now took turns, with the first fully dressed and ready for a fire fight, while the second stood down to get some sleep. This rotation carried on throughout the night. One of the Bulgarian soldiers on a mobile patrol in the immediate area was shot and wounded by a sniper, but luckily, his wounds were not life threatening and he stayed in the camp on light duty, sporting the bandage on his arm like a badge of honour.

The following morning at 01:10 hours, multiple grenade flashes and explosions were reported nearby, followed by heavy small-arms fire. None of the patrols reported being attacked, so we put it down to infighting between the local warring factions. We received more intelligence from our local informers that IEDs had been placed on the road covering our likely evacuation routes; it seemed they intended to keep us boxed in. This was definitely starting to look like the Alamo all over again. At 01:15 we were stood to as heavy firing was coming in over the camp, and tracer criss-crossed the night. There wasn't a cloud in the sky and against the back drop of millions of twinkling stars the green and red streams of tracer made a very pretty firework display. People would pay good money to see this, and I sat on the sandbagged machine gun emplacement above the main gate and watched the show. Not one round hit the camp though, and the tracer seemed to be targeting buildings either side of us: more local infighting - I was all for it! The more of each other they killed the fewer there would be to fire at us. By 01:30 it was patently obvious that none of it was aimed at us and K2 stood us down.

This built the pattern for the next few days. We were getting used to sleeping as much as possible during the day because we knew we wouldn't get any sleep at night. The next night, I was doing my rounds of the Chilean positions when a huge fire fight erupted a couple of miles to the north and Zeppelin and I climbed the stairs to the roof to see if we could identify its location. We saw the occasional mussel flash and spurts of tracer, but couldn't really make out the target. The most likely position in that area and at about that distance was the CPA building. Our principal had wanted us down there at night guarding his bloody furniture. I for one was glad we weren't there, and I knew the others felt the same way. I went back to my hooch to try to get some sleep; unless something happened in the meantime, I would be called at 05:30 hours to stand my men to.

The Iraqis don't usually like fighting at night - not proper fighting. They might fire from the relative safety of a window and put a few rounds our way just to remind us they are still there, but they don't like coming out in the open. Even so, in the age-old tradition of warfare, the possibility of a dawn attack was very likely. It was at times like this I realised afresh how much I loved my wife and family. Still, I had come into this work with my eyes open, knowing what I was getting into. Pushing these thoughts to the back of my mind, I attempted to get at least a catnap before morning. As I drifted off I wondered if this would be a good time to ask the Company for a pay rise and then the next thing I knew, Minotaur was banging on the door signalling it was time to stand to.

I had slept fully clothed with my rifle beside me so that I could get a head start. I splashed water on my face from the sink, looked in the mirror at the apparition sprouting a shaggy growth of white beard and bags under its eyes, and thought 'scary!' I walked down to the main gate where we had a sandbagged machine-gun post covering the right side of the gate; if the outside positions were in danger of being overrun, they could fall back inside and we could cover their withdrawal. Zep and Joker and Carlos, one of the Chileans, were already there. Judging by the state of them, I hadn't been the only one sleeping fully clothed. Zep poured me a cup of coffee from his flask, and as I sipped the welcome hot brew I listened on the radio to the other positions reporting in that they were manned and ready. After 30 minutes, we got the order from K2 to stand down, and now just the skeleton crew manned our positions.

As the day wore on and we continued our in-camp routine, sporadic reports filtered down to us. An Iraqi Police Station approximately seven kilometres from our camp had been surrounded by Mahdi Militia and called upon to surrender. This they did without firing a shot; they then opened up their armoury and promptly handed over all their automatic weapons, ammunition, uniforms, and police cars. Now no one could be trusted, and everyone would have to be treated as an enemy until proven otherwise.

The CPA buildings down town had been heavily attacked with RPG, mortar, and automatic small arms fire. The Iraqi Police on the position were reportedly ready to surrender until a combined Polish and Bulgarian quick reaction force arrived on the scene, dismounted, and used RPG and machine-guns to drive the attackers off and give them a taste of their own medicine. It was suspected that the Mahdi Militia was trying to break the prisoners out of jail, but they weren't allowed to get that close.

That night we had incoming sporadic sniper fire but no one was injured, though a Polish sniper reported engaging an armed Iraqi near the corner of the amusement park. A later patrol couldn't find a body, but they did find traces of fresh blood on the ground where the target was reported to have been. The Special Forces team was in the compound that night eating MREs (Meal Ready to Eat) while they sat on the roofs of their heavily armed Humvees and listened to the radio. I recognised some of the call signs and chatter and the continuous drone coming from the dark clouds above was a giveaway. It meant that we had a C-130 Spectre in support, and he was hungry and hunting.

Another Special Forces team on the ground, hidden somewhere in the city, could be heard giving coordinates over the radio, and the crewman in the C-130 gunship overhead repeated them back. There could be a fireworks display tonight if we were lucky. The C-130 gunship was taking on the role of *Puff the Magic Dragon*, the Dakota DC-3 of Vietnam fame that was immortalised in the John Wayne film *The Green Berets*. It was an airborne artillery battery with 20mm Gatling guns protruding from fire ports and a howitzer mounted in the door. Apparently the gunners had an easy job; all they had to do was clear stoppages and sweep up the empty cases, with the additional task of making coffee for the rest of the crew in their spare time. The navigator executed the actual firing with a joystick and a TV screen. He probably trained on his PlayStation back home!

After a while I could see the Special Forces guys were getting really pissed off over something. I didn't want to speak to anyone who was involved in the mission, but I was curious to know what was going on. I spotted one of their crew who seemed disinterested in the radio and was quietly drinking a Coke on the bonnet of his vehicle. I walked over to him, ready to act completely nosy.

"So, what's up mate? Your people don't seem too happy."

"They're not," he sighed. "We spent a week risking our necks downtown at night, positively identifying groups of armed militia and the houses they're in. We've got a team out there now, painting targets. The Spectre's confirmed our targets with its heat-sensing equipment, but Baghdad won't let them open fire. They cancelled the fire mission on these bastards in case a fucking mosque got damaged. Well, if they're using it for cover, it's a legitimate target. Even under the Geneva Convention it's a legitimate target! Whose fucking rules are we playing by?"

He was one really pissed off operator - his whole team were pissed off. I wouldn't like to be the Operations Officer back in Baghdad if these guys caught up with him.

I let him go back to his Coke and walked away into the darkness towards my hut. I didn't want to upset him any more than he already was, but like him I was under the impression that we were the only people playing by the rule book. I think he knew that already. John Wayne's hooch door was open and he stood outside with a cold one in his hand, waiting to see if the fireworks display was going to start any time soon. I told him what I had heard; bit of a bummer really.

"Want a beer before you turn in, Pops?" he asked. Ok, he had twisted my arm.

I lay in my pit half hoping there would be a sudden ripping noise, signalling the opening fire of the Gatling guns and the demise of the bad guys. As I listened, the drone disappeared into the distance and I felt really pissed off. I couldn't believe those idiots in Baghdad were missing a chance to rid this country of a lot of its pain. Why didn't they trust the guys on the ground to do their job? Maybe they were judging them by their own standards. What a way to fight a war!

The site teams were in good shape, but I did need to find a way to stop the Chileans from talking continuously while on duty. The guys had filled more sand bags, and we had repaired some of the Polish positions as well. If only there were an Olympic category for sand bag filling, we had a team that would beat all comers. It was now a quiet night and a cold one - too cold for the bad guys - and so we had a respite from the usual sniper fire.

\*\*\*

Dingo got an email from Bill in Najaf. There were two photos entitled 'Priceless'. The first showed a load of bad guys with AKs firing at the Spanish camp from behind a semi and a trailer. At the extreme left edge of the photo was a guy of about eighteen looking straight at the camera. He had a look of shock on his face as he realised they had not seen the Salvadorian camp on their flank. Apparently Bill had taken the photo, put the camera down, picked up his weapon, fired off a burst, and then picked up his camera again. The second photo showed the same group, but now they were carrying three bodies away and running in all directions. There was no sign of the youth who had appeared in the first photo. Now that's what I call priceless!

In Najaf they had come close to being overrun and were making every shot count because they were low on ammunition. The Mahdi Militia had made it easy for the Salvadorians, as they had attacked in daylight and across open ground. The Militia at the rear didn't have weapons and were keeping close to those that had, so they could pick up the weapons of the fallen. Very noble, but very stupid! One U.S. Marine was badly wounded and one Salvadorian was shot in the face and killed as the battle wore on. The U.S. forces couldn't get a Blackhawk medevac in to retrieve the body and casevac the wounded. In addition to being hot and under continuous direct enemy fire, the area was not suitable for a large helicopter LZ.

As darkness fell, the Company's three Little Bird helicopters, flown on NVG (Night Vision Goggles), swept into the area like the good old U.S. Calvary. With their door gunners laying down fire support they landed in a cloud of red dust directly in the centre of the compound, to evacuate the casualties. It took an extremely skilled pilot to do this, and Blackwater's pilots ranked among the best. They dropped extra ammunition and heavy weapons to troops and contractors alike and continued to fly missions until dawn. This broke the back of the attack. The Militia fell back in total disarray, having had their arses well and truly kicked and leaving many dead and dying in the kill zone. The Spanish camp was in a good position to help with fire support, but didn't fire a single round to help the Salvadorians. Bremmer ordered the immediate replacement of the Spanish commander, and Spain promptly complied. In the morning, over 50 bodies were collected from the killing area surrounding the camp. An estimated 100 had been hit, judging by the blood trails and other debris scattered about the battlefield, and we hoped the number of enemy casualties would rise a lot higher.

Over 200 wounded were recorded in the local hospital, although by this time the media were calling them innocent civilians caught in the crossfire. Like hell they were! You get very few innocent civilians in the street in the middle of a gun battle. Also, if anyone had bothered to check how old they were they would have found that they were all of military call-up age, between 18 and 30 years old. A couple of battalions of Republican Guard had taken off their uniforms and melted into the local population at the end of the Gulf War, and I had no doubt that they formed the nucleus of the enemy we were now fighting.

***

A dust storm broke over Camp Juliet. It was so thick that you couldn't see your hand in front of your face. It was very much hit and miss trying to find your way around anywhere, and even getting to the cookhouse meant feeling along the side of the huts until you came to the end: feel your way across the short gap to the sandbag air raid shelter at the corner; turn right, feel your way past the two large tents, and then take a gamble and head out across the helipad, hoping you were going towards the entrance to the DFAC. The sand not only blinded, it stung like hell. As anyone who has been in any desert will tell you, the sand gets everywhere - and I mean everywhere! Dust goggles and a shemagh around the face were the only way to protect yourself. The one good thing to come out of it was another day of peace and quiet, although everyone still had to be on the lookout for Militia trying to breach the walls in the bad visibility. The following day we had another report that didn't speak too well for our so-called allies. It was believed that a Ukrainian position had been given up to the Militia without a shot being fired, and at least three police stations and several IP check points had reportedly gone the same way. We had no other information on this, and I hoped it was wrong. This sort of report didn't help the Coalition and it gave the enemy a morale boost.

We were now manning all our new fire positions. The Poles were grateful for the help and clearly saw us as fellow combatants, not just a bunch of hired guns. They also knew we would stand and fight. This must have been reassuring for them, as I'm damned sure the Iraqi Army attached to our camp would not have defended it. Things must have been getting bad because the Poles sent a couple of senior NCOs round to our quarters to teach us how to use their hand grenades. There were several different types, and they showed us the best way to use each kind. They also left us several boxes of fragmentation grenades and some more ammo for our Soviet-made automatic weapons.

A message from our Operations Manager, Dave Jackson, told us to expect a re-supply by chopper that night of a load of goodies, including a couple of SAWs. With only a 5.56 round, a SAW does not have the stopping power of the GPMG, but it has a fast rate of fire. What it lacks in one way it makes up for in another. We cleared the LZ (Landing Zone) within the camp, and waited - and waited, and waited. Finally we got the message that the chopper would not be able to get in because it was getting too dark to operate safely in our area. It would try to get in tomorrow, but they couldn't give us an estimated time of arrival. We needed that extra firepower, and we needed it quickly. Sitting on the roof in the GPMG Sanger, I heard a chopper overhead. I couldn't see it: there were no navigation lights. Suddenly against the moon I caught a glimpse of one black shadow, then another. Seems we had two Apache gunships flying CAS (Combat Air Support) out of Babylon. Now, that was comforting!

I pulled the graveyard shift with my team, working from 02:00 hours until 04:00 hours. A chill wind was getting up and the temperature was dropping rapidly as I came on duty and started checking my guys. A few of the Chileans were not dressed for a cold night, so we sent them back to their tent one at a time to get warm clothing. This might be a hot country during the day, but after dark the temperature could easily drop to below zero; to see ice on the sand at night was normal. I wanted all my team awake and concentrating, not worrying about their extremities dropping off.

With all positions manned and everyone alert, I sat on the roof with two of my team. Using the sandbags to keep out of the wind, I hunkered down and called a radio check. All positions answered up OK. The sound of small arms fire and exploding RPGs echoed in the distance in the direction of Camp Kilo, the Bulgarian base. The CPA complex was also under attack, but there was lots of outgoing tracer so the Iraqi Police were giving it out for a change. Seeing a few dead Mahdi Militia around the place would give them the morale boost they badly needed. Unfortunately they also had a habit of firing lots of rounds into the air. This gave the impression they were in a fire fight, but the truth was they had mates amongst the enemy, sometimes brothers, so they didn't want to hit them

Below me in the compound, two Bulgarian jeeps with their lights off roared out of the gate. I watched their progress until the buildings hid them from view. A few minutes passed and I listened to the noise of the battle above the shrill sound of the wind. Suddenly tracer lit up the sky. A few rounds whistled in our direction and then beyond, disappearing upwards and into the night like so many fireworks. Coming up on the radio, I told everyone to keep low. As I had already found out, stray bullets can ruin your entire day: it's best to stay out of their range. Dawn broke with all our positions intact and no injuries. Even the CPA and prison guards had fought well and scared off the Militia.

General Abbas and some of his entourage moved into our camp for safety and were given a couple of spare hooches near ours. I wasn't worried about the general, but some of his people looked a bit iffy. One of them was always on his mobile phone, which should have been confiscated when he came into camp. With a mobile he could happily call in mortar rounds onto our camp and correct the fire. We would be in deep shit if that happened, and as far as we were concerned it was bad security. I just hoped he was on our side.

I had the day off and slept most of it. At 15:30 hours Joker woke me up and said we had a Blackhawk bringing in a re-supply of ammo. I thought I'd better check the positions, as helicopters are bullet magnets and it would need maximum cover from us. A lot of vehicles were taking up space in the compound, so K2 decided to use the adjoining schoolyard as an LZ. In order to make the area safe, the Poles blew down a lamppost with a small explosive charge. The lamp didn't work and was beyond repair, so it was no loss. K2 and the PSD cleared the schoolhouse and surrounding area, and the Poles and Bulgarians sent out additional mobile patrols. They wanted to discourage the Mahdi Militia from getting too close and to keep them wrong-footed. They were trying to deny the enemy ground and vantage points.

The first chopper came in after about an hour's wait. Spotting the team's fluorescent panels, the pilot circled once and then lined up for his approach. Kicking up a huge cloud of dust, it came in fast and hard, bouncing on its undercarriage. The pilot throttled down, but kept the rotors running and turning. The crew chief threw out stores and our people and a few soldiers moved them to a safe distance.

I was moving up to the roof to take a look around when an explosion shook the air. It must have been fairly close by, as I felt the shock wave and I heard glass tinkling to the floor from some already broken window panes. I ran up the stairs two at a time onto the roof and into the first Polish fire position. Still gasping for breath from my exertion I asked if they knew what the explosion was. One of the snipers had a single radio earpiece held to his ear and was listening intently. The report was just coming over the radio, so I waited for a few seconds for the message to end. He tilted his helmet back and wiped the sweat from his forehead. Then he broke the news that one of our combined Polish-Bulgarian mobile patrols had been hit by a rocket-propelled grenade, and there were casualties.

As we found out afterwards, the rocket had missed. But the RPG is designed to self-destruct after it has gone its full range and as bad luck would have it, the rocket exploded immediately above the patrol vehicles, causing an airburst. It was too close for comfort, and the resulting down blast peppered one of the vehicles with shrapnel. All its crew were hit to varying degrees. They had returned fire to discourage the enemy from firing any more RPGs and had managed to break contact. The Polish NCO in charge of the combined patrol destroyed the badly damaged vehicle with a thermite grenade, so it could not be recovered and used by the militia. This was SOP (Standard Operation Procedure). If a vehicle is immobilised and it's considered too dangerous to try to recover it, it is destroyed on the spot. It can be replaced: lives cannot. With a vehicle destroyed, all the soldiers crammed into the remaining one, which was now badly overloaded. They now had to return fire at the same time as rushing back to camp to get help for their wounded.

The patrol was returning with five wounded men, and as I watched from my vantage point on the roof, I saw the surviving vehicle speed towards the main chicane and being waved through. I could also see it was overloaded with bodies. As it approached the chicane, someone in the rear of the vehicle was firing back the way they had come at an unseen enemy. The patrol's priorities had changed. Killing the bad guys was unimportant; saving their mates' lives was what mattered most.

The Polish doctor had taken his medical team out into the compound so that the wounded could be treated immediately. They would have to be prepared for medevac with the least possible movement, in order not to cause them any more suffering. The doc had only a small surgery, and there was no way he could treat all the wounded in there. The first Blackhawk took off to make room for a 'dust off' and cleared the LZ, as the wounded were being unloaded just inside the gate so that the medical teams could get to work on them straightaway.

From my position on the roof, I could see a considerable amount of blood splashed around the back of the now empty vehicle. Three of the wounded lay on stretchers on the ground as the medics worked frantically to stabilise them, and drips were hurriedly inserted into their arms to replace lost body fluids. Shock would be the biggest killer at this stage. It was imperative to reassure the wounded and make them as comfortable as possible as quickly as possible. All were still conscious, which was a good sign. Two were walking wounded and sat on chairs to be treated. The doctor asked one of the Poles, who had a shoulder wound, if he was hurt anywhere else. He said no, just his shoulder hurt, but he coughed as he spoke and the doc saw flecks of red in the corner of his mouth. That should not have happened from just a shoulder wound, so there had to be another injury. The soldier still wore his body armour, and without removing it the doc looked around the corners and edges for signs of another entry wound. Under the soldier's armpit he found another small puncture from a piece of shrapnel that had ricocheted off the armoured chest-plate. The soldier was completely unaware that he'd been hit twice, but if this wound had gone undiscovered the bloke would probably have bled to death by the time they got him to hospital. Now I understood why Dallas had been so insistent I sit down and let him examine me more thoroughly when *I* got hit. Thanks, Dallas!

With the re-supply chopper out of the way, the LZ was clear for the medevac. It was still too dangerous to move the wounded outside the compound, so we had to make space inside. Every vehicle was moved back against the camp walls, as far as humanly possible from the landing zone. The stores and equipment were brought hurriedly into the camp and the additional ammo and weapons were distributed. We were now informed on the radio by K2 that a medevac helicopter was on its way. The compound was a hive of activity as our Chileans and the regular soldiers ran to get as many machine-guns and automatic weapons as they could onto every high vantage point they could find. On the roof it was bloody hot. The sweat dripped off my nose onto the sandbags, throwing up tiny puffs of dust as it landed, and I could feel it running down the back of my shirt. My mouth was dry, but not through the heat: this was pure nervousness. I knew that a 'dust off' or Medevac would be a sitting duck, and I was feeling nervous for the pilot. I looked into the distance over the city and spotted two small dots moving very fast towards us. As I continued to watch, the two dots became two Blackhawk's flying low and fast, the front one sporting a red cross on its nose. I knew from experience that the Iraqis wouldn't think twice about shooting down an air ambulance: they would probably use the red cross as an aiming point. Depressing my transmit button I reported in.

"Hello K2, this is Pops. In-bound in figures, five. Over!"

"K2, Roger! Out!"

The first Blackhawk to reach us was the escort gunship. It came in fast, and executed a very tight turn over our compound; the door gunner was clearly visible, leaning out and looking for likely hostile targets. He was pulling a few Gs in the turn, and you could hear the rotors beating the air like mad to keep the chopper airborne. Looking across the compound, I thought I saw movement on a balcony about a hundred feet away. As I looked again the Blackhawk flying top cover executed a tight turn, and the door gunner put a short burst into the balcony I had been looking at.

"Sniper!" shouted one of the paratroopers on the right-hand side of the compound. An incoming shot ricocheted off a Marine Humvee, causing the gunner to duck down, and one of the Polish paratroopers spotted the muzzle flash and fired back. I saw movement and the brief outline of an AK as the sniper moved his position to get out of the line of fire. Standing upright, I fired aimed shots at the balcony, starting on the left and firing through the support posts. I was trying to force him back into the corner so he would have nowhere left to go.

K2 had reached the roof and started firing rapidly into the sniper's position, and once over the shock of the near miss the marine opened up with a 50-cal. By now everyone knew where the sniper was, and the balcony disappeared under a hail of automatic fire. A pigeon loft on the balcony exploded in a cloud of dust with feathers fluttering through the air as the surviving birds took off in panic. The owner of that loft now had the fastest racing pigeons in Iraq. Hot cases were bouncing everywhere. Plaster from the balcony and burning shrapnel rained down on the brush below, starting minor fires. "Cease fire! Cease fire!" someone shouted, and it suddenly went quiet. The crackle of the brush fire and the sound of the helicopter orbiting at a safe distance were the only things audible. After all that racket, you could have heard a sparrow fart.

The chopper flying cover made one more turn around our position, checking for more snipers and then the second chopper was in, and down in the small LZ inside our compound. The pilot idled his rotors to cut down the amount of dust he was kicking up over the wounded and the medics huddled over the casualties, protecting them as well as they could from the prop wash. The medical team from the helicopter climbed down and hurriedly discussed the casualty state while the second chopper continued to orbit the camp. The casualties were prioritised and the sensitive job of loading them gently into the helicopter and securing them began. This was done quickly and efficiently, and the medevac took off slowly to give its passengers as comfortable a ride as possible.

We held our collective breaths as the medevac cleared the area and sped off, with the other helicopter covering it above and to one side. I only hoped it wouldn't draw any fire, as its passengers had suffered enough for one day. I guess the amount of hatred that one sniper had attracted made any others in the area think twice before opening fire. After another hour the camp returned to its normal routine, while in the background the brush burnt itself out and smoke drifted lazily across the compound. We found out later that thanks to the medics' excellent care, all the casualties survived their injuries, although one lost a kneecap.

At the briefing that evening K2 thanked everyone for a job well done. He went on to inform us that 2,000 Militia were massing a couple of miles away from Camp Juliet with plans to overrun us. Their leaders were whipping them into a frenzy, so it promised to be another interesting night. Small arms fire could already be heard as we went to brief the Chileans on the night's expectations; it was only 20:00 hours, so the bad guys had started early. Back in my room I repacked my escape and evasion kit and then went up to the roof to check on the guys. I decided that if it was going to kick off again tonight, I wanted to be there immediately. Briefing Ghurkha on my location, I put my sleeping bag down behind the machine-gun Sanger covering the gate, and nodded off counting the stars in the cloudless night. I even managed to ignore the continuous low chatter of the two Chilean machine-gun crew. (I really had to do something about that!) At 04:00 hours a heavy firefight started, with the CPA buildings as the target once again, and lasted until 08:00 hours. This time our Iraqi security guards fought back and the Militia left a few of their dead littering the streets. On March 7th I emailed Carol and then read a few nice messages from home; I came off shift in the early hours and got my head down for a bit of shut eye. Having drifted off into a deep sleep, I was a bit pissed off when Tank opened my unlocked door and asked me why I wasn't helping him fill sandbags. A good old Anglo-Saxon "Fuck off!" and he left in a sulk, having got the message. Unfortunately though, I was now fully awake. After a shower and a wash and shave, I sat down to clean the mushrooms out of my weapons and then walked to the cookhouse to get something to eat. We could enter our new DFAC at any time of the day or night for a snack and a brew. It was a godsend, and our KBR Pakistanis and Indians were friendly and always ready to please. Nothing was too much trouble for them, and they certainly earned their money. They were a familiar sight during an attack, huddled in their bunker in their cooks' whites waiting for the all-clear so they could get back to their cooking. As I came out of the cookhouse a truck pulled up and started unloading MREs, Meals Ready to Eat. There was enough for a two-week siege. Did someone know something we didn't?

During the next few days we reinforced the Sangers again. We had a JCB digger at the camp, but for some reason the key and driver were based at Camp Lima and it was considered too dangerous for him to travel here. We needed to use the bloody vehicle, so hidden talents were called for. Sparky, being a good old farm boy, hot-wired the vehicle and Bullets drove it. Suddenly we had become a construction company. Although what we did was highly illegal and KBR, who owned the vehicle, were going to be pretty fed up, everyone wanted sand and other gear moved by our guys. Well, after all, there was a war on! I was sick of filling sandbags, but I guess this was another profession to put on my next CV. I had told Carol in my email earlier that we had kicked the bad guys' arses, so whatever she saw on TV saying otherwise was a lie. It was more to stop her from worrying really, as even I was not totally convinced. I suppose I spoke too soon.

\*\*\*

We had a couple of days of fairly slow and quiet activity but there were always surprises waiting around the corner. This particular day started off like any other. I got up, washed and showered and went to breakfast. Thomas, Derek and John Wayne were already there, eating breakfast and in deep conversation. Their table was empty except for them and Thomas beckoned me over. They were talking about American football, which is a sport that has every Englishman totally baffled. It's a strange game. Just as things get exciting, everyone stops and has a team huddle. Now what's that about? Ghurkha, Pez, Johnny, Minator, Spike, Trala and a few more of the Chileans joined us and soon the table was full and alive with American football and animated Spanish conversation: a real mix of cultures. Crazy! I wished I'd brought my ear defenders - I couldn't hear my breakfast cereal's Snap Crackle and Pop, let alone think. Just as I thought my brain would explode, Tango saved the day. Suddenly appearing at the end of the table he informed us we would be getting a chopper re-supply early afternoon. We didn't know if it would be a Blackhawk or our own 'Little Birds' but it was definitely coming in. We had a priority delivery of ammunition and a couple of extra SAW's which we desperately needed for two of the fixed positions.

After breakfast everyone went about the daily camp routine, cleaning weapons and sorting out their personal combat kit, and K2 briefed us and the PSD on the delivery. It was vital we get the extra ammo and weapons. We had a couple of weak points on our defences, and if the local Intelligence was correct there were a lot of pissed off Mahdi Militia who would be burning to attack us as soon as their leaders had whipped them up into the usual religious frenzy. The extra weapons would certainly be needed. Zeppelin and I ended up on the roof with a couple of the PSD team and everyone stood to, on the alert for enemy fire. Helicopters landing in daylight might prove too big a temptation for the local rabble and we knew they had plenty of RPG's. It was the usual long wait: our air deliveries were never on time. I don't know whether this was planned to confuse the bad guys whose camp spies may have given them the expected arrival time, or just a helicopter pilots' tradition. About forty five minutes after the expected arrival, Zep and I spotted three dots in the distance. There was a blue sky with only a slight heat haze and we could clearly identify three Blackwater Little Birds coming in low and fast.

Zep informed K2, who was waiting at the edge of the LZ inside the camp, that the birds were in-bound. He got a 'Roger!' back and everyone went onto full alert looking for any hostile movement. The choppers made so much noise when they were overhead that you had to watch for muzzle flashes or smoke discharge from the enemy weapons. Otherwise the only way you would know you were being shot at was when the rounds impacted around you. Not a nice position to be in; we had to hope the guy at the other end was a bad shot. The first two Little Birds came in about one hundred feet above the ground. Both went into a left hand high speed orbit with a lot of separation, so that they could cover as much of the area between them as possible. At the same time the third bird approached down the centre, went past the camp, did a pirouette outside the wall, and with a quick burst of speed the pilot put the aircraft down on the LZ centre marker. A quick flare of the rotors, a cloud of dust and it was down. It was impressive flying.

I was surprised to hear the pilot throttle back and shut down the engine. They normally kept the engines turning and got out as quick as they could. As the rotors slowed down and the engine's whine died away, the other two aircraft turned and flew into the distance. "Stay at your posts!" K2 came over the radio. I looked over the parapet at the chopper below and was surprised to see K2 shaking hands with our Dave, Operations Director. He had sat behind a desk in Moyock and I'd worked under his command when I was training there. He was a big bloke with white hair and a pony tail, so he definitely stuck out in a crowd. He was a nice guy to work for too. The rest of the blokes were equally surprised to see him: he didn't have to be here risking his neck, but here he was. Some of the Chileans were unloading the stores and I could see several boxes of ammunition and some weapons being removed. Blackwater had delivered as promised.

I knew the Operations Director was in-country, but with our present tactical situation I didn't think we'd be getting a visit. This was the sort of SF leader you didn't mind following.

We got the call on the radio. "OK, Guys! Stand down!" It took us five minutes to get off the roof, walk down the stairs and join the rest of the team. Our visitor met us at the accommodation block and shook hands all round.

"Hi, Pops! How's the hand?" he asked when it was my turn.

"No problems, Boss! Just stopped me picking my nose for a while."

He laughed and turned back to the half a dozen boxes and assorted items now lying on our patio area. There were a couple of SAW's (Squad Automatic Weapon), loads of boxes of ammunition and a big cardboard box of the sort you would expect a large TV would be packed in. "Oh, a few comforts for the troops!" he said. One of the blokes sliced the tape holding it closed with his K Bar and we found it stuffed with crisps, bags of Haribo mixed sweets, packets of M and M's and enough assorted sugary goodies to keep a large kindergarten happy for a week. To see so many hardened mercenaries fighting over which one would get a packet of Jelly Babies and which the aniseed balls made you forget where you were for a moment.

"OK!" K2 shouted over the free for all that had developed. "Share it out, and make sure half of it goes to the Site Security Team's tent!"

I put my share of the goodies in my room and locked the door as I left. No one was getting my Jelly Babies!

Tango and Joker took the box to our Chilean friends' tent and handed it over to Pancho and Ghurkha. You would have thought it was Christmas, but when you're in a stressful situation, it's the little things that pump up the morale level. I had no doubt this had been Dave's idea, and it had worked. Dave gave us a bit of a pep talk, told us we were doing a good job and that word had got back to the Baghdad Command about our situation and how well we were standing up to the problems. The Polish Commander had spoken well of us - we were famous. Well, briefly anyway. It was a good chat, leaving everyone feeling confident that we hadn't been forgotten after all. With some of the units in the area having given up, Coalition as well as Iraqi, we were proving to be a thorn in the side of the Militia, and we were not about to give in and run away. It was soon time for Dave to leave, and after the length of time his Bird had been on the ground I felt certain he would draw fire as he went.

Everyone quickly took up their previous positions and watched for any movement from our hostile neighbours as the pilot started up his aircraft and his passenger got strapped in. K2 gave a thumbs up as the Little Bird lifted off, then right on the button and as if by magic, the other two Little Birds screamed in from out of nowhere to orbit and give cover. Their door gunners were almost hanging in their harnesses as the choppers leant over and orbited on their sides to give them the best possible shot at any hostiles. Dropping into a triangular formation, all three helicopters now raced off across the roof tops towards Baghdad and the relative safety of the Green Zone. Behind him Dave left some very happy people, and we were not the only ones with a high morale factor that day. The Bulgarians had a good night as well, having ambushed Saddam's cleric, his Second in Command. That pissed the bad guys right off, and they now had ideas of payback. Our intelligence told us that every Mahdi gangster in the area intended to descend on our position that night. They had been promising this for a while, and I wished they would try it and get it over with. Up to this point, they had just been probing our positions, but that night, the base commander decided there would be no patrols outside the camp. I knew he wanted to keep his guys safe, but basics tell you to deny the ground to the enemy. The absence of patrols would allow them to get within shooting range and give them free run of the outer perimeter. Anything too close to the camp that night would be shot, so I hoped that alone would be a deterrent. Maybe the situation would finally bring all this shit to a head.

My escape gear was packed and I was in what was now seen as my permanent position - on the roof with the machine gun. From there I could keep an eye on all the fire positions that were my responsibility. Joker, Tango and Zeppelin had picked out positions for themselves and had sorted out their men and equipment. The Chileans had been briefed, K2 and the PSD had briefed the principal, and I was confident that if push came to shove all our people would give a good account of themselves. That night nothing happened. The enemy were psyching themselves up again. The following day reports came in that the Spectre had engaged a few targets near the government buildings the night before;

the Blackhawks were also active and had over-flown our position a couple of times. Knowing we had air superiority gave everyone a lot of confidence to tackle these bastards, with the Polish and Bulgarian mobiles, now back on the beat, engaging a few probing patrols from the Militia and chasing them off.

At 04:00 hours there was a mob chanting anti-American crap a couple of blocks away, but they didn't come close enough for us to engage them, and they melted into the darkness when the Polish patrol went after them. What were they doing out at that time of the morning? Didn't they have beds to go to! The Blackhawks orbited for a while, but the Militia must have found a deep cellar to hide in and didn't show their faces again. Our intelligence report from the Polish Operations Room told us we had 2,000 bad guys in the immediate area. This included the Iraqi Police from one of the police stations that had surrendered, handing over their 90 AKs, four PKMs and several vehicles. These cowardly bastards were now wearing the black pyjamas and green sash of Muqtada al-Sadr's rabble army. Meanwhile, a friendly member of the public had come by the gate and informed the sentries that the local hospital was treating hundreds of Militia, so it seemed we had hurt them really badly.

U.S. Special Forces and Military Police had reinforced the government buildings, and we were told that the rules of engagement had changed. The CPA complex was to be held at all costs, and there was a list of key personnel to be evacuated from this position if things get bad. We were obviously not on it. That was to be expected, so it didn't come as a surprise to us. I hadn't packed anyway. Our only way out was by road, and we already knew that would be suicide because of the IEDs. The only option was to stand and fight. We had built secondary fire positions inside the walls and compound for use in case the Militia breached the outer defences and some of the regular American soldiers at the base had said they thought it was a waste of time. They changed their tune now, though, and asked us if we had positions they could help reinforce if things went really bad. All guns would be welcome if it turned that ugly. At 21:15 hours, I went back on the roof. One of my Chilean guards climbed the ladder, juggling three cups of coffee on a plastic plate. I wasn't expecting combat Room Service and the coffee was very welcome.

Shit! Got a rude awakening! I was asleep on top of my green maggot behind the machine gun post when one of the Polish snipers fired a single shot. I woke with a start, and for a spit second didn't have a clue where I was. There was no return fire and no follow-up; it looked like the bad guys were still reluctant to play, so I went back to sleep and got about an hour. I was using a sandbag as a pillow and lying on top of my sleeping bag because it was a hot night. The body armour aggravated my back injury a bit, and I had to sleep on my side. They say a good soldier can sleep anywhere, so I guess I was a good soldier. It's funny how the exploding mortars and machine-gun fire emanating from the direction of the downtown CPA building no longer kept many of us awake at night. I found it almost soothing.

At about 03:00 hours we started to get movement in the street below. Mike spotted it at the corner of one of the buildings and called it in. A few minutes later someone else spotted movement. This time the figure was positively identified as armed - it looked as if we were being probed again. A single shot rang out and there was a *whoosh*, followed by the crash of an exploding mortar falling outside the camp, but close to the old hotel. It shook our position, but did nothing else. We heard a track bike revving up and then growing quieter as it disappeared into the distance. That must have been how they were spotting the 'fall of shot'.

Everyone spent the next hour scanning the darkness with NVGs, looking for the enemy, but once again nothing stirred. At 04:00 I decided to spend a couple of hours in my bed before stand-to at 06:00, so I said good morning to the Chilean gun crew and descended the rickety ladder to ground level. Zep and two Chileans were manning positions designated One and Two Bravo at the main gate, and I stopped to chat. Zep was going off duty as well and suggested a coffee before we turned in. It seemed a good idea. KBR had withdrawn their civilian staff from the mess hall and had them sleeping in their bunkers for the night. They had left urns of coffee and soup on the go for the night duty personnel so the guys would have something to keep them warm in the cold early hours. Two of the U.S. Marines had beaten us to it and were already sitting down in front of two steaming cups of coffee. Apart from them the cookhouse was deserted. K9 was awake and joined us for a brew; the three of us grabbed our cups and were invited to sit with the marines.

They had been interrogating a Mahdi Militiaman who had been captured by our Polish paratroopers.

Dressed in the black robes of the Militia, with a green sash around his middle and a loaded AK-47 assault rifle in his grasp, he had tried to climb the wall under the cloak of darkness at a place the Militia had identified as a weak point in our defences. Unfortunately for him it was not a weak point, and the Poles were watching his every movement through their night vision equipment. When he got close to the wall a Polish patrol was lying in wait, and they captured him using minimum force. Personally, I wouldn't have been as gentle; I would have shot him, but they wanted someone to interrogate. He was not being very cooperative, only telling them obvious stuff that they already knew. He claimed to be an innocent local who had been forced to join the Militia a couple of nights before. We believed that story! Of course he was innocent - all these murdering bastards were.

The prisoner was being held in a small outbuilding prior to being moved to another, more secure camp while one of the Polish paratroopers stood guard outside. Our camp commander needed to get as much info as possible from this terrorist. He had very little on the local bad guys, and anything they could get out of him might save our lives. Despite what the general public have read or seen on TV, our people were still working within the guidelines of the Geneva Convention. Frankly, this was a real hindrance when so many of the men we were interrogating were total savages with no morals or sense of decency. The only way to achieve anything was to get into their mindset and beat answers out of them, but of course we weren't allowed to do that.

One of the marines told me he would like to gather together in one room all the do-gooders who thought we should allow these people the same rights as any normal, civilised person. Then he would play all the gruesome footage that gets shown on Al Jazeera of the hostages being beheaded. He would play it to them over and over again until they threw up. Then he would put them in front of the families of those hostages and have them defend their philosophy of treating the terrorists as equals. Of course we could never do anything like that, even though it was a bloody good idea. It would probably infringe the peace activists' human rights, and we couldn't have that, could we! Some so-called civilised people must have been living on a different planet from the rest of us. How do you compare 'humiliating' Iraqi terrorists with murdering - oh no, sorry, wrong word - 'executing' hostages? How do our 'peace activists' sleep at night? They make me sick!

We sat and discussed interrogation techniques with our marine friends. One of the many qualifications I gained in the British Army came from a 'prisoner handling course'. It didn't do us any harm. Every one of us had gone through the 'resistance to interrogation' phase as a prisoner. We were subjected to 'humiliation', put into stress positions, and made to undergo other methods designed to make a prisoner uncomfortable, disorientated and confused - which was just the right frame of mind to get a prisoner in before you offered him the odd 'carrot' that would get him to talk. The course was designed not only to make us better interrogators, but also train us how to hold out longer if we ever became POWs. Psychological warfare is a good way to get a prisoner to crack without actually physically harming him. Just let the prisoner's mind conjure up all sorts of punishments that he thinks may happen to him, and then give him enough ammunition to fuel those thoughts. Everyone cracks in the end. It's just a matter of when.

Many lives depended on the information this terrorist could give us. Our dog was encouraged to bark and growl outside the building where the prisoner was being held. That unsettled him all right. He was told there were contractors in the camp who were friends of the four men killed and mutilated in Fallujah, and who would be happy to get their hands on him and do nasty things - but the Marines were protecting him, so he had nothing to worry about. Maybe he was not convinced that the U.S. Marine Corps had his best interest and safety at heart, as he started to talk, and talk, and talk.

The most worrying thing was the large stiletto knife he was carrying under his robes, and which he had tried to use during his capture. It was not the sort of weapon usually found on prisoners. A stiletto is designed for stabbing, and stabbing only: it is a long, pointed knife that serves no other purpose. The favoured weapon of most SF and commandos, it is used extensively for dispatching guards. The most famous knife of this kind is the Fairbairn-Sykes commando knife used by the British Special Forces and commando units in World War II.

It turned out that our prisoner was hardcore, and considered a bit of a knife expert. The Mahdi and their spies had observed that our principal's body armour didn't fit him, and due to his size could not be fastened properly. This nasty bastard had volunteered to get into the camp and try to kill him. The theory was that once the assassin was in he would lie in wait until an alert was sounded, and then knife his victim when he moved to his bunker. The body armour wouldn't have protected him. Of course, the Mahdi Army hadn't realised that this scenario was doomed to failure from the start because the PSD team would be with the principal during any alert, and wouldn't hesitate to blow any attackers to hell.

We saw the interrogators later at breakfast. They were more than happy with all the information they now had, and the prisoner was still singing. It was to be hoped this would allow the Iraqi Police to make some local arrests - that is, if the police who were still loyal could be identified. The information would definitely save lives. I spoke to one of the interrogators later at meal time. He had been born in America of Iraqi immigrant parents who had genuinely fled Saddam's regime. He was about as American as you could get, but spoke fluent Arabic with a good Iraqi accent. I wanted to know more about our enemies and their philosophies. I wanted to understand why the Iraqi people were so gullible that they listened to and believed the shit their leaders told them, and I considered him the best person to ask for an honest opinion.

He told me we were being too nice to our enemies, and our own sense of fair play was hampering us. Warming to the subject, he went on at length, knowing he had an audience that really wanted to hear what he thought.

"Here's the situation. You capture an Iraqi terrorist on the battlefield; he's armed, and there's no doubt that he's an enemy combatant. But do you behead him there and then and mutilate his body, as a fanatical Muslim terrorist would? No, you restrain him, making sure his bonds aren't too tight! After all, *we* are civilised and to hurt him now when he's just a helpless, unarmed enemy would be against the Geneva Convention. You question him politely but you don't beat him, so he has no fear and no incentive to tell you anything. You treat his wounds and feed him as he's being passed down the line, and he relaxes because he knows he's not going to be killed. Next you take him by plane to a warm, comfortable climate on an island near Cuba, and you put him in a prison cell with four walls and a roof. The cell is climate-controlled so he doesn't get too hot or too cold. Al-Qaeda would have him in a cellar so he couldn't see the sky and he'd be fed on any old shit they decided to throw to him, if they bothered to feed him at all.

Our American friends ask our prisoner more questions, but is he electrocuted or beaten with an iron bar? Hung upside down till he passes out? Does he have his fingernails removed one at a time and then his fingers broken? Holes drilled in his limbs with a cordless drill? No, of course not! You ask him some more polite questions - you may even threaten him, but he knows you're bluffing. You feed him three meals a day and let him read the Koran. Where's the punishment? You have just put him in a Muslim's idea of a holiday camp where he can read and meditate, be fed and watered, and he doesn't have to work. You've just given him everything he could ask for, and what has he given you in return? Nothing! No wonder al-Qaeda is still flourishing. You're too soft - too *civilised!*"

The way he said the word 'civilised' made it sound almost like an insult, but I could find no weakness in his argument. The terrorists were laughing at us.

***

A strange incident happened around this time. We had got to know many of the kitchen staff by now. The Pakistanis were helpful and eager to please and the food was good, but one of the kitchen boys who spoke almost perfect English was getting a raw deal. His name was Mohamed and his story was typical of many of the low paid foreign workers in Iraq.

KBR sub-contracted to outside contractors, who in turn sub-contracted down the line for staff and equipment. These companies then sub-contracted out to Third World countries to hire workers, and more than a few were unscrupulous in their methods of obtaining the quota of staff they needed. This young Pakistani had been recruited in his home town, where he was the head chef of a small but reputable hotel. He had been promised his own kitchen in Iraq, with plenty of staff and more money per month than he could make in a year back home. Who wouldn't jump at a job offer like that! And he had rosy ideas of making enough money to go home and start up his own catering business. With several other Pakistanis he had made the dangerous journey into Iraq by unarmed civilian transport, and finally arrived in Baghdad at the hiring company's offices. There all their passports were taken off them - for 'security' purposes as they were told at the time. From this point it all went downhill. He now found himself in Karbala working as an ordinary kitchen hand, and when he complained he was told to shut up or he would be left on the streets of Baghdad with no passport and no protection. To make matters worse he was also told that he had signed a contract for one year and would have to serve this term before he could go home. The pay he was getting was low, and he reckoned he'd been on better wages as a head chef back in Pakistan.

He had tried unsuccessfully to get transferred to Baghdad, where he had a friend in the company office who reckoned he could get his passport back. As long as he had his passport, he'd got together the money to get to Kuwait or Jordan. Once out of Iraq he could find work through other Pakistani friends and earn enough to return to his home country. He had it all planned: he just needed to get out of Camp Juliet. A couple of us agreed to help and he was given a strong laxative by our medic. A couple of days later I saw him in the compound. He didn't look well but he had reported to the camp Aid Station with sickness and vomiting, which of course meant he couldn't work in the DFAC for fear of contaminating everyone with whatever bug they thought he had. A few days later when it was obvious to his company he wasn't getting any better they sent him to Baghdad in a re-supply mission of military trucks. That was the last I saw of him. I did hear from one of the other kitchen workers that he had made it to Kuwait, though, and I wished him good luck. He was better off out of it.

# Chapter 14

## Blue on Blue

Both Shiite and Sunni factions had agreed to a cease-fire until the religious festival was over. That was really big of them - made me feel really warm inside. We'd heard the occasional crackle of small arms fire, but it seemed relatively peaceful. It was April 12th and I'd borrowed K9's sat phone to call Carol. It was 03:00 hours and our time zone was three hours ahead of England, so it was midnight at home and I knew Carol would still be awake. I'd tried a little earlier but the line was engaged, so I decided to try again once I was on stag and doing my rounds. I knew I'd get a better signal and reception on the roof, so it would be a better time than any other to call.

The only drawback was that the camp generator was positioned directly under the machine gun post and you couldn't hear yourself speak. I had to walk away from our gun position towards the centre of the roof and I could see the silhouette of one of the Polish soldiers on the far side, so I plonked myself down in the middle where my conversation with my wife couldn't be overheard and I would have a little bit of privacy. There was no wind and it was a comfortable night, with very few clouds and the stars twinkling above. Very romantic! I had dialled the number and was waiting for it to connect when out of the corner of my eye I saw the moving shapes of several vehicles advancing towards our main entrance in the darkness. They had just turned into the street and were about 150 feet from the first Iraqi checkpoint. It was too dark to make out who or what they were; I could only see shadows, movement, and the starlight glinting off a windscreen. As I registered this fact, the phone clicked to tell me I had a connection and could send my message, and just at that moment all hell broke loose!

Tracer from two PKM machine-guns on the Polish gate positions sprayed the vehicles, and the other sentries followed with their AKs. The gate machine guns opened fire, as did the Iraqi guards on the flank. Return fire erupted from the vehicles in all directions; there was shit flying everywhere and our Chileans in the closest position joined in with their Bushmasters vehicles. Heavy machine gun fire erupted from the leading vehicle, and tracer flew across my head with a *whoosh*. It was so close I could feel the air disturbed by its passage. By now I had got myself airborne, diving towards the nearest Chilean sandbagged emplacement a few feet away, simultaneously trying to turn off the phone so my wife wouldn't hear the battle evolving around me. The Poles on the roof opened up with their automatic weapons and at least one 84mm anti-tank rocket was fired.

Suddenly 40 mike rounds burst from the second vehicle and flew across the top of the roof to explode harmlessly in the amusement park. More tracer flew overhead from the vehicles. Hang on, I thought, the Militia don't have 40mm grenade launchers! I told the Chileans nearest to me not to fire unless they had positively identified targets, then I doubled over, trying to hide my head between my shoulder blades, and ran to the Polish position on the other side of the roof.

One of the three Poles there spoke English and I asked him to contact his ops room to see if there were any friendlies in the area. The message came back that there were three MP Humvee's which had just been fired on and had broken contact to come to our position because it was their nearest safe haven. The firing was dying down as the message got around, and I said to the Pole with the radio that he had better ask the Ops Room if we had just had a 'blue on blue' - friendly forces engaging each other. Shit! They checked with the MPs and yes, they had been fired on, and one of them was slightly wounded. They were going to sit it out in a nearby alleyway and wouldn't come back in until dawn. Why had they returned fire if they knew it was friendly fire! It had convinced the Poles that they had bad guys in Humvee's trying to gain entry and simply added to the confusion. They were bloody lucky that the Zeus gunner hadn't been at his post; he was taking a leak and could only return fire with his AK. If he had opened up with the four-barrelled anti-aircraft gun there would have been no survivors.

We got the official story the following day, once it was pieced together by Intelligence. A civilian pick-up had accelerated into the checkpoint, was engaged by the sentries and reversed out, turning left as it went and losing itself down a side street. The MP patrol, already breaking contact from one shooting, saw the muzzle flashes and returned fire. This now left the MPs and the Poles engaging each other while the bad guys slipped away. Despite all the shots fired, only one MP was hit - in the finger by a ricochet. There was no doubt that the armour on the Humvees saved their lives.

That morning the Military Police limped into camp. I happened to know the patrol commander and we talked about the shooting the night before. He was shaken up and angry, and I think he was a bit embarrassed as well. Despite all the hits with the AK 7.62 ammo, none had penetrated the vehicles, although the lead Humvee had lost one headlight, its bumper, and some panelling. It had so many splash marks from direct hits that it could have been mistaken for a dot-to-dot puzzle. The other vehicles had been hit too, but not as badly. In the bottom right-hand corner of the windshield was a neat three-round grouping of 5.56 rounds. The shots had been fired by one of the Chileans and were the only ones that had penetrated. Not surprising, as they were armour piercing. Once again it was just lucky no one had been seriously hurt. It was a good grouping though. Our Chilean friend would pass his annual personal weapons test easily with shooting like that.

The night of the 13th March was fairly quiet until about midnight, when we were subjected to harassing fire. At about 02:00 hours, a single RPG was fired from Area Black. All four walls of the camp had been given a different colour so it was easier to report on the radio which direction the enemy fire was coming from. The rocket fell short and exploded harmlessly on waste ground. Two small groups of enemy were engaged in the residential area to the west of the camp, but neither got to within 200 metres of the camp wall before they were fought off by direct fire from the Poles and the Bulgarian mobile patrols. At approximately 04:00 hours we had a long burst of AK fire followed by a deathly silence. The Militia had got tired and gone home to bed.

After a few quiet nights it was decided to scale down the state of alert on the 17th. We were still on lockdown, but considering and planning our next move. The PSD team had a move planned for El Hilla the next day at 05:00 hours and the site security teams were looking at re-occupying the government buildings on Monday morning. There was to be a big local government meeting that day at which all the local War Cabinet, including the bad guys, would be represented in an effort to stop the fighting. 23:55 hours, and I was sitting in John Wayne's hooch watching a film and having a quiet beer with Thomas, Derek and a couple of the other lads. All at once the cabin shook. "What the fuck was that?" someone asked. "Thunder?" Racing outside, I heard several rounds being launched in the distance and the unmistakable plopping sound of mortars leaving the tube galvanised me into action. "Get into the bunker, John!" I shouted, and raced round the corner of his hooch to go to my room about 50 feet away. John and the others dived into the concrete bunker outside his hut, taking the beer with them, while I ran alongside our water tanks with the intention of retrieving my rifle from my hooch and getting to a fire position. I believed this was the prelude to a concerted attack by the Militia. The second shot, which must have been the mortar man checking his range, exploded 50 feet in front of me, but luckily over the other side of the T-wall.

For a split second the shockwave stopped me dead. I felt the pressure on my chest and eardrums, as if I had been hit by a massive fist. In an instant I saw a huge flame flash up the outside of the concrete wall that was shielding me from the shrapnel. Then, as suddenly as it came, the image was gone. My flight had been halted for a split second, but now I was released to continue my mad dash to the hut. I passed the PSD team going in the other direction, hurrying our principal to cover in his bunker. Grabbing my rifle, I raced to the nearest fire position, Position Four, and found Zep already there. We'd been in position a few seconds when another five mortar rounds overshot the camp and exploded one after the other about 300 yards away in the residential area. The last round scored a direct hit on one of the houses, which disintegrated in a flash of burning embers and flying rubble. The silly buggers had adjusted their fire the wrong way - luckily for us. Mentally, I gave them a round of applause.

A truck full of Mahdi Militia was spotted racing away into the darkness towards one of the mosques. The IPs that spotted them radioed in their location, but chose not to engage them. God knows why not! One of the Polish patrols went out to see if they could find the mortar's firing position, but had no luck and returned empty handed. An hour later we stood down and went back to bed. The next night we all went to bed fully clothed expecting another attack, but nothing happened. This was again turning out to be very frustrating.

The 19th rolled round - the day we would be taking back the CPA complex - and we were expecting it to be a bit hairy. The military had not yet properly cleared the roads after the end of the *Arba'een (the Fortieth)* holiday, and 2,000 Militia were reported to be still scattered around the area. The market north of the CPA building was the most hostile location, and it was from there that most of the RPGs had been fired. Fourteen of us in three vehicles were going in first to clear and hold the building. I found it very strange that the City Council called a top-level meeting of all dignitaries and heads of sheds in such an obvious target, especially as the area had not been properly sanitised of all hostiles. I could only hope that we weren't yet again risking our necks for our principal, just so he could blow hot air and screw up.

It was another early start. As we manoeuvred through streets littered with burnt-out trucks, cars, barrels, and burning tyres, people watched us from their doorways, but there were very few of them out in the open. We gained entry to the CPA building easily. There were no guards at the gate and the razor wire was gone. One guard stood at the inner gate, but didn't seem very interested, so we barrelled through and dismounted. There was very little outside damage and we knew that no Militia had gained entry to the buildings during the fighting. Once again, the police had looted the very place they were guarding. Every door was kicked in and every computer stolen. We were wasting our time trying to teach these people anything.

We had backing from Bulgarian and Polish armoured vehicles and soldiers, and now the place was in Coalition hands once again. The meeting came and went with the usual fuss and palaver, and as far as I know nothing was decided yet again. One bit of good that did come out of it was that the locals got pissed off with the Militia. It seemed they were not a cohesive fighting unit but a series of gangs, each trying to get one over on the other. They had started terrorising the locals and they now wanted rid of them. One council member complained that they were using a mosque as cover and wanted to know why the Americans hadn't bombed them. He didn't really mean it: it was just sabre-rattling, and he would probably be the first person to complain if it was flattened. In true Arab fashion, they sucked their teeth and agreed on the date of the next meeting.

The north end of the CPA compound, where the market was, had been completely destroyed by RPG and small arms fire. Blackened windows, bullet holes, and signs blowing in the wind were witnesses to the fierce fire fight that had raged for almost four days. Captain Victor was happy, though. He had received four computers for his unit from the Panasonic shop. He had them on trial to see if they could do the job they needed them for, but with the shop destroyed it didn't look like anyone would be chasing him for payment.

As if to cleanse the place, it suddenly started to rain - lightly at first, and then increasing to a steady downpour. I stood post on the roof, watching the rain slowly wash the dust from the crevices in my rifle. The rain felt refreshing on my face and I closed my eyes and breathed deeply, but then the stench from Sesame Street filled my lungs and I coughed: the moment had passed, the daydream was over, and this was still Iraq. Once the principal and the committee members had gone, we were given the order to bug out. After making our way downstairs to the lobby, we remounted our waiting vehicles and with horns blaring hurtled out into the chaos that was a normal day in Karbala.

*\*\**

After our evening Orders Group I sat down in John's hut to watch a film with a few of the blokes. No sooner had it got interesting than the steady *crump* of mortar rounds exploding told me it was time to man the fire positions again. Déjà vu! We stood to for about an hour, and from my vantage point on the roof I could see a 360-degree panorama of the camp. One of our Polish patrols went to investigate three mortars that had landed short of the west wall and on their way to the suspected launch site they spotted another Mahdi Militia member on a motorbike carrying an RPG. They gave chase and fired at him, only to see him disappear, bike and all, down an alleyway. The jeep couldn't follow him and he got away, leaving them with the frustration of listening to the bike's motor fading into the distance.

The latest intelligence told us we were about to be mortared somewhere between 02:00 hours and 04:00 hours, so I went back to my cabin and decided to get a good night's sleep for as many hours as I could. If they fired on us, I had no doubt I would be woken up. Dumping my gear in a hurry where I could, I stripped off and climbed into my sleeping bag. The noise of people moving around outside woke me: it was 08:00 hours. Almost seven hours of uninterrupted sleep! Looks like Intelligence got it wrong again.

***

April 21st, and another good night's sleep. I could get used to this! We were ready to move to the CPA building at 09:00 hours when we were told to stand down. One of the Polish patrols was shot at on the way to Camp Lima. They had taken some heavy fire in the form of RPG and machine-gun fire. The patrol had dismounted and engaged the enemy positions, hoping to keep them busy until reinforcements could come to their assistance. As we walked back to the billets to stow our weapons half the Polish paratroopers in the camp, supported by BMPs, were racing out of the gate to do battle. Within an hour they were all back in camp. There were no casualties on our side, but the militia was chased off, there was no follow-up and no arrests made.

This war could get extremely frustrating. All convoy movement had been suspended for the time being due to this incident. Hollywood and Stingray were due to rotate out on the 25th and I was leaving on the 30th. Time was getting short, and so far we had no idea how the Company intended getting us out of there. We had also heard there was a problem with Kuwaiti visas, but we were all confident that Blackwater would have that sorted out by the time we were told to move. The latest Intel was that heavy fighting had broken out throughout Fallujah, with at least eight bombs exploding in three different Iraqi Police stations. Most of the dead and wounded were Iraqis, although first reports said that two British soldiers were among the wounded. These attacks were really pissing us off and we would have loved the opportunity to go proactive. If only we'd been allowed to do the occasional foot patrol, we knew we could have accounted for some of the local bad guys.

The Polish commander asked K2 if we were trained in house clearing, and of course he said yes. If we were given the opportunity, would we be prepared to take out a couple of houses that the bad guys were using as a base? He had jumped at the chance, so a combined operation with the Poles making the cordon and our people taking out the militia was discussed. Preparations and planning were well underway when our politician found out about the plans and threatened us with jail if we went out of the gate. It was explained to him that with just one surgical strike against these bastards we could stop the camp being attacked, but he would have none of it and said he'd have us jailed as mercenaries if we attacked the Militia. I was all for climbing up and painting a big white cross on the roof of his hut so the militia would know where to drop their next mortar rounds. The idea was still being bandied about when Joker reminded me I only had a few days to do if all went well, and I shouldn't think about doing anything stupid. Still, it would have felt really good to know I could do something to make an impact before I left this shit hole.

One of the Chileans came around looking for K9. There was a water tanker at the gate and although the paperwork seemed in order, it was a different crew from usual and the Polish guards were suspicious. It was halted outside the camp gates in an area that was specially built for just this contingency - a square of land hemmed in by four high dirt banks. If anything blew up in there, the earth banks would contain it with minimum damage. Simple but effective! Unfortunately, it would not be healthy for whoever was doing the searching.

K9 got Roy out of his kennel. "Hang on, Mate! Let me get my gear on and I'll give you a hand," I found myself saying. My dad always said never volunteer for anything, and here I was volunteering again. I had done enough searches in my time in Northern Ireland, though, so it didn't bother me unduly. It took a couple of minutes to put my body armour on and grab my long gun and pistol.

The three of us walked to the gate and met a very relieved paratrooper. He was a young lad and not looking forward to searching the tanker. A few weeks previously, another camp in-country had been badly damaged when their usual sludge tanker turned up on schedule to clear their cesspit. It was searched and let in. Once inside it exploded, killing a couple of sentries and wounding many more. On examination of the debris, forensics had found there had been considerable preparatory work done on the tanker. Careful welding had produced a separate, hidden compartment containing the bomb. It had been fixed in such a way that inspecting the top hatch would have shown water present, and opening all its pipes would have produced the shit you would expect from a sludge tanker. Now all tankers were checked with a depth gauge, newly welded panels on the tank were treated with suspicion, and the tankers were always checked with either a dog or mechanical sniffer.

Our Chileans and the Polish sentries positioned themselves where they could cover the nearby rooftops and windows. We also had cover from the front Sanger and forward Iraqi Guard, so I didn't think snipers would be a problem. I did a search of the driver and his mate and signalled for them to stand to one side where they could be covered and observed for any suspicious behaviour. Checking the vehicle cab was not so easy. These guys must have lived in there, judging by the rubbish, dirty clothing, and junk that littered the place. Nevertheless, it took only a short while to confirm the cab clear, at least of explosives.

I gave K9 the all-clear and he went to work underneath the chassis and on the body of the truck. Using his rubber toy as an incentive, K9 encouraged the dog to give the truck a thorough going over. I think the Iraqis were impressed. It took about five minutes to clear the vehicle and then the Poles allowed it to leave the quarantine area and enter the camp. K9 told the Poles to call him if there were any other vehicles they were not sure of.

It was time for a coffee, so we both walked off to the DFAC for a brew.

*Iraq Coalition Casualties: PSD, Convoy, and Site Security April 2004.*

| Date | Name | Nationality | Incident |
|------|------|-------------|----------|
| 01/04/2004 | Unknown | Czech | Accident, Southern Iraq |
| 03/04/2004 | Emad Mikha | American | Killed by small arms fire, Muqdaiyah |
| 06/04/2004 | Gray Branfield | South African | Killed by small arms fire, al-Kut (Gray was part of a PSD team working for Hart Security. His body was mutilated and hanged by the terrorists.) |
| 06/04/2004 | Mario Manchev | Bulgarian | Killed in convoy attack, An Nasiriyah |
| 08/04/2004 | Tim Smith | American | Killed in a convoy attack, location unknown |
| 08/04/2004 | John Michael Blos | British | Killed by small arms fire, Hit. (John was a retired British Parachute Regiment soldier defending workers repairing overhead power cables to bring electricity to the local schools and hospital. He was working for the American firm Custer Battles.) |
| 09/04/2004 | Shiva Prasad Lawati | Nepali | Killed when vehicle hit a landmine, Northern Iraq |
| 09/04/2004 | Ram Bahadur Gurung | Nepali | Killed when his vehicle hit a landmine, Northern Iraq. (Both men were retired British Army Ghurkhas working for Global Risk Strategies as site security team and were in transit to their place of work when attacked.) |

| Date | Name | Nationality | Incident |
|------|------|-------------|----------|
| 09/04/2004 | William Bradley, | American | Killed in a convoy attack, Baghdad. (William was a truck driver working for Halliburton/KBR.) |
| 09/04/2004 | Scott Steven Fisher | American | Killed in a convoy attack, Baghdad. (Scott was a truck driver working for Halliburton/KBR. He was a retired U.S. Marine.) |
| 09/04/2004 | Duane Tony Johnson | American | Killed in a convoy attack, Baghdad. (Duane was a truck driver working for Halliburton/KBR.) |
| 09/04/2004 | Jeffery Parker | American | Killed in a convoy attack in Baghdad. (Jeffery was a truck driver working for Halliburton/KBR.) |
| 09/04/2004 | Jack Montague | American | Killed in a convoy attack, Baghdad. (Jack was a truck driver working for Halliburton/KBR.) |
| 09/04/2004 | Stephen Hulett | American | Killed in a convoy attack, Baghdad. (Stephen was a truck driver working for Halliburton/KBR.) |
| 09/04/2004 | Stephen Hulett | American | Killed in a convoy attack, Baghdad (Stephen was a truck driver working for Halliburton/KBR.) |
| 11/04/2004 | Henrik Frandsen | Danish | Killed by small arms fire, Baghdad. |
| 11/04/2004 | Aron Alexandru | Romanian | Killed in a convoy attack, Baghdad |

| Date | Name | Nationality | Incident |
|---|---|---|---|
| 12/04/2004 | Vis Visagie | South African | Killed in an RPG attack, location unknown. (Vis was a retired SA Policeman from the Pretoria Police Task Force. He was working for Erinys as part of a PSD team escorting diplomats from Amman in Jordan to Baghdad.) |
| 14/04/2004 | Fabrizio Quattrocchi, | Italian | Kidnapped and executed, location unknown. (A very brave man. He tried to remove his hood as the terrorists held a gun to his head, and shouted, "Now I will show you how an Italian dies!" He was shot in the back of the head.) |
| 22/04/2004 | Francois de Beer | South African | Killed by small arms fire, Baghdad. (Francois was working for Meteoric Tactical Solutions.) |
| 25/04/2004 | Thomas Carter | American | Killed by an IED. (Baji. Thomas was a retired Delta Force soldier working for Cochise Consultancy protecting demolition workers clearing explosives to make the area safe for the locals.) |
| 25/04/2004 | Vincent Foster | American | Killed by an IED. (Baji Vincent was a retired Marine Corps veteran.) |
| 28/04/2004 | Rodrigo Reyes | Filipino | Killed in a convoy attack, Abdali |

| Date | Name | Nationality | Incident |
|------|------|-------------|----------|
| 29/04/2004 | Unknown | South African | Killed by small arms fire, Basra |
| 29/04/2004 | Mike Price | American | Killed by an IED, Basra |
| 30/04/2004 | Unknown | South African | Killed when he stepped on a landmine, Fallujah |

# Chapter 15

## Casevac

On April 23 a bomb exploded in Fallujah, killing 36 Iraqis. I was finding it very hard to be sympathetic any more. If only the locals would inform on these bastards instead of turning a blind eye, we could finish this war and bring peace to the country. Another couple of explosions occurred at about 22.00 hours; we felt the shock waves, so they were pretty close to the camp, and everyone stood to. Apparently they'd been aimed at Camp Kilo, but they overshot and fell towards us. It went quiet and nothing came in our direction; the usual drill followed, and after an hour we stood down. When dawn broke, I decided to get on the computer. I managed to IM Carol back in England for a ten-minute chat, but had only just signed off when we came under direct mortar fire - the first time they had tried to hit us in broad daylight. Luckily the rounds overshot again! I ran to the hotel and was on the roof in record time; our Chileans and Poles all ran for their individual fire positions, and were in place and looking for targets within a few minutes. Once again it sounded like the CPA compound was being attacked. Sporadic fighting broke out around the camp, but that was the usual Iraqi way of fighting. Hold your rifle above your head over a wall and let off a 30-round magazine in the general direction of the enemy - you might get lucky and hit something! I don't think they had been taught anything about aimed shots.

There was a loud explosion not too far away and black smoke billowed above the roof tops not more than 400 feet from where I stood near Red Sector of the compound. Tango, Mike, K2 and I, supported by a Polish soldier with a PKM, prepared to fire on the Militia if the fire fight came around the corner of the block in our direction. As we watched, a mixed Polish and Bulgarian Army convoy of pickup trucks, BMPs, Jeeps and trucks hurtled around the corner towards us, the rear armoured car returning fire in the direction of an unseen enemy. They were still firing at an enemy that had ambushed them a few minutes ago on the approach to the camp, and had already destroyed a Bulgarian truck. One of the lorry drivers, a young Bulgarian soldier, had been hit in the head and badly wounded. He had been rescued from his vehicle, which was then set on fire by his comrades to stop it falling into enemy hands. The black smoke we could see over the rooftops was from the burning truck.

Our medical team had been told he was in a bad way and they had already ordered a medevac for him. As soon as the convoy got through the camp gates, the Polish medics started working on the poor lad, while everyone watched their sectors to protect the helicopter on the way in.

The U.S. Marine detachment was controlling the LZ, and we had given them one of our radios so we could be in direct contact with them in case of an emergency. I came up on the radio to tell our marine mate Gonzo that I could see the bird inbound from my position at about five clicks out. Down below us, the medics tried hard to save the young Bulgarian, but with the head injury he had sustained they were fighting a losing battle.

The Blackhawk came in fast and the pilot kept his rotors at full throttle while the medics and chopper crew loaded the soldier as gently as they could into the dark interior and secured him there. The helicopter stayed on the ground for longer than normal on a potentially hot LZ, so that the onboard medics had time to make the wounded man as comfortable as possible and stabilize him before they lifted off. Everyone was working to give him at least a fighting chance of survival. Finally, slowly and steadily, the medevac took off. The pilot made no evasive manoeuvres: they were being very brave, risking their own safety to give the casualty as smooth a ride as possible.

Now the lives of the helicopter crew and the casualty were in our hands. Everyone in the camp kept their eyes on the surrounding area, watching rooftops and windows, and in particular the area where he had been shot. We all wanted to even the score, but in the circumstances no one really wanted an incident now. By the time the chopper and its supporting gun ships were finally specks in the distance, the dust had already settled in the compound. All that was left of the drama that had unfolded a few minutes before was a bloodstained field dressing hanging from a telephone cable where the chopper's downdraft had blown it. A large patch of drying blood marked the area where the young Bulgarian had been treated.

We were getting pissed off playing duty targets. I climbed down the ladder from the roof with a couple of the Chileans, and as we were reaching the ground, I could see through the window of a Polish soldier's room. His TV was on, tuned to the BBC, and it was showing the Bulgarian vehicle burning in the street. Bizarrely enough, I was watching it on TV and could see it for real at the same time, the smoke rising over the rooftops. The TV was showing locals with AKs waving the young soldier's helmet in the air and chanting. If I'd gone back on the roof with a grenade launcher, I could have put a round down in the middle of them, they were that close to us.

It continually baffled the soldiers on the ground how the reporters always seemed to be where the action was. It was obviously just a coincidence - wasn't it? The media wonder why we don't like them. It might be something to do with paying the local rabble to jump up and down on burning Humvees to sell copy.

I remember patrolling as a young paratrooper through Belfast, Tail End Charlie of a British patrol, and suddenly spotting someone step out of a doorway behind us with what I thought was a weapon. I took up the first pressure on my SLR trigger and was about to shoot the bastard when I realized it was a reporter with a camera. I had him pinned up against the wall and was going to shoot anyway when my corporal dragged me off him. The reporter turned out to be from some German newspaper. Our patrol commander took the camera off him, exposed his film, and then told him to fuck off before he let the rest of the patrol loose on him. I went off the media from that day, and in every war I served in they proved a pain in the arse.

The Poles requested an air strike. They'd identified the building that was the source of the fire that had wounded their Bulgarian comrade, and at 22.00 hours that night we heard the Specter orbiting overhead. It circled the town center for about 30 minutes at a height of a few thousand feet. Everyone expected the usual fireworks, but suddenly the plane banked and was gone, its engines receding into the distance. We heard later that the crew had used the aircraft's heat-seeking capabilities to pinpoint several groups of armed men in and around the previously identified building, but no one in Baghdad had the guts to authorize the aircraft to engage. Once again they didn't want any collateral damage: a building was more important than the life of a Bulgarian soldier.

A good result was later confirmed on the daily CNN television report. It seems our Specter pilot must have been pissed off as much as we were for being denied permission to engage positively identified targets. Some armchair warrior, warm and cosy back in the Green Zone, was obviously more worried about public opinion and his career than actually doing his job. So the pilot had orbited wider and wider, looking for enemy targets of opportunity, and on the outskirts of Basra he found one - over 40 militia manhandling a Russian-made anti-aircraft gun into position. He confirmed the target and got permission to engage. The result was the recovery of the remains of the gun the following day and 36 confirmed dead bad guys. That went some way to even the score.

We later heard that our young Bulgarian had died, but that he carried an organ donor card. His parents had given their permission as well, and his body would be put to good use saving other lives. Little consolation, I thought.

At 0200 hours we were engaged by enemy fire. We could see the tracer but not where it originated, (although it was coming in from somewhere to the north) and we couldn't return fire without a confirmed, identified target. During a routine mobile patrol, the Poles chanced upon a group of terrorists setting up a mortar base plate. A running gun battle started and the Poles stayed in pursuit; eventually the Poles were credited with five dead terrorists and two captured. The downside was that the mortar tube had not been recovered.

*** 

The 24th started off very dry and hot, but by early evening we were in the middle of another raging sandstorm. If this kept up, the Specter would be unable to engage any of the targets it had identified the night before. The plus side was that the bad guys didn't like operating in bad weather. Their mortar men would not be able to fire at us in the gale force winds, and the storm would keep their snipers indoors. The high T-walls gave the camp a little protection against the sandstorm, but it still wasn't a good night to be out.

It was another quiet day on the 25th. Stingray caught me at breakfast and told me we were to have our kit packed and be ready to move at a moment's notice. We were receiving intelligence from our local friendlies confirming that the Militia was still in positions all around us.

Their main group was massing near the hospital and controlled most of that area. Stingray, Hollywood and I were due to go to Baghdad to fly home at the end of our contract, but we still had to get out somehow. We hoped Blackwater's helicopters could get in to lift us out, but there was a real danger of them being hit. I for one didn't want to put anyone at risk just to get me out so I could go home on time.

I was prepared to stay until it was safe to move and the others felt the same way. The PSD team couldn't escort us out: there was always a risk of danger to the principal, so they had to stay. We were now in a Catch 22 situation. The original plan was for us to get to El Hilla near Babylon and catch a ride on the chopper out to Baghdad International Airport. Unfortunately, there was a lot of enemy activity in and around El Hilla, making it a very dangerous route to take.

An hour later, one of the Chileans told me a Blackhawk was coming in on a re-supply run and it had been arranged for the three of us to get out on that. After another half hour we found out the mission was cancelled because the area was too hot to bring the chopper in. Gonzo, our marine sergeant friend knocked on my hooch door; he couldn't find K2 and asked me to pass on a message. Would I let him know that Route Tampa had been retaken and reopened by the American 1st Armored Division.

That was good news. The armored boys had taken the route, despite a couple of suicide VBIEDs and the fact that some of the fly-overs had been mined or destroyed by the Militia to prevent troop movement. The Americans had now positioned tanks and troops on all key points and had fought off a few local counter attacks. I heard of one idiot of a suicide bomber who walked up to an armoured Bradley and blew himself up against it. The explosion scratched the paint-work and shook the vehicle, and the crew later washed off the remains of the bomber with a high-pressure hose.

We still had to get from Camp Juliet to either El Hilla or the main Babylon camp before we could pick up the route to Tampa, which meant we would have to run the gauntlet of the Mahdi Militia groups between here and the El Hilla area. We hoped to have good news the next day, though. I had my kit packed, so I spent a quiet night watching films in John Wayne's hooch with several of the guys. Two crates of beer were produced from somewhere, and a happy group whiled the night away. There were no contacts, no RPGs, and no mortars that night.

The Militia members were busy arguing among themselves, and proving they were nothing more than gangs of criminals joined together in a loose alliance. Even that was now breaking down as they got their arses kicked in more and more engagements against the Coalition Forces. They were not getting the spoils of victory their clerics had promised, and they were becoming demoralized. At the end of the day they were just cheap hoods, gangsters, thieves and murderers. Muqtada Al-Sadr had used his influence to bring together all the rabble in the area; he gave them a common cause, put them in a uniform, and promised them the opportunity to rape, loot and pillage, and all under the banner of Allah's will. A lot of the attacks had been the work of Iranian-backed al-Qaeda insurgents, who were not under Al-Sadr's control but were simply using his uprising as a cover for their own agenda.

Most of my gear was in my footlocker and crew bag: I would believe I was going home when I saw my transport outside and waiting! Meanwhile, I caught up with John Wayne and asked him to do me a favour. All through the tour our Chileans had been told they were on a dry contract. This meant no drinking, and as far as I was aware they had obeyed this rule. From my personal experience I knew that soldiers would always do the opposite of what they are told. Tell them they can't drink, and they will find a way to get alcohol. Treat them like adults and they usually behave like children. I, however, was British, not American, and we Brits always manage to get a beer for special occasions. I considered my leaving to be a special occasion, and so I asked John if he could use his contacts to get me a couple of crates of beer for the Chileans. They had been a good loyal crew throughout my tour and I wanted to show them I appreciated it. What better way than with a couple of crates of beer! I knew they wouldn't tear the arse out of it: a couple of crates would only give them a beer apiece anyway. It was a time-honored airborne tradition and one I was not going to break. John promised me he would get the beer and I handed over enough dollars to complete the transaction.

I was going to miss the KBR guys. They had made a crap tour bearable. Thomas, who came from a very religious family, was convinced with the help of Derek and John that I was a Satanist. It used to wind him up something terrible! I'm not sure how it started off, but it was a joke that carried on, and was kept up even after I left Camp Juliet. Sorry, Thomas! John Wayne was a good friend to me and many others, and nothing was too much trouble for him. The countless other guys who also helped us are too numerous to mention. Everyone had worked together, and I had actually enjoyed my tour at Juliet.

# Chapter 16

## Escape from Karbala

More bad news! Our Blackhawk taxi was re-tasked and we had no lift out. At first I thought it wouldn't bother me, but now it was beginning to get on my nerves. I was lying on my pit about midday when Dallas stuck his head round the door.

"Twelve minutes, ready to move! You're going home."

"You're fucking winding me up!" I replied, a bit pissed off at the obvious stitch-up. "No, really, Pops! You're going out with a convoy of Humvees. We're just sorting out a spare hard car."

It took me five minutes to finish packing and drag my gear down to the end of the patio, ready to load into whatever vehicle we were using. A military convoy of four National Guard and Special Forces Humvees had fought their way down from the North on their way to Baghdad; they'd got a bit lost but found their way to us. They had popped off a few rounds on the way in, but hadn't met any real resistance as the Militia's resolve had been well and truly broken by that time. They'd asked for directions to the main supply route, and K2 had been on hand to strike a deal with them. We would show them the way through the surrounding area if they would escort and cover us in our hard car on the way to Baghdad. We now had some serious hardware as escorts! I don't know who was the more relieved, the SF section commander now that he did not have to blunder through the badlands to get to the main supply route (MSR) or us, as we now had a chance of getting our flights out of Baghdad on time.

We were moving so quickly that I wouldn't have time to say goodbye to many of the friends who had made this a decent tour. They wouldn't even be aware that I'd gone, and I felt bad about that. I was lousy at good-byes anyway. Some of my Chilean team who were not on duty came out to wave me off. Gurkha thanked me for being his friend, and all of them pushed forward to shake my hand. I was a bit choked. I was going to miss these people.

Gurkha leaned forward and whispered in my ear, "We're going to miss you more than you know."

"Why? I didn't think I was that good a team leader!"

"It's not that," he said, keeping a straight face. "It means now we'll be getting an American!"

A few members of the bodyguard team had not been very helpful towards the Chileans, and they were disliked for it. The Chileans were very pro-British. Throughout their history they had been led into battle by British mercenary generals - against the Argentinians for instance - and on at least one occasion by a British pirate moonlighting as an admiral in their navy. I was sure they would get a good team leader, and I knew all my team would be just as hard-working for him as they had been for me. Of all the site se-

364

curity guards provided by other countries I considered the Chileans to be the best.

We had borrowed a hard car from KBR, which would be left in our safe compound in Baghdad until the team could pick it up and bring it back to Karbala. K2 briefed the SF team leader and the rest of us on the proposed route and on emergency RVs. Hollywood gave the order to saddle up, and we made our last quick goodbyes. I shook hands with Zeppelin and Joker and promised to keep in touch. Mounting up, I covered my arc from the right rear seat of the borrowed hard car as we sped out of the gate with the Humvees and into the debris littering the street. It would be bloody unfortunate to get ambushed now.

The Polish paratroopers moved their truck out of the way and waved to us as we negotiated Camp Juliet's chicane for what we knew would be the last time. As we turned into the local residential area, the Militia's presence was all too obvious. Burnt-out barricades and collapsed houses spread debris and rubble across the street, and recently destroyed cars still smouldered. Our hard car had the lead as we doubled back onto the main road, navigated the roundabout, and accelerated towards the main route out of the city. The big green water tower that had been our reference point for so long was soon swallowed up by the rest of the city and left far behind.

There were very few people on the streets. The Militia were not too fussy about who they killed, and even the locals thought it too dangerous to be out. The turret gunners on the Humvees swung their 30 and 50-cal. machine-guns left and right looking for targets, but the bad guys were in no mood to oblige. With any luck, the Militia had taken the day off.

Between our location and the MSR were at least two villages known to harbour terrorists; one was a pretty nasty choke point where we expected to have trouble. We had surrendered our Bushmasters prior to leaving Juliet and now carried an AK-47 each and a few magazines. Our weapons had stayed at the camp for our replacements and with only a couple of magazines apiece, we couldn't afford a stand-up fight with anyone. The advantage was the ammo: the AK's 7.62 rounds had more stopping power. If attacked, we would have to get off the X and fight through, relying on the SF Humvees to give the bad guys a headache.

As we progressed through the villages at speed towards Baghdad we saw nothing, not even a kid with a slingshot. Even the local dogs were keeping out of the way. It looked like the Militia really had lost the will to fight, at least for the time being. Running up the on-ramp to the motorway, we passed a concrete block with the words "Route Tampa" painted on it. So far so good, and not a shot fired.

It was soon evident that the 1st Armored Division had been very busy. The first thing I noticed was an American tank to one side of the road, its commander still in the turret clutching his 50-cal. machine-gun. Some yards away was the still burning wreck of a Mahdi Militia pick-up truck that had tried to take on this heavy armoured monster. Bad mistake! David and Goliath sprang to mind, but this time David had lost. Travelling at speed down the MSR, now sandwiched between the four Humvees, we passed more evidence of the hard-fought battle for the route. A blown up overpass had a hole the size of a small house gaping in its centre. Twisted metal reinforcing rods protruded at strange angles from the rubble at its edges, the result of a huge car bomb. Another hole further along was spanned by a Bailey bridge guarded by armoured engineers, and the occasional wrecked civilian car bore witness to attacks on military targets.

Strangely enough, there was a conspicuous absence of bodies; either the Militia had taken their dead with them, which was highly unlikely, or our people had rushed them away for Forensics to work on. Even against the backdrop of all this shit, the Military Police and their supporting branches still viewed these incidents as crime scenes, and carried out exhaustive tests to gain as much information as possible from the debris. They were able to trace explosives and ammunition, identify Insurgents, and get all the usual results you would expect from a crime scene in a civilized country. The Mahdi rabble had lost heavily this time, and a lot of the explosives were being traced back to Iran through good police work.

As we got closer to Baghdad, we passed more and more armoured vehicles and their support arms holding positions on flyovers and on and off ramps. All key positions needed to take and hold the main supply route, and life was beginning to return to normal, thanks to the 1st Armoured Division. The locals obviously felt reassured by their presence because the stallholders were now opening up at the side of the road and we were passing market traders who filled the roads with battered, overloaded trucks and horse drawn carts. It was strange seeing combat air patrols of Blackhawks, Apaches, Hinds, and Havocs, which a few years ago would have been trying to shoot each other down and were now protecting us against a common enemy.

We reached the suburbs of Baghdad without incident and immediately entered the usual traffic jams and chaos that you find in any big city. It was as if the fighting on the MSR was happening in another world far away instead of on their doorstep. Despite the very present danger, everyone visibly relaxed a little. It was funny how you could bring your personal alert state down a couple of clicks, but still be ready instantly for a fire fight. I suppose it's the built-in safety valve we all have. On the left, we passed the huge scrap yard that had become a famous landmark. Most of Saddam's wrecked Armoured Division lay there in ruins, a reminder of two previous wars fought in this country. If peace was ever brought to Iraq, it would be a vehicle collector's paradise. In his day, Saddam had amassed an army of vehicles brought from all around the world. Not all had been destroyed by enemy fire, and many had just been captured and thrown in the dump. Your average poor Iraqi is an expert at scavenging and improvisation, and many combat vehicle parts now powered generators, had become water pumps, or had been commandeered for any of the other 101 uses they could find for them. Everywhere you looked, horse-drawn carts were using tyres from Jeeps. In the meantime the hulks sat there rusting, waiting for someone to find a use for them and what was left of their parts.

Our convoy passed the outer defences of the Green Zone, once again without a shot being fired. Three of our escorting vehicles peeled off towards their own camp, blowing their horns as their crews gave us a farewell wave. The leading Humvee took us into the Baghdad central parking lot and pulled to a halt. Everyone dismounted to stretch their legs and thank our escorts. We had done them a favour by showing them the way and leading them through the hostile villages, so they had been only too happy to help us. The lieutenant in charge said to let him know if there was anything at all he could do for us. They weren't just empty words: he meant it. That was how things got done out here - favours for favours. We shook hands with him and his crew and remounted for the short drive to the Company's safe house.

# Chapter 17

## Downtime

We were welcomed back to the safe house by the familiar young Iraqi security guards we had met weeks before. They smiled as they recognised us and waved us through. Stingray parked up outside the front gate and we walked through into the house. The light was failing as we arrived, and the house cook was busy making the evening meal. Kiwi and a few of the other permanent PSD crew came in, and old acquaintances were renewed. The fridge was well stocked with beer and we sank a cold one as the local team brought us up to speed on the happenings in Baghdad.

We were sitting in the lounge telling war stories when Cory and some of the Bremmer PSD team arrived. We shook hands: it was good to see him again. He was still running the team at the principal's house and wondered if we'd like to come over and have a look at the security systems in place. It would be a good experience and all three of us agreed. We put the body armour back on and got our AKs out of the armoury. Climbing into Cory's two vehicles, we left the safe house and ventured across the Green Zone to Mr. Bremmer's house.

The Suburban drivers identified themselves at the main gate to the villa and moved slowly up the driveway. With cameras and alarm systems everywhere, there was no way anyone could get access to the compound without being seen and engaged by several guns. The vehicles parked up and we entered the main hall, coming face to face with one of our own guys armed and alert. Behind him was a bombproof door that gave us entry to the house.

The villa originally belonged to one of Saddam's two sons, Uday, and was christened his 'Pussy Palace'. It was a large and imposing building, simply decorated compared with Saddam's usual taste, but I thought it had a strange, cold feeling about it. If walls could tell stories, this place would have some tales to tell. Uday used to send his bodyguard team to the university to pick out the prettiest females. They were brought to his house, where he indulged himself in whatever sadistic pleasures took his fancy. Once he tired of them, or if they complained, he had them taken to his private zoo and fed alive to his tigers. Nice guy! He obviously didn't want a permanent relationship.

I thought Mr. Bremmer was a very brave man to live there. I'm sure I couldn't have done it: there was no way I could have stayed in a place that had seen so many horrors. The house had its own Operations Room manned by well-armed guards. Closed circuit television covered every angle of the house, both inside and in the grounds. Let a bat fart anywhere near this place, and it would be spotted.

Bremmer was well protected by a guard force that respected their principal, a completely different situation from ours with the bloke we had been looking after. One guy told me he was present when the boss was informed of the Spanish commander's request to leave his camp to the Militia and withdraw to safety. Bremmer was on the phone to the Spanish military immediately, demanding that they instantly sack and replace the officer concerned. Under no circumstances, he told them, was the camp to be surrendered. The result? The offending officer was replaced, and his replacement held the camp. Some weeks later, the Spanish bottled it and withdrew their troops from Iraq altogether. Just as well, was my personal opinion. No good having allies you cannot rely on to watch your back.

The tour over, we thanked the residential team for the informative look-see and got a lift back to the safe house from Cory and his team. The rest of the guys were watching a war film on TV when we arrived, and I was just about to grab a beer from the fridge when a burst of automatic fire whistled across the roof of our building. Everyone made a dive for their weapons and ran to prepared firing positions in and around the house. There was nothing: no follow-up, no explosions; even the once familiar Blackhawks did not turn up. No one seemed interested. It was probably yet another negligent discharge from a trigger-happy gunner or the celebrations at another bloody wedding. There was some Iraqi tradition whereby the bridegroom had to prove he was a man by firing into the air. Unfortunately, this led to wedding parties being mistaken for terrorist ground fire and they were then engaged by Apache gunships. Would these people never learn?

We were told to stand down and everyone went back to the TV. The welcome hiss of a Charlie being opened was the signal for the party to start again. Beer cans were passed out to all present, and with the war film once more blasting from the TV, everyone relaxed and carried on with the evening's entertainment.

Our small group was to fly out the following morning. Cory came round to let us know his guys would be escorting us down the BIAP road and waiting with us to make sure we got our flights okay; his team had volunteered, even though it was not their job. Everyone appreciated the need for our people to get out safely and on time at the end of the tour. Our departure time was to be 05:00 hours, to enable us to catch our flights. However, the U.S. Military Operations Room in the Green Zone had advised us not to travel at that hour. They couldn't guarantee our safety that early in the morning because they would still be clearing the road of IEDs. Could we postpone our flights? That was impossible, so Cory's team had still volunteered to move us to the airport. The U.S. military had good reason to be wary. The day before, 16 devices were found on the first morning sweep of the airport road - all that in just a few short miles. Cory's guys knew the risks, and they also knew we would have done the same for them. 04:30 hours saw us loading our personal equipment into the Suburban. After Cory's briefing on the route and the usual actions on, Stingray, Hollywood and I once again thanked the safe house staff and the resident PSD team for their hospitality and climbed into the vehicles. Watching our arcs, we drove out of the safe house and headed for the BIAP road. There was very little traffic at that time of the morning, but that was to be expected. It meant we could get the speed up, but we wouldn't be any safer because we still made an obvious target. We stood the chance of being hit by al-Qaeda and the Mahdi Militia - or worse still, by friendly fire from half-asleep Iraqi guards.

I looked at the city of Baghdad, now slowly recovering from the ashes of war and the destruction that had been inflicted on it, and guessed that in another ten years no one here would recognise the place. Unfortunately the only people who could stop the war were the Iraqis themselves, and at the moment they were showing no sign of doing much that could be considered constructive.

At 140 kilometres an hour, we were not that easy a target for a terrorist with an RPG, and this did make our ride a bit of a fast and furious affair. We got through the corridor of Iraqi checkpoints, followed by American checkpoints, followed by Global Security guards, and finally our vehicles screeched to a halt outside the airport terminal. We had 20 minutes before check-in time for our flight.

Things had changed in the short time since we had flown into Baghdad: it was starting to look more like an international airport. Customs and Security now manned their posts and airport workers were at their jobs. There were even a few porters, but Hollywood grabbed a trolley and told the Iraqi porter to go away; we could manage on our own. He gave us a look of disgust and wandered off to pester someone else. With all our gear unloaded from the vehicles and now balancing precariously on the trolley, we shook hands with

Cory's team and thanked them for the lift. Cory asked us if we would be coming back, but we all agreed it was too early to think about that. We needed a break first and time to reflect, but I thanked him for all his help and the opportunity to break into this type of work. He smiled and said, "I'll see you when you come back!" I cleared my weapon, showed it was clear to one of Cory's guys, and then handed it over with the ammo.

Clearing customs was no problem. It just seemed strange standing there without a weapon after three months of being permanently attached to mine. We had all been booked onto Kuwaiti Airlines and would spend one night in Kuwait before flying on to London Heathrow. Loading was pretty quick, but the usual chaotic Arab affair. The airliner took off and banked sharply as it climbed away from Baghdad, so I was able to look down and watch the city slowly disappear into the distance.

The flight to Kuwait was uneventful and the Company's representative met us at the airport. My two companions decided they wanted to spend their last night in Kuwait booked into a hotel. It was a dry country, and I could see no good reason for spending all that extra cash I had worked so hard for. Call me tight if you like, but I had plans for my money. I had already opted to stay in Blackwater's villa, so once the others were dropped off, we drove over to get me settled in for the night.

I thought I was going to be in there on my own, but I discovered a dozen replacements waiting to fly into Baghdad. So much for a quiet night! Some of them had never seen action, and a few had spent hardly any time at all in the Military before opting to get out and try for this kind of work. On the whole, they were not as experienced as our batch of potential PSD had been. The majority seemed keen enough and they would learn quickly if they survived long enough. They fired questions at me left right and centre and I gave them the most honest answers I could: I only hoped what I had told them would help.

I left early the next morning on a British Airways flight to Heathrow, but not before the Kuwaitis had stung me for excess baggage. Evidently they'd gone back to their old ways pretty quickly and were determined to make money out of the war; they'd forgotten in the blink of an eye who it was liberated them. The airport staff was just another typically ungrateful bunch of Arabs, and contractors going home were any easy pinch. I didn't care! They could do what they liked: I was going home, and my money was in the bank.

I watched my footlocker and kit bag roll down the conveyor belt, through the rubber curtain and out of sight. A Scottish bloke from *Krull* stood at the next counter. "You want how much? Bollocks! No fucking way! I'm taking less out than I came in with, and I didn't pay a penny then, you robbing bastards!"

All this was said in a strong Glaswegian accent, so I'm not sure if the Kuwaiti on the checkout understood any of it but I guess he realised from the tone that this was not a happy customer. The airline official on the other side of the check-in desk didn't bat an eyelid. He was going to make this Infidel pay, no matter what he said. He looked surprised when the Scottish lad opened up his kit bag and threw out dirty combat boots, soiled briefs, socks, and some other bits and pieces. The pile of dirty gear sat next to the counter as he once again put his kit bag on the scales and demanded it be weighed again. This time it was well under.

"Right! Put that through!"

The bag rolled down the conveyor after my gear as the guy accepted his receipt and walked towards the departure gate.

"But, but, you can't leave that here!" stammered the check-in clerk. Too late! The Scottish lad was gone, leaving a festering pile of gifts for the Kuwaitis. Nice one, Mate, I thought. Wish I'd done that - but then I just couldn't be bothered.

I slept most of the way back to Heathrow. I think everything had just caught up with me and I needed the rest. Three quarters of the people on the plane were Arabs from one country or another, and I felt a little unsettled travelling unarmed. Still, I'd get used to it; I had grown too used to wearing a side arm. Just before we landed I got up to use the toilet. One of the Muslim male passengers had decided he was going to say his prayers in the aircraft - bearing in mind that Muslims pray five times a day. He had put his prayer mat down in the crew area at the back and was kneeling down, concentrating on sending his prayers to Mecca. I wondered if he realised the aircraft was in a holding pattern circling London, so his prayers were only getting through if he happened by chance to be pointing in the right direction. I couldn't help smiling.

Our aircraft landed and taxied to the gate. It took me ten minutes to get my gear and clear Customs, and the hustle and bustle of Heathrow took me a little by surprise. As I walked through the airport I spotted two London coppers wearing body armour and carrying MP-5s - now there was a reassuring sight! Then I saw my wife waiting for me over on the other side of the airport foyer. I was home.

# Afterword

## Kidnapped from the CPA Karbala

Blackwater had handed over the security of the CPA to the United States Army and moved to various other locations. Most of the Karbala team moved to Babylon, El Hilla to protect the US Embassy. Karbala became a hub for American patrols in the area, offering a safe haven to convoys and patrols during their breaks and 'piss stops.'

On the 20th of January 2007 all that changed. The US forces had decided to withdraw from Karbala and hand over the reins of the area to the Iraqi Police and Army. This was a decision made at top level, despite the fact that the troops on the ground had voiced their reservations feeling that the local Iraqi forces were still a pretty apathetic bunch, and despite several murders in their own forces still didn't get the real idea of 'Security' or how to implement it. Still, what did the Americans care? They would be going home to their loved ones early.

It was 17:45hrs and the offices had wound down for the day. The civilian staff had gone home, leaving thirty US soldiers scattered throughout the large, three-block government building now renamed the Provisional

Joint Coordination Centre, or PJCC for short. The soldiers carried out their various tasks ready for the withdrawal the following day. I wouldn't say they had 'switched off', as I wasn't there and haven't spoken to anyone who was, however most soldiers in a situation like this tend to get a bit relaxed and maybe not as alert as they should be. This is understandable. Some of their own guys stood watch making sure that the Iraqi police on duty did their jobs and didn't fall asleep on duty. There had been no major incidents in the area for a while and they were going home. What could possibly go wrong? Down in the outer courtyard a convoy of five black GMC Suburban

SUVs pulled up, of the type used by State Department bodyguard teams and most of the PSD teams in country. The man in the front vehicle passenger seat was later described as a blond white male who spoke English. The men in each vehicle wore American army uniforms and carried American weapons. The passenger in the front vehicle greeted the Iraqi policeman on sentry duty and showed his ID. He was waved through to the second checkpoint which would give them access to the inner courtyard and the entrance to the main HQ building. Once again the passenger flashed his ID and was waved through. Having cleared the last checkpoint, which separated them from the main building, three vehicles then parked up very close to the entrance and the other two parked further away. This in itself was not unusual, as there were many high buildings surrounding the government buildings and any one of them could hide a sniper, and had done on several occasions when I had been there. The idea was to give your principal and his bodyguard team as short a walk to the safety of the vehicles as you possibly could. But the fact that there were so many vehicles should have rung a few alarm bells. A normal team is three vehicles, not five - unless you have a very important passenger, and as none was expected, and there was no one in the building who warranted that type of escort, someone should have asked questions. When the twelve attackers made their move they first destroyed two Security vehicles outside the building, setting them on fire with improvised explosive devices. Then as a group of them raced into the entrance to the PJCC they tossed fragmentation grenades killing one American soldier, Pvt. Jonathon Millican, and wounding three others. Their aim was to separate the two duty officers in the Operations Room from the other soldiers in the building, which they succeeded in doing very quickly. It's interesting to note that no Iraqi police or army were targeted during the raid, and that the attackers knew exactly where to go and where the various soldiers were: not a raid that could be executed this professionally without inside help and up to the minute intelligence. The attackers took time to throw grenades into the living accommodation area and followed up with short bursts of automatic fire, classic room clearance techniques. They did not hunt down and kill any American soldiers in the building, but seemed happy causing maximum chaos in a short space of time. While this was going on part of the assault force captured the two duty officers, 1st Lt Jacob Fritz and Capt. Brian Freeman together with their lap top computers and bundled them out of the building.

As they withdrew to their vehicles they also dragged PFC Shawn Falter and SPC Jonathan Chism out of one of the stationary Humvees and took them captive. All five vehicles and the twelve attackers then drove out through the Iraqi checkpoints with their prisoners and made a clean getaway.

I know this should not have been allowed to happen. The checkpoints guard a narrow driveway through a series of Hesco walls, and any Iraqi sentry with a set of balls could have dropped the barrier, put their cal-trops into play (metal spokes designed to puncture tyres) and stopped the vehicles escaping. Of course that didn't happen, and there is no detailed record of exactly what the Iraqi police were doing while this attack was taking place. At approximately 18:00hrs, fifteen minutes from the start of the attack, the attacking force was clear of the government compound. They made their way out of Karbala province and into the neighbouring province of Babil. By now the Iraqi police had begun trailing the convoy after they had aroused suspicion at one of the many checkpoints they passed through. Obviously not all Iraqi police are corrupt - just enough to make you unable to trust any of them. Near the town of Mahawil the Iraqi police found the five vehicles stationary. Cautiously they closed in on them, only to find a pile of US Army uniforms, abandoned non-US made weapons and radios. The two officers were found murdered, handcuffed together in the back of one of the vehicles. Both had been shot in the chest. A short distance away another soldier was found shot dead and the fourth was found alive with a gunshot wound to the head, but died of his wounds on the way to hospital. Judging by the direction the attackers had been travelling in, it was surmised they had been making a run for the Iranian border.

During the next few weeks there was a lot of speculation. The full report of the raid was not released - just enough to be classed as misinformation. It was later taken for granted that the Iranian Special Forces had instigated the attack in retaliation for the US raids on the Iranian diplomatic missions in Baghdad and Irbil. In these raids the US had captured five Iranian Quds agents, together with documentation that clearly showed Iran's support for Shia death squads, Sunni insurgents and al Qaeda. In fact they seemed to be supporting everyone from both sides who had an axe to grind with the USA. Once again it was surmised that the Americans may have been captured by forces loyal to the Iranians to be used as a bargaining chip to get back their own agents. They may have hoped they could recover computers with information that could have been embarrassing to the US government. We shall probably never know the truth, but it was a huge embarrassment that enemy forces could carry out a raid like this and get away with it. A short while later at least four local Iraqis, including at least one senior policeman, were arrested for their involvement in the incident. Implicated as the mastermind behind the attack was an Iraqi terrorist known as Azhar al-Dulaimi. On the 31st of January 2007 the Iraqi Prime Minister Nouri al-Maliki stated publicly in a speech that Iran was in fact supporting attacks against the Coalition Forces in Iraq. This was already common knowledge for virtually everyone on the ground: he was stating the bloody obvious. Iran as usual denied any involvement.

In May of 2007, working on a tip-off, American and Iraqi Forces surrounded an area of North Baghdad where it was believed Azhar al-Dulaimi was in hiding. After attempting to avoid capture he was finally killed in a short but ferocious fire fight. This evened the score a little for the dead American soldiers, and gave the Coalition Forces a sense of 'pay back'.

To carry out the raid the attackers would have needed up to date, minute by minute intelligence and specific training in order to pass themselves off as American soldiers. They would also need a pot full of money and the resources to provide enough weapons of a similar type to give the impression of uniformity. The Iranians were known to have carried out similar raids against the Israelis, but as a result of this one they had shot themselves in the foot: the United States had now authorised the death or capture of any Iranian agents found inside Iraq. This order covered Afghanistan and Lebanon as well, and now we were involved with Syria and several other countries in the area it would be interesting to see if the order was rolled out further.

On July 2nd 2007 a captured Hezbollah terrorist, Ali Moussa Dakouk, revealed a link between the Quds Force of the Iranian Islamic Revolutionary Guard and the Karbala raid. This terrorist had supposedly acted as the go-between for the Quds Force and Shia group. There is no way any Militia Shia group could carry out such a raid without expert help and training from elsewhere. They were just not that bright or resourceful. This was more or less the last piece of the jigsaw puzzle needed to confirm everybody's theories that Iran was indeed responsible.

I am only glad that by the time all this took place not only my team, but Blackwater itself were long gone.

# Glossary of Terms

| | |
|---|---|
| AK-47 | Russian designed, fully automatic assault rifle |
| APC | Armoured Personnel Carrier |
| BIAP | Baghdad International Airport |
| BMP | Soviet designed armoured vehicle |
| BRDM | Soviet designed armoured vehicle |
| CAS | Combat Air Support |
| Casevac | Casualty evacuation, to remove the wounded from the battlefield |
| CIMIC | Civilian, Military Co-operation |
| CO | Commanding Officer |
| CPA | Coalition Provisional Authority |
| CQB | Close Quarter Battle |
| Debus | To dismount from a vehicle |
| Demob | To demobilise |
| DOD | Department of Defence |
| EndEx | End of exercise phase |
| EOD | Explosive Ordnance Disposal |
| EOTECH | Manufacturer of Instinctive reaction weapons sight |
| ETR | Electrical Target Range |
| FIBUA | Fighting In a Built Up Area |
| Five by five | Radio procedure - receiving loud and clear |
| 40 Mike-Mike | 40mm grenade launcher |
| Gimpy | General Purpose Machine Gun |
| GPMG | General Purpose Machine Gun |
| GPS | Global Positioning System |
| IED | Improvised Explosive Device |

| | |
|---|---|
| IP | Iraq Police |
| IRA | Irish Republican Army - Northern Ireland terrorist organization |
| JCB | Joseph Cyril Bamford - Heavy Plant manufacturers |
| KBR | Kellogg's Brown and Root - suppliers of catering and other services to US forces |
| K9 unit | Dog handler and dog |
| LZ | Landing Zone |
| Mercenary | Soldier of Fortune - a retired soldier who sells his services to the highest bidder |
| MP | Military Police |
| MOB stock | Mobilisation stock |
| MSR | Main Supply Route |
| NAAFI | Navy, Army, Air force Institute - equivalent of the US PX |
| NCO | Non Commissioned Officer |
| NVG | Night Vision Goggles |
| OC | Officer Commanding |
| PKM | Pulemyot Kalashnikova Modernizirovanniy – Soviet de-signed general purpose machine gun |
| PLO | Palestine Liberation Organization |
| Pro-active | To take the fight to the enemy |
| PSD | Personal Security Detail - bodyguard team |
| Piss stop | A safe haven or area where a patrol or convoy feel safe enough to take a quick break and empty their bladders |

| | |
|---|---|
| PT | Physical Training |
| Recce | Reconnaissance - to have a close look at a target area |
| RCT | Royal Corps of Transport |
| RPG | Rocket Propelled Grenade |
| RV | Rendezvous - a meeting point |
| SAM | Surface to Air Missile |
| Sanger | Defensive position or bunker |
| SAS | Special Air Service - top British Special Forces unit |
| SEAL | Sea, Air, Land - US Navy Special Forces |
| SF | Special Forces |
| SITREP | Situation Report |
| SLR | Self Loading Rifle |
| SOP | Standard Operation Procedure |
| Stag on | To complete a tour of sentry duty |
| S-Type | Enlistment or attachment into the regular army by a reserve soldier |
| SWAT | Special Weapons and Tactics |
| TA | Territorial Army |
| Teeth arm | Front line troops - tip of the spear |
| VBIED | Vehicle-Borne Improvised Explosive Device |
| VCP | Vehicle Check Point/Vehicle Control Point |
| Your Twenty | Radio procedure - your location |
| WASF | World Wide Association of Special Forces |
| X | Centre point of an ambush |

**'Keepers of the gateway to hell'**
**is the second book by Simon Chambers**

To be published by Percy Publishing in 2015
**More Real Life Stories from Percy Publishing**

# The Middle Man
# by Philip J Howard

MrH was 'The Middle Man' for some of the biggest underworld factions in the world of crime. For over twenty five years he was the link and negotiator to the deals. From an eighteen year old kid to middle age there is nothing in life he hasn't seen. His motto is "let nothing in life surprise you" Here is his true view of events that took him to deaths door and almost beyond to eventually changing his life around and making him the renowned Film and TV Director he is today.

**A book and film being produced in 2015.**

# 'A Sketchy Life'
# by Kevin Paul.

**From trouble to notoriety.**

To be published in 2015

# Thrilling Fiction Titles
# from Percy Publishing

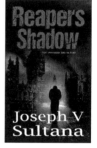

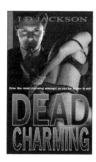

## PERCY
## PUBLISHING

Visit www.percy-publishing.com for more information.

Facebook: www.facebook.com/percypublishing

Twitter: @percypublishing